# BESTSELLING
# BOOK PUBLICITY

## The Insider's Guide to Promoting Your Book—and Yourself

Rick Frishman and Robyn Freedman Spizman
*with Mark Steisel*

Adams Media
Avon, Massachusetts

Published by
Adams Media, an F+W Publications Company
57 Littlefield Street, Avon, MA 02322
*www.adamsmedia.com*

ISBN: 1-59337-524-7

Printed in the United States of America.

J  I  H  G  F  E  D  C  B  A

**Library of Congress Cataloging-in-Publication Data**
Frishman, Rick
Author 101 : bestselling book publicity / Rick Frishman
and Robyn Freedman Spizman.
p. cm. — (Author 101 series)
ISBN 1-59337-524-7
1. Books—Marketing—Handbooks, manuals, etc. 2. Book industries and trade—
Handbooks, manuals, etc. 3. Authors and publishers—Handbooks, manuals, etc.
4. Publishers and publishing—Handbooks, manuals, etc. I. Title: Author one-on-one.
II. Title: Author one hundred one. III. Spizman, Robyn Freedman. IV. Title. V. Series.
Z283.F68 2006
002.068'8—dc22
2006004164

This publication is designed to provide accurate and authoritative information with
regard to the subject matter covered. It is sold with the understanding that the publisher is not engaged in rendering legal, accounting, or other professional advice. If
legal advice or other expert assistance is required, the services of a competent professional person should be sought.
—From a *Declaration of Principles* jointly adopted by a Committee of the
American Bar Association and a Committee of Publishers and Associations

Many of the designations used by manufacturers and sellers to distinguish their products are claimed as trademarks. Where those designations appear in this book and
Adams Media was aware of a trademark claim, the designations have been printed
with initial capital letters.

*This book is available at quantity discounts for bulk purchases.*
*For information, please call 1-800-872-5627.*

All it takes to get a book published is getting one person to say "yes." We dedicate this book to the editors, publishers, and individuals along the way who said "yes" to us and hopefully will say "yes" to you too.

■ ■ ■

To my wife, Robbi, with love and thanks.
—*Rick Frishman*

To my husband, Willy, and our children, Justin and Ali.
You make life a bestseller!
—*Robyn Freedman Spizman*

# Contents

# Foreword

CONGRATULATIONS! YOU JUST took a huge step toward making your book a big success. You hold in your hands the final elements to having a bestseller. However, let's not forget the word "sell" in "bestseller." Writing a book is only part of the journey. Getting people to take notice and to buy it is the other half. Thankfully, Rick and Robyn are here to help and make this stage of the process both exciting and productive. They tell you that you can have *fun* making yourself a success. This really can be enjoyable.

For starters, you already did the hardest part . . . writing a book and getting published! You should be proud of what you accomplished. Take *joy* in letting the world know about this great new book that they can't ignore. The second leg of your journey is not overwhelming once you know what to expect and then how to do it. The scariest part for authors is the unknown. This book is your system, your crash-course guidebook to getting and using publicity to achieve your goals. These seasoned authors will help you walk the walk and talk the talk! They give you all the details and get you on your way. All you need to have is the *want*. Do you want to be a success?

Everyone may have a book inside them, but you brought yours to life and made it happen! This is your "product." Don't forget that. People need to be informed when a new product comes out. Don't be bashful! You didn't write a book for the sole purpose of giving it to your family and friends. Your book, your product, is the key to your future. It can open up doors you never imagined. If you believe you have something the world needs to hear about, stand up and be heard. For many authors though, it is sometimes tough to talk about yourself. Are you afraid of being too self-promotional? Do you feel like you are boasting? Well, I say get over it! This is your success. Promise yourself right now to get out there and do it!

I have a unique perspective on the content you'll be reading. I am currently an associate producer with Fox News Channel's number-one rated cable morning show, *Fox & Friends*. My job is to find interesting guests, book them, and produce all the elements that go into making it a compelling and interesting segment. Over the course of my career at Fox and elsewhere, I've booked and produced over 4,000 segments on the national level. One could say that I understand how the process works. The information in this book will help you navigate through the process with ease.

My side business as a media trainer also gives me an interesting perspective on this world. I have talked to countless authors at different stages of the process who share a need for one thing: guidance. Authors have many questions about what follows when their book is done. Consider the authors of this book your virtual tour guides. Like them, I came to a similar point in my life. In the process of doing what we do each day, we realize that there is a wealth of knowledge we can pass on to others. As a media trainer who works with authors, experts, and executives on how to make the most of media interviews, whether it be for print, radio, or television, the greatest thanks I get is seeing people who were scared and unsure of themselves begin to shine. Part of what I teach is controlling the media. Right now, you hold the power to make yourself a superstar. *You* have the greatest control over your future. Get out there and start doing it!

Rick and Robyn wrote this book hoping to help make your job as an author easier. They have seen it all! They have been on both sides of the fence and realize once you know how publicity works, it's just a matter of getting it to work on your behalf. As experienced authors and publicists, they are some of the dedicated few who have decided to share this information, to teach others, and I commend them!

Remember, the media is looking for content, that is, *you!* Newspapers, magazines, TV, and radio eat up content like fast food. Their need is insatiable. They are always on the lookout for more and more content to fill up their publication or show. Make yourself a resource, be multiversatile, and let the media see you as an expert. A little secret on how it really works with the media: If you provide interesting and compelling content, the media will be more than happy to not only promote what you want, but help make you famous and successful.

That sounds like a pretty good deal! People talk about investing in stocks and bonds. You have made the greatest investment, the investment in yourself. It's all up to you. You are in control of your fate. Now, go and *make* opportunity knock.

That's what this book is all about!

—Jess Todtfeld
President of Success in Media

# Acknowledgments

OUR WARMEST THANKS to Gary Krebs and Scott Watrous of Adams Media, who gave us the green light when we presented this book series. Their steadfast enthusiasm for the project and encouragement has lit a fire under us. We also want to express our appreciation to our wonderful editor, Paula Munier, for her guidance and support, to Beth Gissinger, Karen Cooper, Gene Molter, Jason Flynn, Laura Daly, and the entire staff at Adams Media.

We especially want to express our deep appreciation to David Hahn, David Thalberg, Sharon Farnell, Joel Roberts, Randy Gilbert, Willy Spizman of the Spizman Agency and Jenny Corsey who generously gave us their time and invaluable expertise. Their contributions have greatly enhanced this book and we are extremely grateful.

Thanks also to our many and gifted literary and publicity contacts whose help and wisdom made this book possible. When we asked them to help us, these friends consistently came through and shared their remarkable knowledge, experience, and insights with us. They selflessly took time from their busy schedules to help us and the readers of this book.

So, to all of you who have given us so much, please accept our heartfelt thanks. We are extremely grateful for your help! We would like to especially acknowledge and thank the following people.

| | | |
|---|---|---|
| Jamie Brickhouse | Steve Harrison | Jill Lublin |
| Alex Carroll | Paul Hartunian | Peggy McColl |
| Danielle Chiotti | Douglas M. Isenberg, | Penny Pollack |
| Jenny Corsey | Esq. | Karen Quinn |
| Richard Curtis | Hillel Italie | Diane Reverand |
| Barbara De Angelis | Dan Janal | Joel D. Roberts |
| Sharon Farnell | Lloyd J. Jassin, Esq. | Jeff Ruby |
| Brian Feinbaum | Jerry Jenkins | Willy Spizman |
| Randy Gilbert | Brian Judd | David Thalberg |
| Beth Gissinger | Deborah Kohan | Patti Thorn |
| David Hahn | Gabrielle Lichterman | Jess Todtfeld |
| Bill Harrison | Steve Lillo | John Willig |

We would like to thank and acknowledge David Hahn, senior vice president of New York City's Planned Television Arts for his great help in writing and consulting with us on some of the business book sections of this text.

We would also like to thank David Thalberg, former senior vice president of New York City's Planned Television Arts, for his great help in writing and reviewing Chapter 13.

*From Robyn:* To my wonderful family—my amazing husband, Willy, I am eternally grateful to you for your unwavering encouragement. Thank you for your endless support and loaning me the Spizman Agency whenever I needed their public relation's help, guidance, and endless PowerPoint presentations! I am one lucky girl to have married a guy like you! To our children, Justin and Ali, who fill our lives every second of every day with laughter and love. You are the best chapters we've ever written. To my parents, Phyllis and Jack Freedman, who have cheered me on to success my entire life. You are my greatest fans and I am yours. To my brother Doug who said, "Real authors have agents." To Genie, Sam and Gena, my devoted family Lois and Jerry Blonder, Ramona Freedman, and my wonderful group of friends and Dr. Ava Wilensky, who encouraged me to write this series. Plus, a special thanks to the Spizman Agency, Jenny Corsey, and Bettye Storne for your unending devotion and continued support. You are the absolute best bar none!

To my coauthor, Rick Frishman, who is genuinely one of the finest human beings on this planet. Thank you, Rick, for being such a remarkable friend and coauthor and to the talented Mark Steisel, who is a total literary genius in our book! A special thanks goes to our wonderful editor at Adams Media, Paula Munier, and to Scott Watrous and Gary Krebs, who brought this series to life and to Beth Gissinger, Karen Cooper, Gene Molter, and all the amazing folks at Adams Media for your hard work and efforts on our behalf.

Thanks also to my readers, who continue to grace me with their presence. I am most fortunate to have all of you in my life.

*From Rick:* The first thank-you goes to my wonderful coauthor, Robyn Spizman, who I've known for over twenty years and is one of the finest coauthors a guy could ask for!

Mark Steisel—your help and wisdom have been invaluable. Working with you has been a joy.

Thank you to our super editor at Adams Media, Paula Munier, and to Gary Krebs and, of course, the man who made this happen, Scott Watrous. Thank you, Beth Gissinger, publicity guru at Adams, for all of your hard work and Karen Cooper and Gene Molter.

I have to acknowledge Mike (Manny) Levine, who founded Planned Television Arts in 1962 and was my mentor, and partner, for over eighteen years. Mike taught me that work has to be fun and meaningful and then the profits will follow.

To my exceptional management team at PTA—David Hahn, David Thalberg, and Sandy Trupp—your professionalism, loyalty, and friendship mean more to me than you will ever know. To Hillary Rivman, who helped build PTA and is still an affiliate and friend of our company. To Bob Unterman—you are always there when I need you and are truly a best friend. To the staff of PTA, you are the best in the business.

Thank you to David and Peter Finn, Tony Esposito, Richard Funess, and all of my colleagues at Ruder Finn. It is an honor to be part of this amazing company.

To my friends Mark Victor Hansen and Jack Canfield. Making the journey with the two of you has been incredible, and your friendship and advice have been invaluable.

To Harvey Mackay, for the lessons about networking and for your amazing support. You are in a class of your own.

To my mother and father, for keeping me out of the fur business and helping me discover my own destiny. And to my brother Scott, who has always been there to support me in whatever I do.

To my children, Adam, Rachel, and Stephanie. Watching you grow into fine young individuals has been the highlight of my life. And to my wife, Robbi—you are my strength.

# Introduction

YOUR BOOK MAY BE the best and most important title of its time. It could contain groundbreaking information, ideas, and approaches that could dramatically improve people's lives and even change society. Isn't that the true wonder of books—that they can alter the lives of readers and the world?

In order for people to read your book, they must first hear about it, learn that it exists. If they never hear about it, all the amazing information you compiled, all the new ideas you explained, and all of the poetic descriptions you composed will never penetrate their minds. If readers don't know about your book, your words won't have a voice.

Books exist to be read; that's their primary purpose. However, the competition for readers is fierce. And, unlike other forms of communication, such as radio and television, reading takes a special effort; you can't get information from books by simply pressing a button. Since readers must make an effort, you must get them interested in your book. To do so, you have to get their attention and convince them that reading your title will be worth their time, money, and effort, and that it will give them something of value. That's where publicity comes in. Publicity singles out your book for attention. It convinces readers to give it a try, to make that special effort. Publicity announces that your book is available, what it's about, and the benefits received by reading it.

Every author—from the most noted, perennial bestseller to the complete novice—needs to publicize his or her book. Even if your publisher's in-house team is promoting your title full steam, you also must promote. It can be the difference between its being widely read and not read at all.

## Bottomless Pit

To publicize your book, you can employ an endless assortment of tactics; the options are virtually unlimited—a bottomless pit. No single formula, guaranteed method, or foolproof recipe can make every book succeed; however, many approaches do work. As professional publicists and authors, we've used those approaches. They have succeeded for our clients and us big-time. Now, we want to teach them to you in this book.

All publicity experts have their favorite methods and tactics. Some of their methods may do wonders for them but flop for others. Or, they may work on some campaigns but not others. The trick is to know the approaches that you can use and then find those that will be best for you and your book. In this book, we'll show you how.

When we agreed to write this book, we fully understood that we couldn't cover all of the bases; that it would be impossible to teach you every book-publicity tactic that has ever worked. You see, unlike base-ball, publicity doesn't have just four bases, it has thousands of them, and publicists—a remarkably inventive group—keep devising more every day. So, we decided to zero in on those areas that we considered the most important and that could be the most valuable for you.

In the pages that follow:

- We explain the basic ingredients needed to get publicity, such as writing a silver bullet, preparing press releases, compiling media lists, getting media coverage, handling interviews, and much more.
- We also venture into exciting areas that most others barely touch, including building bridges with the media, media training, Web sites, and blogs.

■ Plus, we have devoted entire chapters to special niches that others have rarely addressed, including e-mail blasts, business books, books of faith, campaign timelines, and how to hire publicists.

This collection of invaluable information is the product of our years of experience as book publicists and authors. It has been enhanced by the generosity and wisdom of our friends: other top and highly successful publicists and authors, legends in the field, who have contributed to this book. For this volume, we compiled an all-star cast of experts who have graciously shared their time, insights, and remarkable expertise with you. Furthermore, they've broken down the information they contributed so that you can adapt it to your book and your own special needs.

## Creativity and People

Publicity is a business in which creativity, inventiveness, attention to detail, and people are more important than rules. It's a business that lets you break old rules, go against the grain, and formulate new ones. Publicity is a people business that is built on building close relationships and on being true to your word. If you let it, it can be a wonderful, productive, and exhilarating journey.

Just as each book and author differs, so do all publicity campaigns. Each campaign must be sculpted to fit the needs of the individual book and author and then follow its own path. When campaigns reflect and are outgrowths of the personalities and spirits of their authors, they usually work best and take on successful lives of their own.

As you read this book, keep an open mind and take it all in. Consider all of the different approaches that you could use. Let them stimulate your imagination and trigger your resourcefulness so that you come up with the best tactics to make your campaign a thundering success. Customize them to suit your personality and the realities of your life, values, and goals. Remember that the essential product you're selling is you. So, create a campaign that truly reflects you, because when you do, people will be more likely to respond.

## The Bonanza

Before we get into the heart of this book, we would like to briefly address your expectations. Your book can become a bonanza for you, but not necessarily for the reasons you may think. If you have visions of seeing your name at the top of the bestseller lists or appearing on all the major talk shows, we wish you well, but we must point out that the odds against you are steep. While the chances are remote that you will become a celebrated, bestselling author who makes money from writing, your book can generate other benefits that can be equally great, if not greater!

Few authors actually make money from the sales of their books. Most, especially first-timers, receive meager royalties and they don't get them until their publishers recoup whatever advances they paid. In addition, publishers' discounts, reserves for returns, and literary agents' fees are deducted, which may leave little or nothing for the authors.

The best way for authors to strike it rich is to harvest other benefits from their books; for example, by establishing themselves as experts, becoming celebrities, getting wide media attention, boosting their businesses, and refocusing their careers in new, more lucrative directions. If they wish to continue writing, they must use each forthcoming book to boost their literary careers.

In creating the campaign to promote your book, think beyond this current book. Always plan for the long term. Build a campaign that is consistent with your values and ambitions, and position yourself to reach your goals—including your nonwriting goals. Your campaign to promote your book, important as it now may be, is only one piece of the puzzle, one step in your rise to the top!

Enjoy this book!

—Rick Frishman and Robyn Freedman Spizman

**CHAPTER 1**

All publicity is good, except an obituary notice.
*Brendan Behan, playwright*

# The Publicity Party

**THIS CHAPTER COVERS:**

▶ Make publicity fun
▶ Be imaginative
▶ Publicity campaigns
▶ Planning
▶ Take the reins
▶ Make it great
▶ Passion

HOW MANY TIMES have you heard so-called experts on book publicity solemnly warn, "Now that you've written your book, the hard work begins." We've all heard that comment over and over again, but don't listen to it! Don't let the doomsayers scare you off! We're here to show you the other side of the picture, the bright side—that promoting your book can be lots of fun. And, when it's fun, it can be more successful, considerably more successful.

After authoring and promoting many books, we're here to testify that the writing is the hard part; it's slow, solitary, exacting work. It's constant writing, rewriting, checking, rechecking, editing, and re-editing deep into the night until your mind is mush and your fingers feel like linguini as they bounce off all the wrong keys. Writing a book requires intense concentration, dedication, and discipline. Plus, when you reread it in the morning, it often makes no sense. After you've written your book, the real fun begins—if you let it. The load gets lifted, the juices kick in, the adrenaline flows, and the best ideas come screaming out of your mind at incredible speed. Your focus becomes sharp, all that creativity you had when you began writing (and you feared was lost forever) pops back up and soars to absolute peaks. Finally, after what seemed like eons writing your book, you're no longer glued to your computer; you can break loose and end your confinement. Suddenly, excitement reigns, and it's time to throw off the shackles and have fun.

## Be Imaginative

Yes, promoting a book can be a big, even a huge job. Jerry Jenkins, chairman and CEO of JGI, a family of publishing service companies,

**Robyn Says**

My appearances on an Atlanta talk show helped to position my career in the media. After paying my dues with many highly rated appearances and years of hard work, a CNN producer contacted the local talk show I was on to find a seasoned gift and toy reporter and my producer recommended me.

I prepared nonstop for my CNN debut. I made sure that I knew my material cold, that I triple-checked all facts, and that my delivery was crisp and had pizzazz. The news anchor introduced me as the author of my latest book, and we had a terrific interview. After my appearance, congratulatory calls poured in and I began receiving invitations to appear repeatedly in the national media. Five-minute segments turned into hour-long shows on *Talk Back Live* and even specials with me focusing on my books.

If your take-away message is strong and you provide a prescriptive insight into a subject area, that's the key to being a success in the media. It's also a marvelous opportunity to connect with wonderful individuals who are dedicated to educating others. I feel truly lucky to be an author and am grateful to all the talented people who have helped me throughout the years.

says, "Producing the book is 5 percent of the work, but promoting it is 95 percent." Why does it take so much? Because creating and running a publicity campaign involve planning and focus and require you to seamlessly execute a million coordinated steps. Yes, it can be plenty of work, but it may be the difference between making your book, and your writing career, a success or a bomb.

The key to successful book publicity is approaching it positively, with excitement—to open up and expand that creativity that you may have suppressed or never even knew you had. Turn the work that lies ahead into an enjoyable, creative experience, to eliminate the drudgery and increase your chances of doing a fabulous job. Break free of your chains and open up your mind by following these simple guidelines:

1. Forget about reality, logic, and limits. Instead, focus on your dreams, your wildest, craziest, most unrealistic ideas.
2. Expand upon those thoughts. Let your imagination fly.
3. Picture yourself on *Oprah,* being featured in *People* magazine, presenting at the Academy Awards or being honored as the person of the year. Unleash your imagination, break through all boundaries, shoot for the stars, and go for the gold.

## You, You, You

Yes, it could happen to you. So, think big; picture the top of the mountain before you start to climb. Have a clear and precise vision. Know your objective before you begin laying out all of the little steps you'll have to take to strike the mother lode. Don't let anyone dampen your dream! Stimulate your creativity by brainstorming with friends.

- Come up with crazy, wacky ideas, ideas that make you laugh and stay with you.
- Explore interests, impulses, and feelings that excite you, not those that you think or are told you should do.

### Visualize Your Dream

Actually see and feel every detail of your vision. Picture yourself in your dream situations: standing in response to thunderous applause from the balcony of the Kennedy Center while your three favorite entertainers salute you from the stage before they begin reciting passages from your books. Seated around you are the other award winners, the president, and the first lady; they're all smiling, staring admiringly at you, and clapping loudly.

Visualize what it's like to sit behind a table at a bookstore and see a long procession of people waiting to have you sign their copy of your book. Imagine the thrill of seeing your book being read by total strangers and stumbling across rave reviews in the press. What could be better than hearing Katie Couric tell you how hard she laughed at page 43? Think how proud and happy your mother would be!

- Experiment, be daring, chart your own course, and don't be afraid to remove barriers and to break the rules.
- Play around until you find your special and unique voice, a voice that people will respond to because it's really you and not some pale imitation of everyone else.
- Record your brainstorming sessions and follow up on those ideas that continue to excite you days later.

Expose yourself to the new and different. Break your routines and open yourself up. Let new stimuli, ideas, and approaches into your life. Read magazines you normally don't buy, turn to different radio stations, and visit new Web sites. Examine them closely. What items do they promote? List what grabbed your attention, identify the strong points of the best presentations and which of their features you could copy or adapt. How could you make them better, funnier, or more interesting?

Give your campaign authenticity by making it reflect you. Capitalize on your strengths and special abilities by weaving them into your campaign. Build upon your sense of humor, insistence on excellence, love of meeting new people, shyness, fears, creativity, and drive.

# Publicity Campaigns

We live in celebrity-obsessed times. The public gobbles up products created or endorsed by their favorite stars; people they like, believe in, or respect. The publishing industry has capitalized on this fact by publishing books by many celebrities and building its bestselling writers into celebrities. The industry knows that star power sells. So, if you want to sell lots of your books, follow the same formula and become a star—whether you write fiction, nonfiction, or both.

That's where publicity comes in. A well-planned and implemented publicity campaign can give you exposure and help you build name recognition and a following. A book-promotion campaign should consist of a series of events, each of which is coordinated to capture the attention of the media and the public. Each event in the campaign should strengthen and reinforce the impact of each of the other events in the campaign. The ultimate objective is to create a strong cumulative impact, which translates into a continuing public interest in the book.

The individual events in a book-publicity campaign don't have to be big blowouts. Often, it pays to take a smaller but sharper focus on your target readership. So if your book has a clearly defined but limited audience, it's usually better to target that particular group than to squander your resources in areas that your core readers won't see.

A campaign should be built to give the book a continuing presence with buyers. It must be more than a one-shot event. Unfortunately, many campaigns start with a bang and then peter out. Even when they get strong media coverage, they generally don't follow through and disappear.

*As the word* campaign *implies, book publicity efforts must be planned in detail and executed with precision.*

# Planning

The media constantly needs stories for its publications and shows. According to radio expert Alex Carroll, "Radio needs 10,000 guests every day to fill up the airways." So, the media needs you. Getting the media to know that you have a great story, that you would be a great guest or subject, usually doesn't happen by accident. It takes precise and detailed planning; it takes publicity. Sure, great opportunities may occasionally fall into your lap, and if you hustle like crazy, you may be able to make the most of them. But without planning, those bonanzas are rare and they can appear so suddenly that you're not prepared to take advantage of them. However, when you've laid the groundwork and devised terrific plans, you create opportunities and are in position to promptly capitalize on them.

An effective publicity plan must have staying power; the longer it runs, the better. It must be designed to run for months, even years, after your book is released. If you start with a big salvo, follow up; capital-ize and build upon its success so that your name and the name of your book continue to generate interest. Otherwise, your book will probably fade into oblivion and onto remainder tables.

Although we'll discuss the media in greater depth in Chapter 6, "Build Bridges with the Media," one introductory concept is crucial for you to clearly understand from the start. It is that the media oper-ates on a herd mentality. Although everyone in the media constantly searches for scoops and exclusives, once a story is out, the rest of the media piles on, and they all seem to dash madly to cover the identical story. Publicity begets publicity, and each new exposure can improve your performance and your desirability to the media.

If you and your book get good buzz, others will jump on the band-wagon. Everyone will be looking for something different, a unique angle or new twist, which is when you can shine. You can attract coverage if you're prepared to give the media new slants, something different that will whet its appetite and build its interest in you. That takes planning.

Finally, it's essential to remember that the media is fickle. When your story is hot, the media will court you and lavish attention on you. You will become its best friend, its darling. But when the media feels your story is played out, it will move to the next hot story so suddenly and fast that you'll feel abandoned and let down. Plus, it rarely looks back.

**Rick Says**

Running a publicity campaign is like surfing, riding a series of waves. Riding each wave is an event, an exhilarating adventure that has several distinct purposes. They are to:

1. Put on a great show that will make people sit up and notice,
2. Put on each show in a fun-filled way that will make your life enjoyable, and
3. Make all the shows work together so you sell tons of books.

For each wave, produce a terrific show; pull out all the stops and always try to top your previous effort. If you produce a great show for every wave, the overall impact will be powerful and memorable. It will bowl them over and be all they can talk about. The word will spread.

When you deal with the media, you have only a brief window of opportunity, a short period in which to get coverage. So, you better have a plan and be ready to make the most of it!

## Take the Reins

Publicity works best when you distinguish yourself and your book and show others why it's so special and a must read. It's the perfect opportunity to be creative; your only limits are those you impose on yourself. Unfortunately, many of us have been sold the bill of goods that publicizing our efforts or ourselves is crass, undignified, and not what respectable people do—which is just plain wrong. According to that thinking, we should sit back and wait for the world to recognize and applaud us; do nothing but let nature take its course.

However, doing nada doesn't sell books! So take control. Start by changing your attitude and your approach. Adjust your thinking; become positive, optimistic, and active. Commit to vigorously promoting your book and yourself. If you want to sell books, it's a must!

Start by blowing blow your own horn. It doesn't have to be loud, brash, and dissonant; it can be musical, lyrical, and enchanting. To be a Pied Piper, potential followers must hear your tune.

Concentrate on stripping the negativity out of your reluctance to get publicity. Here's how we do it. When we publicize books, we approach it positively, joyfully, and with excitement—as if we were planning a series of parties. Although each event will be special, they all must be coordinated so they build an overall effect that shows the book in its best light. When planning each publicity party, ask the following questions:

- Who would you invite?
- Why would you invite them?
- How would you invite them?
- What would you tell them?

Think about your answers; let them settle in because they will form the basis for your book-publicity campaign.

## Make It Great

Before we tell you how to begin your book-promotion campaign, it's essential to stress how crucial it is that you write a first-rate book. Quality really counts; your book must be terrific!

If your book isn't great, the word will get out. Doors will slam in your face, and it will become increasingly difficult, if not impossible, to change people's minds. If your book doesn't deliver, the world's best publicity efforts won't bail you out. They may generate some initial success or notice, but readers will soon feel ripped off, and they won't support your book.

Word-of-mouth publicity is critical to the success of books; book sales depend on chains of recommendations—recommendations from reviewers, family, friends, and teachers. So, give readers high-caliber products that they will eagerly share with others.

## Passion

Publicity must start from within; what you say must be heartfelt or it will be short lived. To persuade others to read your book, they must feel that you're passionately convinced that it's great, that it will offer readers substantial benefits that will change their lives.

People have extraordinary sensors. They quickly perceive when you don't believe what you say, when you're simply going through the motions or trying to sell them something. When they don't believe you, they quickly tune you out because they've been burned too often by too many false promises and claims. Plus, they have better uses for their valuable time.

The public can sense when you truly believe and it will respond. Your passion will generate passion in them. Deep down, most people want to believe, so you have to allay their doubts. Passion, your total belief in your book, will make them stop, lower their guard, and listen. And if they believe you and like your book, they will praise and recommend it to everyone and work tirelessly to see that it becomes a big success.

If you are not totally convinced that your book is special, that your audience truly needs it, identify why. Then fix it before you try to promote your book. Promoting what you honestly don't believe in is rarely successful; it feels dishonest and people catch on. Promoting what you adore is easy, natural, and produces fabulous results.

## Books of Fiction

Some authors mistakenly think that it's unnecessary to promote books of fiction. They believe that once their novels, short stories, and poetry are published, literary acclaim, huge book sales, and big advances for subsequent books will automatically follow. Sorry to say, they're wrong—very wrong.

The market for fiction is densely crowded, and the competition for readers is fierce. Without publicity, first-rate fiction can get lost in the crowd, languish, and not sell; it happens every day. Lack of sales can hurt authors' careers because when publishers make their acquisition decisions, they consider how the authors' prior books sold.

So, as you read this book, keep in mind that the information will be beneficial to both fiction and nonfiction books.

## Action Steps

1. List three creative ways to promote your book without the help of others or spending much money.
2. List three ways that you could follow up on the answers you gave for item 1.
3. What is the most important benefit you would like to receive from the publication of your book?
4. Who would you invite to your first publicity party?
5. What would you tell those you invite to your publicity party?

### Remember

⚠ **Although publicizing your book can entail a lot of work, it can be great fun, which will make the work easier and more successful.** Be creative, even if you don't consider yourself a creative person. Find ways to publicize your book that can capitalize on your book's concept, the people you know or current trends, news events, and you.

⚠ **Planning is the key to effective publicity, and your campaign should run for at least a few months.** Understand that the media has a herd mentality. Write the best book possible. If your book isn't good or does not deliver what is promised, the best, the most expensive publicity efforts may not be able to help it sell. All books, fiction and nonfiction, will benefit from promotion.

**CHAPTER 2**

Imagination is the beginning of creation. You imagine what you desire, you will what you imagine and at last you create what you will.
*George Bernard Shaw*

# Authors—It Starts with You

**THIS CHAPTER COVERS:**

► About publicity
► Publishers' efforts
► In-house publicists
► What publishers provide
► Authors' platforms
► Finding your niche

PUBLICITY IS THE ART of creating favorable interest in your book. It's getting the word out, informing the public about your book and drumming up interest in it. It's telling the world:

■ That your book is available,
■ What it's about,
■ Why it's important, and
■ The specific benefits it will provide.

Publicity differs from advertising. In advertising, you pay media outlets to run your message. You write the message you want the public to receive and you pay publications, stations, Web sites, and other outlets to deliver it. According to the old adage, "With advertising, you pay for it; with publicity, you pray for it." In publicity, your message is delivered through the media and through channels such as your networks and your contacts' networks. In contrast to advertising, you don't pay the media to deliver your message, but convince it to deliver it in its articles, reviews, and programs. The media may deliver the exact message you provide, or present the information in its own words, style, or format.

Publicity is effective because the public tends to think of information it gets from the media as news. So, it gives publicity more credence than advertising does, which the public knows is bought and paid for by advertisers. Advertising is perceived as being big on hype and short on truth, while information provided by the media is generally accepted as true.

In comparison with advertising, publicity:

- Is less expensive.
- Provides wider exposure.
- Has greater credibility because, unlike advertising, people usually consider the information provided to be news.
- Tells your story in greater depth, which is ideal for creating interest in your book.

**Rick Says**

To be successful, all books need publicity. Readers are swamped with books. According to estimates, 195,000 books were published in 2004, which breaks down to several new titles being issued each minute. That's an awful lot of books competing for booksellers' shelves and readers' attention. Plus, books face stiff competition from movies, television, newspapers, magazines, sports, the Internet, games, and more.

Publicity is the most effective way to single out your book for recognition and to build its identity and visibility. In publishing, they refer to "breaking a book out," which means getting it noticed so that it can emerge from a sea of competitors. Through the wonders of publicity, weak books have been built into huge successes, and great books that lacked publicity have not been widely read.

## In-House Publicists

Writers frequently think that the mere fact that an established house is publishing their book will guarantee big sales. They believe that their publisher will share their belief and passion for their book and roll out the heavy artillery to promote it. Not so!

"The biggest myth authors make the mistake of believing is that you can count solely on your publisher to help you publicize your book," bestselling author Barbara De Angelis, *How Did I Get Here?* (St. Martin's Press, 2005), advises. De Angelis operates Transformational Communication (*www.transformationalcommunication.com*), which trains writers and speakers to be more successful and effective. We're sorry to tell you that publishers, even the biggest of them, don't promote all of their books. And, they probably won't publicize yours, except perhaps for the first few weeks out of the gate.

The top brass at publishing houses usually determine which books and authors they will publicize and how extensively. Publishers also don't invest the same amount for publicity in all titles they release. For example, they may authorize extensive campaigns for Books A, B, and C, but provide little, if any, publicity for the other new releases on their lists. They may not even send out a press release when a particular book is about to come out. Furthermore, if a publisher decides to promote a book, its efforts may not prove sufficient or successful, and you might have to jump in and try to save the day. Although the amount of promotion a publishing company provides will differ from house to house, book to book, and author to author, most publishers will usually:

- Announce the deal to publish the book in Publishers Lunch.
- Announce the publication of the book in their catalog for that season.
- Include the book on their publication list.
- Solicit endorsements or blurbs for the book.
- Send free advance reader copies to selected reviewers, the media, and those who could influence book sales.

Unpublished writers frequently assume that publishing companies employ large, in-house publicity departments that create extensive campaigns, lavish attention on their authors, and send them on glamorous, high-profile, national tours where they're shuttled around in limos and feted at the best restaurants. They get this impression from constantly seeing celebrities and well-known authors plugging their books on TV and other media outlets. So when these novices sign on with publishers, they often expect to receive the same treatment.

Wrong, wrong, wrong! Unfortunately, for most writers, that's no longer how it works. Today, publishers usually earmark the bulk of their promotional budgets for their biggest, most highly recognized authors, those who pull down the biggest advances, not for the rest of the pack. Writers who are not yet established or don't have big names usually have to fend for themselves.

Six huge, multinational corporations now control about 80 percent of the book-publishing industry and a seventh is Disney Publishing Worldwide, a subsidiary of the giant Walt Disney Company. Their publishing divisions must adhere to strict corporate guidelines and no longer operate as looser, less formal businesses. Every facet of each publishing entity is now required to contribute to corporate profits.

To achieve this objective, cost-cutting measures have been imposed and in-house publicity departments have been trimmed drastically. The dynamic publicity machines that houses once maintained are now skeletons of their former selves, so they don't have the staff or the budgets to promote lots of books.

Publishers understand these realities, so they concentrate on putting their in-house promotional resources behind a select group of books and authors, and not all of their titles and writers. They may announce each of their new publications in their catalogs, mention them in other releases, seek endorsements and blurbs, and send out advance reader copies, but often, that's all they do, and many don't even do that.

Publishers expect authors to be their "publicity partners," Jamie Brickhouse, vice president and executive director of publicity at the Perseus Books Group, tells us. "They expect authors to be actively involved in promoting their books."

If you want to go on a national book publicity tour, your publisher won't stop you. It may even suggest bookstores and venues where you could appear, help you plan your route, and give you names of local contacts. It may also arrange to have books on hand wherever you appear, but it usually won't foot the bill. Usually, however, you must pay all these travel expenses.

## Authors' Platform

When publishers are contacted to determine their interest in a particular property, most now ask, "What is the author's platform?" As we stressed in our previous Author 101 books (*Bestselling Book Proposals*

**Robyn Says**

Many publishing houses have shifted the responsibility of providing publicity from themselves to their authors. If, prior to or upon its release, a book shows promise, publishers may decide to crank up their publicity machines and put greater effort into promoting the book.

However, if you want your book to be successful:

- Accept that your publisher probably won't promote your book.
- Create a book-promotion plan.
- Incorporate your promotion plan in your book proposal.
- Keep your promotion plan in mind as you write your book.
- Think beyond this book and shape your promotional efforts to lay the groundwork for sales of books you may subsequently write.

and *Bestselling Secrets from Top Agents*), a platform is the author's continuing national visibility and following—in other words, his or her celebrity. Most publishers now require aspiring nonfiction authors to have national platforms, and they generally won't sign those who haven't firmly established themselves through speaking engagements, writing, teaching, media and Internet presence, government posts, faculty positions, large mailing lists, and professional affiliations. Although a platform isn't as essential for fiction writers, it's still helpful.

Publishers now want authors who can market their books; many now insist on it. Today, for authors to get nonfiction book deals, they need more than good book ideas; they must be entrepreneurial, promotion minded, and willing to energetically sell their books.

For business, psychology, parenting, and relationship books, a national platform is now virtually mandatory. It's no longer enough to be an expert, even a published expert. To be published today, nonfiction authors must be experts who also have national platforms, who beat the bushes to sell their books. Publishers want authors who are well known, admired, and have followers in their fields.

"It's not enough to just have the great idea or to have that great idea and be a great writer. Today, you also have to have a platform, which is a word taken from the IT world," John Willig, president and founder of Literary Services, Inc., explained. "A platform translates to publishers as energy behind the book; it tells them that the author, the author's company, the author's e-mail community, and the author's following will help move the book in an extremely crowded marketplace."

Like so many other businesses, publishing has become hit dominated. So publishers seek out books that have the potential to become bestsellers, generate large profits, and spawn series of related books. They want more than books; they want books that can become brands. Publishers justify their insistence on platforms on the ground that it's hard to break out a book—for it to become a bestseller—when the author doesn't have a strong platform. So they look for writers who have followings that will buy their books and who have proven that they have the ability and experience to vigorously sell their books.

## Finding Your Niche

Before you begin to create your promotional plans, identify and understand your niche. Distinguish your book from the 195,000 titles that will be published in the same year; find the special features that make your book unlike anything else on the market. Research the competition and all similar books in your field to understand why yours is special, how it's different, and why it's better. Then concentrate on that niche in writing your book.

"Every day, the media receives tons of calls regarding authors," New York City publicist Brian Feinblum, of Planned Television Arts, disclosed. "They're contacted about diet books; first-time novels; tomes on how to make money, improve relationships, and cook up 500 tasty recipes. In one week, it's not uncommon for a writer or producer to be hit on by several people regarding each of those genres. So make your book stand out by knowing and being able to explain its uniqueness. Think about linking it to your work, to who you are, to your experiences, your credentials, uniqueness, and personality. If you want to stand out, speak with a unique voice."

Writers who understand how their books fit in the market usually write and promote their books more successfully. "An author who understands where his or her book fits is a total asset," Danielle Chiotti, senior editor at Kensington Publishing, revealed. "My most successful authors are the ones with the clearest visions. They understand who their competitors are and what their market is."

## Action Steps

1. List three reasons why publicity is important to authors.
2. Why is publicizing books more effective than advertising them?
3. List three items that you can expect from publishers' publicists.
4. Explain what the term *author's platform* means.
5. Explain why it's important for authors to know their niches.

### Remember

⚠ **Publicity can inform the public that your book is available, what it's about, why it's important, and the benefits it will provide.** Publishers don't provide strong promotion for all of their books, and the fact that an established house publishes a book doesn't guarantee the book's success.

⚠ **Most publishers now want aspiring authors to have national platforms.** Many of them generally won't sign those who haven't established a following by speaking, writing, teaching, their media and Internet presence, government posts, faculty positions, mailing lists, and professional affiliations. Authors now bear the burden of publicizing their books.

**CHAPTER 3**

Eighty percent of success is showing up.
*Woody Allen*

# What's Your Silver Bullet?

**THIS CHAPTER COVERS:**

▶ What is your book about?
▶ Identify your book's niche
▶ How will your book benefit others?
▶ Connect with the media
▶ Writing your silver bullet
▶ Backup material

THE BOOK-BUYING MARKET is densely crowded and difficult to crack. When you try to enter, you'll be thrust dead center into an information-intensive world in which everyone is competing for the attention of those who have endless other options. When you try to tell them about your book, many won't listen. They may be busy or just numb from being constantly besieged by endless messages from advertisers; charities; political, educational, and community organizations; as well as their families, neighbors, and friends. They may even act as if they're listening and never hear a word.

The problem is that everyone has been overwhelmed by "media noise," that blare of unending messages that try to convince us to buy or support something. And, essentially, that is what you must also do to promote your book. To publicize your book, you have to dive into tightly crowded waters and try to get through to people who have virtually stopped listening. And those who are still open to listening tend to have very short attention spans. They protect themselves with super-sensitive filters that automatically switch off if the first five or six words don't grab them.

Getting people to listen to your message has become more than a challenge; it's become a feat, and many don't succeed. However, we know how to get through. We've taught it to thousands of authors and know how it can work for you. By following the guidelines in this book—with planning; attention; and a positive, creative, and orderly approach—your message can be heard.

To get your message heard, you must know exactly what you're selling, which will make it music rather than noise. If you know what you're selling, you can target your message so that your audience will hear and respond to it. If your message isn't targeted, it will be swallowed up and lost in the media noise.

Describe what you're selling in your "silver bullet": the sharply focused pitch that you can deliver to cut through the media noise. Your silver bullet can also be called your elevator speech, pitch, sound bite, or message. It's called an elevator speech because it should be delivered in the time it takes an elevator to rise from the lobby to the fourth floor.

Think of your silver bullet as the verbal business card for your book. It's a brief, memorable description that you quickly give people you meet or those who may be interested in your book. Your silver bullet is your core message, the unique selling proposition that you must get across if you hope to successfully promote your book. It must

In publicizing your book, your objective must be to get more than just ink. Some authors excel at generating tons of publicity, they get loads of media coverage, but their books languish and don't sell.

The object of publicity is to sell your book, so you need to generate media coverage and build strong word-of-mouth sales. Your silver bullet must do more than produce media coverage; it must make people want to buy your book.

penetrate your target market and be delivered rapidly and powerfully before your small window of media attention slams shut.

Your silver bullet must clearly explain in the most palatable terms

- What your book is about,
- Why it's special, and
- Precisely how it will benefit your audience.

Without these ingredients, few will listen. Before you try to write your silver bullet, take a few preliminary steps. They are:

- Come up with a plan that will sell.
- Understand your book's niche.
- Define your book's specific benefits.
- Understand the media and how it works.

### Your Book's Niche

To clearly describe your book, you must know what it's about and whom it targets. What it's about will be what you're selling, and whom it targets identifies the audience to whom you hope to sell it.

Agents and editors tell us that a surprisingly large number of writers can't clearly explain what their books are about. These authors usually can detail their motivation, philosophies, and their personal dreams, but they can't describe the specific benefits their books will give their readers. For example, they don't say that it will teach novices to hook up computer networks, to bake mouthwatering lemon squares, or to design stylish children's sweaters.

When authors can't clearly describe their books, agents and editors usually conclude—with good reason—that they can't write a salable book. And if writers can't describe their own books, how can they expect agents or publishers to sell them?

Instead of describing their books, many authors tend to litter their descriptions with unverified, and often unbelievable, superlatives. They might say, "This is the best, the most informative, the most up to date, or

**Robyn Says**

After you've defined your audience, identify the benefits that your book will provide to them. State that by reading your book, readers will learn to network at business events, to prevent disputes with teenage children, or to respond promptly to life-threatening illnesses.

Some book titles clearly explain the benefits they provide, such as *The Everything® Guide to Writing a Novel,* but most are not that clear. In an attempt to be catchy or clever, many are vague as to what they provide. Many books overcome the problem by explaining the benefits in their subtitles. For example, in Rick's *Networking Magic,* the subtitle is *Find the Best—From Doctors, Lawyers, and Accountants to Homes, Schools, and Jobs.* In my book *The GIFTionary,* the subtitle reads *An A–Z Reference Guide for Solving Your Gift-Giving Dilemmas . . . Forever!*

the only book on. . . ." Or, they will claim that it will become a runaway bestseller, an all-time classic, or a great TV series. In describing your book, forget the hype and stick to the facts. Simply state what it will do.

To create an effective publicity campaign, understand your niche. Since the public has so many options and listens so selectively, your first big hurdle, which can be huge, is to get their attention! To make them stop and listen, you must know:

- What your book is about.
- Exactly for whom it was written.

Clarify who your audience is; identify the specific group or groups that will be most likely to buy your book and why they would buy it. If you believe that your book has a broad or universal appeal, name the demographic groups that would be most interested in it, according to their size. Don't fool yourself into thinking that it will appeal to everyone, because it probably won't, and it will distort who your audience actually is.

Authors tend to mistakenly believe that it's better to appeal to wider, broader-based audiences than smaller, more defined groups. They don't want to overlook any potential buyers and think that if they pitch larger groups, more people will buy their books. However, publishing experts tell us that the opposite is true: The shotgun approach seldom attracts as many readers as tightly targeted methods do.

Know your niche. Identify the principal audience that will most likely read your book, and then focus your publicity campaign on it. Then, if you believe that your book will appeal to additional audiences, decide what resources, if any, you will commit to reaching those additional groups.

## Your Book's Benefits

Readers buy books because of the benefits they hope to receive. They may want news and information, mental stimulation, or just to escape. Often, they may want to learn how to solve particular problems such as putting up a Web site, making electrical repairs, or preparing holiday dinners.

When you're competing in such a crowded market, tell potential buyers the precise benefits they will get from your book. Explain specific problems your book will solve, new information it will provide, or hidden secrets it will reveal. Draw up lists of the important facts contained in your book, and material that is controversial, shocking, or groundbreaking. Be prepared to rattle off a dozen specific issues that your book addresses.

Don't fall into the trap of generalizing or being vague when you can be precise, even if you think it could attract more readers. In reality, readers whom you address specifically are usually the only ones who listen to your words. So, be specific, exact, and leave no room for doubt.

## Connect with the Media

In our information-intensive society, the media controls the channels through which information circulates. Those channels include print publications, television, radio, and the Internet. The media finds, shapes, and disseminates most of what we read, see, and hear. So, to publicize your book, you virtually always have to go through the media. Although we will discuss connecting with the media in detail in Chapter 6, "Build Bridges with the Media," it's important to start thinking about working with the media now.

Since the media is in the information business, it continually needs a steady stream of new information to survive, and it receives tons of it. Usually, far more than it can use. This requires people in the media to take time from their already jammed schedules to continually sift through stacks of leads with the hope of uncovering items they might use. Basically, they quickly scan for flags, key words, or phrases that attract their attention, and if they don't immediately find them, they quickly move on to the next lead.

The media is interested in news. It will cover you, your book, or information in it if it considers you or it newsworthy. Demonstrate to the media that the items you submit are newsworthy, that a significant segment of the public will be interested in them. See Chapter 6 for information on how to work with the media.

## Writing Your Silver Bullet

Your silver bullet should serve the same purpose as a newspaper or magazine headline: to grab people's attention and compel them to want to learn more. Make your silver bullet the centerpiece of your promotional campaign; the initial piece you put in place to clarify, define, and give your campaign direction. Frequently, your silver bullet will be the first impression you make, the attention-grabbing device that will get you and your book noticed, covered, and remembered.

Writing your silver bullet is an important exercise because it forces you to examine your book and identify the features that your readers will find most interesting. Define those features as specifically as possible and then encapsulate them in a short statement that quickly, clearly,

> ### *Expand Your Audience*
> Different people often have different takes on similar matters. So, people outside your target audience might recognize potential benefits that you may have overlooked. Speak with those who are not in your target reader groups and who are outside your area of expertise. Tell them about your book and the its specific benefits. Answer their questions and get their reactions. Frequently, their input can expand your perspective and inform you of benefits of your book with which you may not have been aware.

and compellingly describes your book. Be creative. Make your silver bullet a grabber, a memorable message that will make listeners want to buy your book and talk about it.

In your silver bullet, the two most important ingredients are:

- **Clarity.** Your silver bullet must clearly explain what your book is about and the benefits it provides so that your audience recognizes that it contains something of interest to them. If buyers purchase your book and subsequently feel that it did not deliver what you promised, they will feel deceived and ripped off and won't support your book. In fact, they may even badmouth it. Since the success of books depends on recommendations, you want to build reader support, not antipathy.
- **Brevity.** In most cases, you get little time to make your pitch—so be quick. Expect your targets to be busy, have other voices vying for their attention, and have short attention spans. So, to get them to listen, use short pitches that go straight to the point, headlines, and quick overviews, and avoid long, protracted stories. The more you can say quickly, the better—but don't ramble; if your silver bullet is too long, they will stop listening.

Write a description of your book that you can reel off in twenty to thirty seconds. Then, trim it to about twenty seconds, and ten to fifteen seconds for the media. Radio news segments come in ten-second increments, and if you can't say what you need to in ten seconds, media people will stop listening.

Make your elevator speech interesting enough to attract immediate interest, powerful enough to be remembered, and convincing enough to stir overloaded listeners into action. Explain in twenty seconds or less (1) what your book is about and (2) the benefits readers will receive. As much as you may be tempted, don't go into why you wrote it.

Examples of effective silver bullets are:

- At 350 pounds, I nearly broke the scale. Now I'm a size 8. My book, *Lopping It Off*, will show anyone how to lose and keep off weight. Guaranteed!
- Filled with exotic, heart-stopping, erotic adventure, my new novel, *Paris to Hoi An*, will leave you breathless and glued to your seat. It will make every part of your body tingle.
- Fire employees without being sued. Avoid costly, time-consuming, and disruptive lawsuits—even in the most contentious situations.
- Save lives in the most critical medical emergencies with *Dr. Fischer's Little Book of Big Emergencies*. It easily fits in your pocket or purse.
- Reading *Trapped Underwater* will keep you awake all night and gasping for air the entire next day. It's the thriller lover's thriller!
- Literary agents sell books. Find the right one for you in *Author 101*, where top agents tell writers how to identify, interest, and sign with the best agents.
- *Everything for Love* tells the heroic, heartwarming, and inspirational true story of a man who walked across two continents to find the woman he loved.

Take a closer look at your book. Then answer these questions:

*What is most interesting or unusual about your book?*
*What makes your book most memorable?*

*What three important benefits will readers receive from your book?*

*What differentiates your book from titles on the same or similar subjects?*

*What are the responses you receive when you tell people about your book?*

*What causes people to stop, listen, or say "wow"?*

*What questions do people ask when you tell them about your book?*

## Writing and Making It Great

Compose and perfect your silver bullet by following these guidelines:

1. Write the first ideas that come to mind without worrying how long they run or how much space they occupy. Don't even worry about whether they make sense. Be honest and truthful, but take the most positive, rosy approach. Get your thoughts down on paper, raw as they may be.

2. When you finish listing your ideas:
   a. Circle each descriptive word you wrote.
   b. List all the circled words on a new sheet of paper.
   c. Place all those words in the order of their importance to readers.
   d. Question whether each word you selected is the most descriptive and colorful word available.
   e. If not, add or substitute more colorful, illustrative or hard-hitting words.

3. Draft a silver bullet that consists of one or two short sentences. Initially, don't worry about length. Make sure that you include the most important words and that you clearly communicate your message. Clarity is paramount—don't sacrifice clarity to be clever.

4. Read your silver bullet aloud five to ten times and listen to it closely. Then, change anything that feels awkward. Trust your ear.

5. Recite your silver bullet to others, solicit their input, and consider making changes they suggest. Ask them to be totally honest with you, but understand that they probably won't want to hurt you.

6. Recite your silver bullet aloud until you can say it smoothly, comfortably, and with ease and assurance every time. When you believe it, others will also. You will also be more confident and convincing.

7. Time how long your silver bullet runs. If it's more than thirty seconds, first cut it to thirty seconds or less. After you've got it below thirty seconds, try to lop off another ten to fifteen seconds without weakening your message.

8. Don't memorize your silver bullet; instead, picture the key words and recite them as if you're telling friends what you ate for lunch.

9. Practice, practice, practice. Recite your silver bullet until you can do it perfectly every time. Practice before a mirror, in your car, and tape yourself. Don't act, emote, or be dramatic. Speak conversationally, with sincerity, and be prepared to be interrupted.

When you state your silver bullet, maintain eye contact and smile softly. Show listeners that you're eager to deliver your message and that you believe in yourself and your message.

Speak with authority, excitement, and passion. Excitement and passion are contagious. Your audiences will sense your conviction, feed off it, and want to share their feelings with others.

Look for opportunities to give your silver bullet and recite it frequently. Carry plenty of your business cards to distribute with your pitch. Also have on hand your brochures or other materials that you can distribute liberally. Make sure that they each give the name of your book and your contact information. Work your way around rooms; approach new faces and introduce yourself by reciting your silver bullet. Repetition reinforces name recognition and brand identity and builds confidence.

Customize your silver bullet for specific audiences and situations. For example, if you're at an auto dealers' meeting, sprinkle in terms relating to that industry, like "on all cylinders," "out of gas," or "cruise control." Using their language breaks down barriers, lightens the mood, and makes groups feel that you're speaking directly to them. In doing so, you become one of them, at least for the time you're together.

Prepare an alternate silver bullet. Use your alternate if your original feels inappropriate, if someone else in the group has a strikingly similar pitch, or if it doesn't seem to be going over.

Write ad-libs that you can add to sound spontaneous. Comment on or work in references to hot news items, scandals, or events that will make your sound bite more relevant and up to date. However, since your main objective is to get your message across, don't make alterations that could take away from the clarity or impact of your message.

Trust your instincts. You'll quickly learn how and when to alter your silver bullet. Sometimes, you may find yourself altering it just for your own interest or amusement.

## Backup Material

After you recite your silver bullet, be prepared to answer questions or provide additional information. Answer all questions fully and directly. Occasionally, when appropriate, tie an answer to your book, but don't force connections that don't fit smoothly. It will make you seem manipulative,

---

### Author 101 Advice

Since newspapers understand the importance of headlines, they employ individuals who specialize in writing them for the articles they print. The papers have taken this extra step because they understand the importance of headlines and know that the feature writers may not come up with outstanding headlines or that they may be too close to their stories. Well, you can suffer from the same problem.

Fortunately, most of us know people who have a real knack for coming up with clever names and titles. So call upon them. Make them a part of your team and consult closely with them on writing your silver bullet. Also enlist their help in writing the title and subtitle of your book and headlines for your press releases, Web site, and other promotional materials.

insincere, and a huckster. Avoid referring to your book, and never state "As it says in my book" or "As I wrote on page 93." It will turn people off, especially the media. Print a handout containing frequently asked questions and their answers, fact sheets, and/or an interview with you.

Prepare information that expands upon your silver bullet or introduces secondary points that were not included. Facts and statistics make great supplemental materials. Write up your secondary information and distribute it in handouts. Write it as a news release and use your silver bullet as the headline or lead sentence. Then, bullet-point five to seven additional items and address each of them in a brief sentence or two.

Carry plenty of copies of your news release, brochures, information sheets, or other written material and freely give them out. Make sure that the name of your book and your contact information are clearly listed on every page. Also have ordering information for your book with you. Limit all handouts to a page or two.

Since everyone has different interests, some may ask about or comment on subjects that catch you completely off guard. Their inquiries and interests may be tangential to yours or involve things you don't know or about which you don't care. They may also be looking for you to provide answers that will solve their special problems. In these situations, don't bluff. When you don't know the answers, explain that you don't know, but volunteer to check into it and get back to them. Make a written note so you won't forget to find and get them the answers as promised. Getting back to them could gain you ardent supporters.

## Be Patient

Finding your silver bullet and mastering how to deliver it to others usually takes time, trial, and error. Your initial ideas may not work, so be open to other approaches. Pay careful attention to anything listeners don't seem to understand or believe and then fix it.

Keep trying to come up with different and better ideas until you find those that work. Test your silver bullet on your family and friends.

Send up trial balloons and observe their reactions. Ask for their opinions and make sure that you're getting your message across.

When you're convinced that your message is consistently getting through, consider adding another thought or concept. Operate on a two-step approach: First, give your basic, stripped-down, core silver bullet; then, follow it up with additional information that is no more than twice as long. Proceed cautiously and abandon providing any additional information if listeners' eyes glaze over or they seem to stray.

## Action Steps

1. Write a silver bullet that you can recite within twenty seconds.
2. List the two most important requirements for your silver bullet.
3. Describe what your book is about.
4. List the precise benefits your book will give readers.
5. List three ad-libs that you could add to your silver bullet.

### Remember

⚠ **To publicize your book, you must capture people's attention in a world filled with media noise.** The best way to do so is to write a silver bullet—a clear, sharply focused description of your book that can be recited in the time it takes an elevator to go from the ground to the fourth floor. Your silver bullet must clearly explain what your book is about, why it's special, and the precise benefits it will provide to readers.

⚠ **Learn how the media operates because it controls the channels through which information is dispensed.** Make yourself valuable to the media by becoming a media resource. Have additional information on hand that you can distribute after you've given your silver bullet.

**CHAPTER 4**

Give us the tools, and we will finish the job.
*Sir Winston Churchill*

# Your Book Publicity Tool Kit

**THIS CHAPTER COVERS:**

▶ Inventorying your tools
▶ Web sites
▶ Media lists
▶ Media kits
▶ Press releases
▶ Authors' information
▶ Additional items

PROFESSIONALS ALWAYS come prepared. Good plumbers don't show up at your home unless they have all the right tools with them. And, they keep their equipment in shipshape condition so repairs go smoothly.

Well, the same holds true when you want to publicize your book; you need to have the right tools and they must be ready to use. Having the right tools is an indispensable part of being prepared.

Numerous tools can help you publicize your book. However, for our purpose, lets classify them in two basic categories. They are:

1. Primary tools, items that are essential and that no promotional campaign should attempt to proceed without, and
2. Secondary tools, those that are not essential but can help your campaign be more productive.

# Inventorying Your Tools

In Chapter 3, we discussed the author's silver bullet, which is an author's number one publicity tool. No book publicity campaign should proceed without a silver bullet. In addition, every campaign should include the following primary tools, which we will subsequently address in greater detail. The primary tools include the following.

- Web sites
- Media lists
- Media kits
- Press releases
- Biographies
- Photographs of the author in color and black and white, including one of the author in an action shot, perhaps signing the book or doing something that relates to the book
- Question-and-answer sheets
- Business cards
- Newsletters
- Promotional materials

### Additional Tools

The number of additional tools that you can use in your campaign is as extensive as your imagination. Finding them can be an exercise in creativity. Unlike the primary tools, which are a must for every campaign, additional tools should be plugged in only when they can be helpful, because adding tools you don't need can clutter your campaign and weaken the impact of initiatives that could be more productive.

The following items are examples of some of the additional devices you can use. Be creative and come up with other promotional tools of your own that could help you publicize your book. Additional promotional tools include the following.

- Articles
- Blogs
- Book excerpts
- Bookmarks
- Brochures
- Clippings
- Contests
- Endorsements/recommendations
- Fact sheets
- Gimmicks
- Graphics (photographs, charts, diagrams, lists, illustrations)
- Handouts
- List of top topics for the media
- Op-ed piece
- Pitch letter
- Postcards
- Puzzles
- Quizzes
- Quotations
- Reviews
- Sample chapter
- Stories about the book
- Toll-free telephone number
- Videos

## Web Sites

Web sites are more than extensions of individuals' or businesses' identities; they are major parts of their identities. When parties are interested in an individual, a product, a service, or a business, they frequently go to its Web site. At the least, the Web site tells them about their target's accomplishments and how they present themselves.

New York City literary agent Richard Curtis told us that when he first speaks via telephone to editors about an author and the author's book, he frequently hears their keyboards. The editors, according to Curtis, go straight to the author's Web site and then frequently discuss information it provides with Curtis.

Well, the media operates similarly. When it hears or receives information about authors or books, it visits their Web sites. The media searches for insights on who the authors are, what they look like, their backgrounds, interests, expertise, accomplishments, writing, and how they present themselves. It looks for information that could help determine whether an author or a book is worth pursuing.

Your Web site should include everything that is in your media kit, including your press release, biography, questions and answers, excerpts or sample chapters of your book, and book ordering information. Web sites and blogs, which are online logs or diaries, will be discussed in more detail in Chapter 10, "Web Sites and Blogs."

## Media Lists

Media lists are databases that contain the names of media contacts that can promote your book and information about them. Build large, comprehensive lists in terms of both the number of contacts you include and the information you record about them. Add entries for anyone who could conceivably help promote your book because the least likely contact might be the one who latches onto your book and does the most to publicize it.

At a minimum, your media list should include each contact's:

- Name
- Employer or business
- Work address
- E-mail address
- Telephone numbers

- ■ Job title
- ■ Specialty areas or interests
- ■ Credits

In a media list, the more information you collect, the better. Additional information can help you break the ice with contacts, warm them up, or help you to become a more valuable resource. This information includes:

- ■ How you got their names.
- ■ How and where you met.
- ■ Common friends, associates, experiences, hobbies, and interests.

On the entry for each contact, note the projects you pitched him or her, the dates, when you last spoke, and the specific outcome. Also list anything you sent the contact and how you sent it so you don't duplicate the effort.

Study the media to discover who's covering your field and related areas. Check out writers, reporters, editors, radio and TV producers, publicists, and interesting individuals such as experts or authorities in similar or allied fields. Research these individuals by reading their stories and watching or listening to their programs; then add their names and information to your media list.

Contact local newspapers and magazines, radio and TV stations, and online publications to get the names of those who cover areas that could help promote your book. Collect business cards from everyone you meet, and add entries to your list for those in the media.

Subscribe to Internet services that provide names and information on media contacts. Books that list media contacts quickly fall out of date because so many people in the media are on the move. Although Internet services, which are updated frequently, may be more reliable, verify all information that they provide before making contact.

Internet services that furnish media contact information include the following.

- Bacon's MediaLists Online—*www.medialistsonline.com*
- MediaMap Online—*www.mediamaponline.com*
- Online Public Relations—*www.online-pr.com*
- BurrellesLuce—*www.burrellesluce.com*

Since the turnover is so great, update your entire media list regularly—at least every three months. As soon as you hear about a change, update your list. Keeping your media list current is essential in order to reach contacts when you need them. Otherwise, you may end up wasting time and energy trying to connect with people who are no longer at their old jobs.

An easy way to check whether information on your list is current is to send a postcard to each contact. Make sure to include a return address, and when cards are returned undelivered, delete those entries from your list. To more sharply focus aspects of your campaign, prioritize the entries in your list. Create three separate categories.

### A-List

In this group, list only the top sources that can give your book the most or best publicity. Usually, this category includes national media or national trade/industry media, outlets that have the most power and reach. Think of biggies like *Oprah*, the *Today* show, and the *New York Times*, to name just a few. Make a list of your best sources.

### B-List

The B-list consists of other, less powerful, national media and the top media in large metropolitan areas. These outlets may be great for focused local campaigns. Repeated coverage by B-list media can be equivalent to A-list coverage. List your secondary sources.

### C-List

Local or regional media. For local promotions, this group can be ideal, and it may be more willing to give you coverage. In some campaigns, concentrating on local coverage can provide better value. List other sources that could help.

Don't discount the value of building a strong media base in your hometown. A supportive local base can be extremely loyal and helpful in expanding your contacts. Usually, locals will take special pride in your success and go to great length to boost your career.

## Media Kits

Elaborate media kits that high-priced PR firms traditionally produce are seldom worth the cost and they usually don't help to effectively publicize books. The media has seen it all and has little time or patience for overstuffed packages, no matter how beautifully they're written, designed, and produced.

In a media kit, which is also called a press kit, all you really need is:

1. A killer press release.
2. The author's biography.
3. The author's photograph.
4. An excerpt or sample chapter from the book.
5. A list of suggested questions to ask the author, with their answers.

If you want to sweeten the package, throw in a list of the author's articles and appearances. You can also provide the book's brochure,

Rick Says

If you're on a limited budget, sending a bulky media kit probably won't be cost effective. Instead, just send your press release and bio. Then, if anyone from the media requests additional information, send a media kit loaded with everything you've got. When additional information is requested, you can't overdo it.

copies of articles and reviews, endorsements and testimonials for the book and author, quizzes, quotations, trivia, and giveaways.

The focal point of a media kit is the press release, which is also called the news release, and it must be outstanding. The press release may be the only item in the media kit that is read. If your press release isn't terrific, the media could stop reading and toss your entire kit in the trash. Place your press release in your media kit package face-up so it can be immediately seen when the kit is opened. And make it look and read great!

## Press Releases

The media gets flooded with press releases, so it doesn't give them much attention. At best, the media quickly scans press releases, sets aside a few that may be intriguing, and discards the rest. At first glance, it may seem foolish to go to the trouble of writing a press release when few people will actually read it, but the cost isn't great and you can never be sure whom it will excite. All it takes is one person to be intrigued by your book and decide to cover it, because when he or she does, others frequently follow suit.

The objective of press releases is to be informative, to provide information that stirs up interest and generates responses. Hopefully, someone will contact you and say, "The item you sent sounds interesting. Tell me more about it." Even though it may not read press releases, the media wants to receive them because they're a good source of information. The media gets lots of good leads from press releases.

Since the media receives so many press releases, it tends to be picky, and it looks for information in a particular format. Sending press releases in the right format tells it that you know the rules and that your release is more likely to convey information of interest. Releases that are not in the proper format usually won't get much of a look.

To increase your chances of getting your press release noticed, consider the following guidelines.

- Keep it to one page. Publicists refer to press releases as "one sheets," so don't make them longer. Remember that the media has little time to read and wants to get information succinctly.
- Print it on white 8½" by 11" paper with no letterhead or designs. Releases on colored paper with borders and designs may get attention but probably won't be read.
- In the upper left-hand corner write, "For Immediate Release," which makes it clear that the information sent may be used. However, if you don't want the information used until a certain date, write, "For Release on May 15, 2006."
- On the first line in the upper right-hand corner, state, "For further information contact:"
- Then under it, on the second line in the upper right-hand corner, give your name, phone number, and e-mail address. If you want them to contact someone else, give that person's name and contact information.

### Headlines

Start your press release with a great headline that will convince the media to read further. "The headline of a press release has one job and one job only," according to press release guru Paul Hartunian. "The only job of a press release headline is to force the reporter to keep reading. The headline has no other job. Don't force your press release headline to do anything more than force the reporter to keep reading. That's a big enough job!"

In press releases, headlines are critical. They're the first, and often the only, thing the media reads. If your headline doesn't immediately grab the reader's attention, your release usually won't be read.

To seize the media's attention, link your headlines to:

1. Money
2. Sex
3. Health
4. Controversy

Compose lively, one-line headlines that will make the media read further. Be bold, daring, and risqué. Take chances; be provocative, naughty, and controversial. Lure readers into reading more.

*"Never Pay Taxes and Stay out of Jail"*
*"Three Can't-Miss Secrets to Looking Younger"*
*"Scandalous, Forbidden Secrets on Every Page"*
*"Make Rich Men Fall in Love with You"*
*"Nothing to Lose, So Desperate Killers Run Wild"*
*"Five Ways to a Free College Education"*

Headlines should (1) be no more than one line and (2) take only seconds to read. When a headline grabs the media's attention, you get additional time to explain further.

### Editing Headlines

Writers frequently can't edit their own writing because they overlook their own mistakes. Whenever possible, have someone else edit your writing.

Read newspapers and magazines and keep copies of headlines you like. Try to determine why you liked them and what interested you in them. Identify words, phrases, or usages that were strong. Then, try to write your own headlines for those same stories.

Visit Web sites. Web sites are headline intensive, so study them closely. Print the screens you like and circle the best headlines and underline the best, most descriptive, and colorful words. Then, write your headlines and bullets using the same techniques.

Often, it's more productive to write your headline after you've drafted the body of the press release. Your headline should tie the content of your release together with a catchy or descriptive phrase that will grab readers and make them want additional information. Headlines must be short, one-line summaries that briefly introduce your book in the most colorful words. Study newspapers, magazines, and Web sites for examples of great headlines. Save them for future reference. Also compile a list of hard-hitting words that create strong impact.

### The Body

The text of press releases should give information quickly, in a short, fast, easy-to-read page written in the "who, what, where, why, and how" format. It should let the media quickly determine why it should carry your story, why it will interest its audience, and what benefit it will get from it.

Write releases in the journalistic style used by the print media because outlets may publish them, or parts of them, with little or no changes, especially when they're faced with tight deadlines. The format of a press release isn't as important for the electronic media because it treats them as leads that it must investigate further. The electronic media is used to getting information in the journalistic format and then shaping it according to its own needs.

Write your press release in three parts: (1) Introduce your book and the problems it will solve, (2) give your credentials, and (3) explain what action you would like the media to take.

For the print media, the first paragraph of your press release is vital. It should run no more than two or three sentences and set forth all the main points covered in the release. Don't clutter up your opening paragraph with details. The press isn't interested in every trivial point and will fly right past them. Unnecessary information can turn off readers, which could kill your more important points. If you must include details, stick them at the end of your release or, better yet, put them in a separate, more comprehensive article that you include with your media kit.

After the first paragraph, amplify your lead, but hold your release to one page. The lead paragraph should inform the media about your book, so treat it as an announcement. Then, explain your lead in the subsequent paragraphs by providing background, more specific or additional information such as points you didn't cover in the lead, and some statistics. A great way to do so is with bullets. You can also place bulleted items in a box or shade them. Prioritize your bulleted items and list them in order of their importance because readers may not get through the entire list. Write five to seven bullets, with five being preferable. Each bulleted item should not exceed two concise sentences, and one sentence is preferable. Write bullets crisply so they are short, clear, and hard hitting.

After you've described your book, give your credentials. Concisely show why you're so eminently qualified to write this book. Stress your experience, but don't list all your degrees, awards, or accomplishments.

---

### Solve, Don't Sell

In your press release, show that you are an expert who can solve real problems. State the name of your book only in passing and just to show your credentials. Don't give its price or ordering information because it will make you look like you're trying to sell your book when your job is to give problem-solving information.

If your release makes it appear that you're just trying to sell your book, you probably won't get an interview or feature article. Instead, focus on problem solving. Think in terms of "Homeowners' Biggest Mistakes in Hiring Contractors," "Sick of Always Being Cheated by Repair Shops?" or "How to Keep All the Money You Earn."

Limit yourself to those that best relate to your qualifications to write your book. If you want to add quotes, press release expert Paul Hartunian recommends, "Always quote yourself. Never quote anyone else. Why give someone else any attention in your release? It's your release. If they want some attention, let them get their own release!"

In the final paragraph, state what you want the media to do: contact you for more information, read your book, or come to your event. Include your contact information at both the top and bottom of each page.

Don't send a contact the same press release more than once unless it's specifically requested. Forwarding the same release again usually wastes your resources and could alienate recipients. Don't send the same press release to more than one online distribution service because they all send releases to the same recipients.

### Radio and TV

As we mentioned, people in the electronic media react differently to press releases than those in the print media do. Radio and TV people seldom read press releases, but when they do, they usually scan the headlines and bullets. Unlike print journalists, radio and TV producers can't simply run your press release in the exact form that it was sent. If they're interested in your story, their work is just beginning. They need to come up with an angle and then line up guests, prepare questions, and produce the segment. Radio and TV producers are interested in story ideas, so frame your press release to list the precise feature stories they would get by covering you. The best approach is usually to point out specific problems and show how you would solve them. Get producers' attention fast because they have loads to do in little time. Sell them within ten seconds or they won't read further. Since radio and TV love controversy, radio expert Alex Carroll suggests including a controversy sheet that lists the arguments your appearance can generate. For example, on one side of the sheet, make your point: "Artificial Sweeteners Help You Lose Weight." Directly next to it, on the other side of the sheet, give the opposing argument: "Artificial Sweeteners Create Health Hazards." Also add a sentence describing each opposing point.

Review the sample press releases below and see how you can adapt them to inform the media about your book.

## SAMPLE PRESS RELEASE NUMBER 1

Media Contact: Willy Spizman
THE SPIZMAN AGENCY
Tel: 770-953-2040
Email: willy@spizmanagency.com

FOR IMMEDIATE RELEASE:

**The Most Dangerous Hour of Your Life**
**Six Essential Tips to Make Your Commute Productive and Less Stressful**

ATLANTA (date)—Do you know which hour of your day is the most dangerous? Which of your daily activities is more stressful than what fighter pilots or what police officers experience in training? Do you know what you do each day that accelerates your aging process and is taking as many as 10 years off your life? The answer is your daily commute.

More than 3.4 million Americans now travel at least 90 minutes each way to work. Some extreme commuters even travel over time zones. Five days a week, morning and evening, we race for the best seat on the train, the last spot on the bus, the fastest lane on the highway, the choicest parking space in the lot. Increasingly, we can feel angry and frustrated at others for being in our way; worse, science tells us commuting is a threat to our health. What can you do to make your commute an oasis? How can you refresh and renew yourself during your drive to and from work?

Stress management expert Dr. Kathleen Hall, founder of The Stress Institute, advises daily commuters to take advantage of a seemingly bad situation by using the time constructively to better themselves. She dedicates

*continued*

*continued*

an entire chapter to commuting in her book *Alter Your Life: Overbooked? Overworked? Overwhelmed?* This arduous chore can be transformed into an opportunity for personal growth and self-development. Use the time to meditate or pray, listen to audiobooks or language tapes, refresh and renew yourself, or simply enjoy having quiet time alone in your mobile oasis.

Gain a new perspective on your commute by discussing:

*The toll commuting takes on our health*
*How to change your commute from a dreaded task to a welcome opportunity*
*Why waving to fellow commuters is better than other hand signals*
*How science tells us that commuters face more stress than fighter pilots*
*Why Monday morning commutes are the most dangerous*

Please contact The Spizman Agency to arrange an interview with Dr. Kathleen Hall. Thank you for your consideration.

## SAMPLE PRESS RELEASE NUMBER 2

Media Contact: Willy Spizman
THE SPIZMAN AGENCY
Tel: 770-953-2040
Email: willy@spizmanagency.com

FOR IMMEDIATE RELEASE:

**Teen Writes Book to Inspire the Art of Saying Thank You!**

ATLANTA (date)—How do you thank a hero? Do they teach saying thank you at Harvard? How do you write a meaningful thank-you note? Teenager Ali Spizman answers those questions and tells today's technologically

*continued*

*continued*

savvy youth why saying thank you and spreading kindness is both meaningful and cool in the newly released and first *Thank You Book for Kids:
Hundreds of Creative, Cool and Clever Ways to Say Thank You!* (Active Parenting, *www.activeparenting.com*, $12.95)

"Saying thank you is a very powerful way to let someone know you appreciate them. If more kids would treat each other with kindness and respect,
perhaps everyone would get along better. Plus, saying thank you reminds
us how many people we have to be thankful for and there are so many
opportunities to express our appreciation," said Ali.

In the *Thank You Book for Kids*, Ali shows how easy it is to turn a thank-you
chore into an activity even the "coolest" kids can enjoy. She offers dozens
of easy suggestions for writing memorable notes, and her Web site, *www
.thankyoukids.com*, is a helpful resource for kids. Ali believes now is the
time, more than ever, to share a thank-you. In her book, she shares her creative tips to inspire other kids to write meaningful notes and express their
feelings year-round. Her book also includes thank-you wisdom from many
noted celebrities and individuals, including Michael Eisner, Wally "Famous"
Amos, R. L. Stine, the president of Harvard, *Apollo 17* astronaut Eugene A.
Cernan, and many others.

Please call if you wish to interview Ali or request additional information.
Her book is available at local bookstores and online at *www.amazon.com*
and *www.activeparenting.com*. See her Web site at *www.thankyoukids
.com* for more information. Media Contact: The Spizman Agency, at *www
.spizmanagency.com*.

## Author's Information

You will need to consider how your personal information is going to
be presented. More so than in other forms of media, a nonfiction book
draws heavily from the author and how they're portrayed.

### Your Biography

Your bio should paint a portrait of you through your accomplishments. Your bio is your opportunity to blow your own horn—tell the media who you are, what you've done, and how you accomplished it. Make its tone light and personable but impressive. Let your achievements show how interesting and accomplished you are so the media will want to cover you and your book. Be succinct and write no more than a half to two-thirds of a page. Be current and also provide some background. Your bio is intended to convey information, so be direct and concise, not verbose; it's not the place for you to be poetic.

Outline your training, experience, and achievements in chronological order. Also list your hobbies; interests; and charitable, civic, social, and athletic activities because readers might connect with them. Remember that you are trying to paint a picture. To get inspiration, read the authors' biographies in a number of other books. Note the type of information authors provide in order to give readers a sense of who they are.

## SAMPLE BIOGRAPHY NUMBER 1

Dr. Kevin Leman
*Making Children Mind While Not Losing Yours,* Revised

Dr. Kevin Leman is an internationally known psychologist, bestselling author, popular television and radio personality, and well-traveled guest lecturer. He has helped millions of parents raise a generation of healthy children, having personally counseled thousands.

Dr. Leman has appeared on all the major national television shows, including *Oprah*; NBC's *Today* show, *Early Today*, and *Later Today*; CNN, ABC's *The View* and *Live With Regis and Kathie Lee*; and CBS's *Early Show*. He was the consulting family psychologist for *Good Morning America* and has also made house calls on *The 700 Club*, *Focus on the Family*, and *Midday Connection*.

*continued*

*continued*

As the host of the new nationally syndicated television program, *RealFA-MILIES*, broadcast on Trinity Broadcasting Network, Dr. Leman continues to inform millions of parents and couples of how to raise their children. He is also the cohost of *Parent Talk,* the nation's first syndicated live radio show in which parents talk to parents.

Dr. Leman is the author of 21 books, with several million copies in print, including bestsellers *The New Birth Order, Making Children Mind Without Losing Yours,* and *Sex Begins in the Kitchen.*

He is the founder and president of COUPLES OF PROMISE, a church-based program seeking to stabilize marriages. He was a keynote speaker for MARRIAGE BUILDERS, a series of large, arena-filled seminars to help couples improve their relationships. Dr. Leman is the keynote speaker at BRING HOME THE JOY conferences sponsored by Women of Faith. His teachings have allowed couples to acquire the tools to strengthen and nurture their relationship to the highest level.

Dr. Leman earned his master's and doctoral degrees from the University of Arizona. He is a happily married husband and father of five children, ages seven to twenty-seven. He resides in Tucson, Arizona, with his family during the winter, and in Buffalo, New York, during the summer.

## SAMPLE BIOGRAPHY NUMBER 2

JAYME BARRETT
*Feng Shui Your Life*

### Biography
Jayme Barrett is a certified Feng Shui consultant, specializing in techniques for personal fulfillment, prosperity, and integrated health. Many of her

*continued*

*continued*

clients come from Hollywood, including actresses and actors Mary Steen-
burgen, Ted Danson, Alexis Denisof, and Alyson Hannigan, as well as TV
directors, successful fashion designers, and movie executives. She holds
"lunch and learn" workshops with handfuls of powerful executives at Paramount Pictures, Warner Bros. Studios, and other busy, on-the-go professionals.

At 35 she is one of the youngest known professional consultants in the art
of Feng Shui. Her new book, *Feng Shui Your Life*, was published in June 2003.
Barrett was recently appointed to the position of Body/Mind Editor for *Ms.
Fitness* magazine.

Raised in a very spiritual family, she has been meditating, practicing yoga,
and studying holistic health, motivational techniques, and energy flow
since she was a girl. She studied Feng Shui and energy healing with Grand
Master Choa Kok Sui, who is an internationally known expert, author, and
teacher of Feng Shui, Pranic Healing, and meditation. Barrett was certified
at the Feng Shui Institute of Physics and Energy and graduated from the
American Institute of Asian Studies under the tutelage of Master Stephen
Co, coauthor of *Your Hands Can Heal You*.

For over fifteen years, she has studied Eastern and Western healing tra-
ditions, life coaching, and spiritual practices from teachers around the
world, including India, China, Korea, and the Philippines. Her inspiring and
transformational work with individuals, businesses, and corporations has
made her a sought-after speaker on Feng Shui and life enhancement. Barrett also consults on residential and commercial properties.

Barrett has recently appeared nationally on TV's *The Other Half*.

She worked in television production from 1990 to 1995. She was an associate producer of documentaries and worked for TV directors, producers,

*continued*

*continued*

and writers for many shows, including episodic shows, sitcoms, and TV movies. She worked for major studios, including Columbia/ Tri-Star, Sony Pictures, and Warner Bros., as well as many independent production companies in L.A.

She is a graduate of UCLA, having earned a B.A. in 1989, graduating cum laude, and is a member of the Alpha Lambda Delta Honor Society.

Barrett resides in Los Angeles, California. For more information, please consult *www.123energy.com.*

### Your Photograph

Photographs give you and stories about you a human face. The media wants to know what you look like because this personalizes its coverage and creates greater interest. If you look good, capitalize on it. When they see your picture, hard-to-reach producers, reviewers, or reporters may recognize you or like what they see and decide to help.

Submit a professional-quality photograph, not a snapshot or some out-of-focus shot your kid took. The point is to give the impression that you are a professional who cares about how you look.

For a press kit, a 5" × 7" black-and-white photograph is sufficient. Color and larger images, which may be more impressive, are more expensive and can get costly if you're sending many media kits.

As we will discuss in greater detail, plan how you want to pose, the clothing you should wear, and the setting for your photograph. If you want to appear professorial, wear your glasses and tweed sport coat and be photographed in an academic setting. For your gardening book, appear amidst your prize-winning roses with a bouquet in hand.

### Question and Answers

Send radio and TV producers a list of suggested questions, but don't send them to print journalists without their consent. Print journalists often want to ask their own questions, not yours. Radio and TV hosts seldom read items in press kits and they generally just leaf through authors' books. Usually, they read only what producers put in front of them, and they don't read that until moments before they go on the air.

If you submit questions that the host could ask you, they may be used if the producer considers them good and in keeping with the program's style. They may rewrite your suggested questions or change their order, but they usually won't stray far from their basic meanings. For each question, state how long your answer will run.

"Submit questions that make the interviewer seem intelligent, like he or she has done research and read your book," Barbara De Angelis, *www.barbaradeangelis.com*, advises. "For example, say, 'In your book, you mentioned that more people are now taking antidepressants. Do you attribute that to the fact that they are now under more stress?' Draft questions that people would actually ask and that are conversational. Include statements that interviewers could also include."

Publishers frequently hire the Los Angeles media trainer Joel Roberts and Associates to write question-and-answer sheets for their media kits. One of Roberts's favorite strategies is to write questions "that challenge what the author has stated in his or her book in order to create a hot show," Roberts confesses. "Naturally, we train the authors to answer those questions in a way that stresses their core message."

For example, a skeptical question to an author who is promoting a book on low-carbohydrate diets is, "Isn't it true that the high-fat foods that you recommend in your book clog arteries and promote heart disease?" These challenging and confrontational questions give authors opportunities to explode myths and misinformation and tell audiences about new positions advocated in their books.

By crafting skeptical questions, you are telling the media, "Hit me with your best shot. Go for it, I can take it. Hosts love this tactic because it generates controversy, makes them look powerful and as though they really did their homework. It also moves the interview to the author's strength."

The following sample Q&A was prepared by the Spizman Agency for Robert L. Turknett and Carolyn N. Turknett, authors of *Decent People, Decent Company* (Davies-Black Publishing, 2005).

**Q: What do companies do wrong? How are they missing the decent corporate environment?**
A: Leadership development typically focuses exclusively on the individual. However, as the book explains, it is just as important.

**Q: Who should read *Decent People, Decent Company*?**
A: *Decent People, Decent Company* was written for CEOs, corporate executives, managers, and individual contributors alike who conduct businesses in any industry. Anyone who desires a corporate culture of decency to be restored or created will benefit from the sage advice found in these pages. This book was written for both the CEO and the administrative assistant. Both of these employees can create change in their organization with effective leadership. Two specific groups that will benefit from this book are top leaders who want to build companies where everyone is excited about working, and where everyone works as hard as they do for success, and individuals who want to make a real difference in their organizations—to lead a project team or a department, pursue a corporate initiative, or simply accomplish something that needs to be done.

**Q: Why did you write *Decent People, Decent Company*?**
A: We wrote *Decent People, Decent Company* because we want to help people grow. We believe that developing the character necessary for leadership can be the most rewarding and profound thing you've ever done. It allows you to accomplish more, to genuinely like your job more, to commit more fully to whatever you're doing—running a *Fortune* 500 company, organizing a PTA fund-raiser, or managing a project at work—and to simply enjoy life more. It allows you to lead in a way

that lends integrity and character to everything you do, and to create organizations where everyone takes responsibility for the financial and ethical success of the company.

American culture is largely shaped by business, and business leaders have a huge impact on the culture at large. Influencing leaders to exercise leadership from a foundation of character is our ultimate goal. From our research and experience, we created the Leadership Character Model as the foundation of our work. We have applied this model with executives and team members for almost twenty years.

The character necessary for leadership is depicted as a scale with respect and responsibility balanced on a base of integrity. When people build relationships based on respect, have a strong sense of personal responsibility, and live with unwavering integrity, they build their own character and foster organizational cultures that encourage decency and growth in everyone. Both the individual and the company come out winners—and so does society as a whole.

**Q: Why do leadership skills have to be developed at all levels within an organization for success to occur?**
A: Due to the competitive demands in today's global marketplace, employers must expect all employees to deliver their absolute best and perform up to their maximum potential. Companies that are going to be the most successful are those that recognize that they have to tap the talent and creativity of every individual. Therefore, in order to succeed, everyone must perform up to his or her maximum abilities. While everyone cannot be a leader by "title," everyone does need to be a leader within one's own realm, effectively producing results and assuming responsibility in one's own department and job as well as adding the most value possible to the organization. Anyone can become a leader in any setting.

**Q: How does a decent corporate culture begin?**
A: One way is to establish a culture that rewards initiative and risk taking. Another way is to bring the whole organization together through the use of communications tools such as TV, satellite, and computer

networks. It's important to communicate clearly, fully, and frequently to employees about what's happening within the company; employees who assert leadership will make decisions, and the more information they have, the better those decisions will be. It also helps them feel connected to the inner life of the organization, and it pays off as far as people feeling involved and having a sense of ownership. It also makes their jobs meaningful in the context of the overall, big corporate picture and helps create leadership awareness at all levels of the organization.

**Q: What are some practical ways to start today?**
A: Assess the corporate culture of the company. If an organization is interested in maximizing its ability to attain its strategic objectives, it must understand whether its culture supports and drives the actions necessary to achieve its goals. An in-depth cultural assessment, based on quantitative data and interviews, can enable a company to determine the difference between its current culture and its desired culture. Take responsibility for the good and the bad. Enact changes to improve effectiveness. Maintain a corporate accountability structure.

**Q: What key message is most important for CEOs and managers to walk away with after reading *Decent People, Decent Company*?**
A: Leadership is a choice, a decision, a willingness to take responsibility. Character is destiny, not personality, the foundation of leadership. Leadership is first about who you are, not what you do. Ask not what they can do for the organization, but what you can do for the organization. Everyone can and should strive to be a leader with character. So many places are hungry for leadership. Real leadership is simply someone who will raise his or her hand and say, "I'll do it." This book teaches readers how to raise their hands and be successful once they take that step. Everyone can and must develop his or her character throughout his or her lifetime—and has a moral obligation to do so. This is particularly true of leaders, since character is the foundation of leadership. The professional and personal results of this life endeavor are absolutely immeasurable.

The following sample Q&A was prepared by Planned Television Arts for Bruce Schwartz, the author of the novel *The Twenty-First Century* (Park Avenue Press, 2004).

Q: **Bruce, you've written a political thriller that touches upon so many issues and fears confronting America today. Is your book, *The Twenty-First Century*, our wake-up call to alert us as to where we fall short as a nation?**
A: Yes, but it's more than us falling short as a nation. We're falling short as a people, all of whom want to rise in class, and a class system unwilling to share the American dream. As a presidential candidate, Sam Howard asks in *The Twenty-First Century*, "Where is all this hatred coming from, and worse, where is it all leading?" It is our country's attitude toward our own people and the rest of the world where we fall short as a nation. My book is a metaphor for what's happening right now.

Q: **What's most intriguing is you wrote this book back in the 1990s, before 9/11, and it now seems almost prophetic, a tale of Middle Eastern terrorists avenging American aggression from an earlier time. Also interesting is that your book's setting is during a presidential election year. Is reality imitating art—or vice versa?**
A: In 1990, I got the idea for writing a book about a second civil war in the United States, but this time it being racial. After the Gulf War and Saddam Hussein's humiliation, I knew a maniacal ego such as his could never accept defeat. I needed a group of fathers who lost their only sons in the Gulf War to carry out Saddam's ingenious plot to secretly take control of the United States economically and politically. By setting it one week before the presidential election, I would say *The Twenty-First Century* is definitely reality copying art.

Q: **You cover the potential for an explosive race war in our nation, a devastating civil war that could yield tens of thousands—if not** millions—of deaths. Why do you believe the circumstances and tensions in the country today are ripe for such a scenario in the not-so-distant future?

A: Because America's values, ethics, and trust have changed. Almost everyone has become distrustful of our government. Yes—something is going to happen in America. It's going to take many lives and divide our country even more. In the 1990s, an average of 200 to 400 black churches were burned to the ground every year. Black children today are still forced to go to terrible inner-city schools with inferior books and activities, while the middle class goes to the schools in the suburbs and gets a better education. We presently have division by derision; if racial relations don't change for the better, we will have division by death.

Q: You also warn that America opens itself up for a terrorism attack—a large-scale annihilation of citizens in their home dwellings. Do you believe it's only a matter of when—and not if—such a thing can happen here?

A: First, we must analyze why we're open to a massive terrorist attack. Is it because America is trying to promote democracy to cultures more than a thousand years old who know only one way to live? America is trying to take these countries' most fundamental beliefs and customs and modernize them so we can sell our products to them, have access to all the oil we need, and also have a closer and more strategic place to defend Israel. The Muslim world (that's one billion people) will stop America the next time she tries to take over another Muslim nation. Iraq has had more than 10,000 innocent men, women, and children killed, not counting their soldiers. They will make America pay one day for this unjust killing spree.

Q: In your book, America's government is nearly covertly taken over by Iraq and foreign figures of power. Can that really happen?

A: I guess it could, but I doubt it will. However, there are many ways, many of which I wanted to use in *The Twenty-First Century* but was afraid I'd give ideas away that could hurt America, so I didn't use them.

What I'm trying to say is anything can happen to our country, and it could happen on an even greater scale.

Q: Revenge is also a theme in *The Twenty-First Century.* Many of the characters are driven to avenge a loss or hurt. So many are filled with hate. How can we stop such a cycle from repeating itself?

A: Revenge can be stopped, but first our government leaders, starting with the president, must set an example for its citizens. The problem, however, is that there has always been revenge in our world, ever since Cain and Abel. It's a human emotion that I don't believe will ever be eradicated from our psyches, which is one of the many reasons I wrote *The Twenty-First Century*—to show Americans and the world that revenge just begets more revenge. Revenge only goes to prove that might wins the fight, no matter who is right. It never solves the problem.

Q: Power is another big theme in *The Twenty-First Century.* Will there ever be a time or place where people who seek to lead a nation are not power driven but service oriented?

A: I believe almost every candidate starts their candidacy with a service-oriented ideology. But then the special interest groups come into the picture. To get money for their campaign, our politicians become pawns to these groups. Of course, the larger problem is that the two biggest self-interest groups, the Democratic and Republican National Committees, dictate the candidate's or elected leader's platform. If it is not in line with their interests, the candidates will have no money to continue their campaign, nor will they get any support from Congress. These groups hold all the power. No longer can a candidate vote his conscience; he or she must vote the party's beliefs. If we didn't have these committees, then maybe we might find a service-oriented candidate. Until then, it's all power driven by the party and its puppets.

Q: While conducting extensive research for your book, I understand you actually asked a friend in government how one could kill the president of the United States and get away with it (from a tactical point of view)—and that the next thing you knew, the Secret Service was knocking at your door. Tell us about that experience.

A: I was near the end of my rewrites, and I needed to know the particulars about Inauguration Day. I called up a friend of a friend in Washington and told him I needed to know about the security surrounding the parade. I also asked him how I can go about killing the president without anyone knowing it was me. He knew I was writing this book, so he felt comfortable answering me and guiding me to other departments involved in the inauguration. Later that day, two suited men appeared at my door asking, "Are you Bruce Schwartz?" They asked me if I recently made a call to Washington, D.C. You see, every phone in Washington is bugged so that if the words *president* and *kill* or *shoot* or whatever are in the same sentence, they're on top of it right away. They then asked me if I was going to the inauguration. I told them I was invited, showed them my gold-embossed invitation and then the manuscript. They warned me upon leaving that every step I take at the inauguration will be watched. I felt like a criminal. My children, of course, thought it was cool.

Q: Bruce, you have a background as an actor and a producer of plays. How did that type of experience and training—coupled with research, current events, and an active imagination—help you write *The Twenty-First Century*?

A: When I write my books, I write them cinematically. I don't mean to do it that way, but being a book, movie, and Broadway fanatic it helped me to visualize and analyze the audience's needs from scene to scene. Characters should motivate the plot, and the plot must motivate the characters. So, if you want to write, you must not only do your research, you must then study: reading every bestseller, seeing Broadway shows, and/or the best movies. After thirty-five years as a storyteller, a former actor, and Broadway producer, I study the characters and plot of a script I'm beginning. So, yes, writing, especially with a background in the arts, opened my eyes and imagination to what makes for great stories and characters that you'll always remember.

**Q: Senator Sam Howard in your book is running for president and he offers some very interesting campaign promises. His platform includes a get-tough measure on crime bill that sounds a little severe. Would it fly today?**

A: That depends on who's in the Oval Office and what political party controls Congress. I didn't want to create a platform that everyone would agree with; after all, this is a work of fiction. Differing opinions to the platform brings reality to the book. Would the Howard Crime Bill be something our politicians can implement now or in the future? If they study each component of the bill, they will see that most of it is logical and reasonable. Everything else we've attempted has failed. Maybe this will change Americans' fear of living in America today.

**Q: He also has interesting ideas on education reform. Please share some of those ideas with us.**

A: In order to build a stronger America, America must change its antiquated educational system. We're now in the twenty-first century, and we have a responsibility to our children, to America's future, to educate tomorrow's leaders and teach future generations the skills they need so they can survive in a world that is becoming increasingly more difficult to survive in. With television broadcasting our every military and political move, and with computers and the information highway, our children are more intelligent and more worldly than ever. We need to treat them as the young adults they are. Therefore, America has to reinvent its schools' curriculum, of which I go into detail in *The Twenty-First Century*.

**Q: Would Sam Howard be electable today, and if so, why?**

A: Yes, Sam Howard would definitely be electable today. However, I must stress upon our listeners that in the 1930s, Hitler was able to manipulate the German people by promising them a solution for the country's problems. Because they were in the middle of the Depression, everyone rallied around him because they were a desperate people looking for someone to guide them back to normalcy. Now, Sam Howard is charismatic, brilliant, and his ideas are new and fresh. With the presidential primaries and conventions near, Sam Howard would be a strong presence, promising to change America into a safer, happier, and healthier society.

## Additional Items

### Copies of Reviews and Articles

Include copies of good reviews or articles about you and/or your book. As we mentioned, the media likes to see and will be influenced by how others covered your book and you.

If reviews or articles have not been published on you or your book, include those that have been written on your subject matter to show the media interest in it. Include them even though they don't mention you or your book. If they were cover stories, include a copy of the cover.

Try to get articles written about you or your book. Start with your local paper and be persistent. Use your contacts to reach them and push the local author angle. The hometown media is usually eager to support area residents. When you receive local coverage, use it to get more ink.

### List of Articles and Appearances

Producers and journalists need subjects that will give them lively, entertaining shows and articles. So, they prefer to feature authors who have strong performance records. They will be more likely to cover you after they read favorable pieces that others wrote about you or review tapes of your appearances. These items may help them avoid asking you what others have fully covered, or assist them in coming up with unique angles or spins. When you list articles, give the name of the publication they appeared in and the dates they ran. For radio and TV appearances, list the program's name and the date it aired and include complimentary quotes from the producers or hosts.

### An Expansive Article

When you want to give the media more information than will fit on a one-page press release, write a separate article to include in your media kit. The press may pick up your article and run it verbatim or use it as the basis for their own pieces.

Usually, it's not productive to send expansive or supplemental articles to radio and TV producers because they generally won't read them. However, on occasion, they may scan an article, be intrigued by it, and consider doing a feature based on it. In those rare instances, they will conduct their own research to develop it along the lines that interest them.

### Business Cards

Print separate business cards for your book; don't use your personal business cards. The business cards for your book can, but don't have to, include the cover image of your book. On your book's cards, list the title and subtitle, your name, the publisher's name, the publication date, and your silver bullet. Also give your contact information.

Business cards can be a terrific promotional tool because they're inexpensive, which allows you to hand them out freely to everyone you meet. They also can be good icebreakers and informational aids, and people generally keep them. Business cards are also ideal places to write personal notes or information.

Consider having the card for your book professionally designed or consult with your publisher's designer because great-looking business cards are an easy way to attract interest and provide a good impression of your book and you.

Some media kit folders come with cutouts, in which business cards can be inserted. Usually, they're on the inside pocket. If the folder has a place for your business card, insert it. If not, attach the card to your press release. Don't toss loose business cards in the pockets of your folder because they may fall out and get lost.

Postcards, bookmarks, decals, note pads, stationery, and similar easily handed-out items can also help to promote your book. When printed in bulk, they're inexpensive. When well designed, they can be eye catching and give important information, including ordering info for your book. These items can also include the book's cover image and the same information that is printed on the book's business cards.

### Newsletters

In your media kit, include a copy of the latest newsletter for your book. Use the book title in the newsletter name. For example, call it the "Author 101, Bestselling Book Publicity Newsletter."

Newsletters are low-cost, high-impact marketing tools that help you publicize your book, stay in contact with those who may be interested in it, and build your list of names. E-mail newsletters are also called e-zines or 'zines. Producing any newsletter can be time consuming and work intensive, but e-mail newsletters are easier to distribute than their print counterparts. If putting out a newsletter becomes a burden, contract out all or some of the work.

Build a subscriber list by collecting lots of names. Also ask your friends and colleagues for names. Your publisher and publicist should be willing to give you access to their lists, and you can buy lists of names from services that compile them by demographics and subject areas.

Don't send your newsletter to anyone who has not requested it because he or she might think of it as spam, which can tarnish both your and your book's reputation. In every issue, give subscribers the ability to easily opt out or unsubscribe.

Try to publish your newsletters on a regular schedule because it helps to maintain subscribers' interest. Also maintain a consistent format because readers are creatures of habit who like the same content to always be in the same place.

The quality of a newsletter's content is more important than its length. Anything more than a printed page or a couple of computer screens is acceptable if it provides valuable information. Don't waste your subscribers' valuable time by filling your newsletters with junk.

Keep them vital and interesting so that subscribers will look forward to receiving them and will tout them to others.

In your newsletter, report on recent news and developments relating to your book, its subject, you, those who contributed to it, or experts in the field. Write articles or regular columns and conduct interviews. Invite guests to contribute and encourage submissions from subscribers that could lead to lively exchanges. Also include reviews of and articles about your book as well as excerpts from the book. Always include a form that lets readers order your book electronically.

Provide a calendar of upcoming events. It should list your schedule of speaking engagements, book signings, and personal appearances. Consider including the schedules of your strategic partners or other experts on your book's topic. You can also provide items such as games, quizzes, contests, and puzzles.

Build loyal subscribers by providing value in your newsletter. Make it interesting, not just a brochure or infomercial for your book or you. People receive tons of e-mail, so distinguish your newsletter by making it outstanding or it won't be read. Your primary object should be to build and solidify relationships with people who will support your work. So lay off the hype and hard sell.

E-mail the first issue a month or so prior to the publication of your book in order to create interest in your book and obtain purchase orders for it. Then, publish a launch issue just before the book is released and periodic issues thereafter to keep on promoting your book and to remain in contact with subscribers.

### Endorsements/Recommendations

Obtain endorsements from well-known people praising you, your book, and your appearances. Send copies of your book to authors in your field and ask them if they could endorse it. Other authors can be surprisingly generous and helpful. Include excerpts of the endorsements you receive in your media kit and post them on your Web site.

Douglas M. Isenberg, Esq., sent letters to the top authorities in his field when he started writing his book, *The GigaLaw Guide to Internet*

*Law* (Random House, 2002). In his letters, Isenberg informed them that he was writing the book and asked if they would consider endorsing it when it was completed. A number of them agreed, which Isenberg believes carried great weight with his target market.

After you make appearances or give interviews, ask the hosts, producers, and interviewers to send you a letter stating that you were a fabulous guest or subject who generated great interest. Ask them to write their endorsements on their official letterhead. Letters of endorsement regarding your past appearances can be extremely important because radio and TV producers often rely on them in booking talent for their shows.

### Ordering Information

Since your publicity tools are intended to generate book sales, give potential buyers easy ways to buy your book. Prepare print handouts that you always have with you. Create links on every page of your Web site that visitors can click to order your book. Get a toll-free telephone number that you can repeat during radio, TV, and personal appearances. Select a number that will be easy for potential buyers to remember.

### Quizzes, Contests, and Giveaways

If you include quizzes and games in your media kit, the media will often use them as the basis for on-air interviews. Quizzes and games such as anagrams and crossword puzzles can draw more attention when you award prizes to the first individuals who solve them.

Small, inexpensive novelty items printed with your name, logo, or motto and contact information can also be included in your media kit. Useful items like calendars, tipping percentage cards, pens, pencils, flashlights, and sewing kits are effective because many people use and hang on to them.

Contests that offer great prizes can attract a lot of attention. To promote the first book in this Author 101 series—*Bestselling Book Proposals*—our publisher, Adams Media, sponsored a contest in which it awarded the person who submitted the best book proposal a contract to publish that book and a promotional package for the book worth $20,000.

**Rick Says**

Print every item that you send in your media kit on your letterhead. Don't use fancy or exotic type or designs that may be difficult to read.

Make sure that your contact information—name, address, e-mail address, Web site address, telephone numbers, and fax number—is on your media kit cover and on both the *top* and *bottom* of *every* sheet. The items in a media kit are usually removed from their folder and often get separated from the rest of the kit. One isolated piece might contain information that arouses interest and prompts someone to call, e-mail, or visit your site.

### Trivia, Quotes, and Anecdotes

Factual information, clever quotes, and intriguing stories attract interest. The best ones are frequently repeated and can create memorable links to your book that the public will remember.

Anecdotes and case studies serve as vivid examples and illustrations. They make concepts and theories more understandable by putting them in a context that people can more readily identify with, understand, and retain. Good, illustrative anecdotes are usually repeated.

### Packaging

Put all your media kit materials in a two-pocket envelope or folder. Place a photograph of the cover of your book on the cover along with your contact information. Place your press release face-up in the pocket that people see immediately when they open your media kit package. If that pocket has a place for your business card, insert it. Put your picture, followed by your biography, in the opposite pocket. They also should face out.

If you use colored folders for your media kit, make sure that they don't clash with your book cover image. Color code and layer any items in your kit that you want to stand out. For example, you could print your press release on paper in the primary color of your book cover.

## Distribution

Send your media kit package by Federal Express, UPS, or priority mail. Overnight packages give the impression that their content is important, that you value what you shipped, and that you incurred expense to ensure that it would be promptly delivered. However, these shipping methods can be expensive for large distributions.

## Action Steps

1. Name an author's number one publicity tool.
2. List four other primary book publicity tools.
3. What items should be included in a media kit and why?
4. What information should be contained in the lead sentence of a press release?
5. Explain why articles about you should be included in your media kit.

### Remember

🔺 **To conduct an effective book publicity campaign, you need to have the right tools.** Start with your silver bullet and then assemble a great media kit that features a killer one-page press release with a fabulous headline. Write the headline and press release to capture your readers' interest and make them want to learn more about your book and you.

🔺 **Include in your media kit a photograph of you and your biography.** In your bio, describe yourself through your accomplishments and experience and don't be verbose. Also include in your media kit good reviews of your book, articles about your book and/or you, a list of features written about you and of your personal appearances, and complimentary letters about you from radio and TV producers and/or hosts.

**CHAPTER 5**

I had grown tired of standing in the lean and lonely front line facing the greatest enemy that ever confronted man—public opinion.
*Clarence Darrow*

## Slicing and Dicing

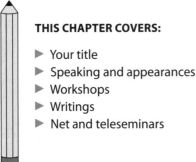

**THIS CHAPTER COVERS:**

▶ Your title
▶ Speaking and appearances
▶ Workshops
▶ Writings
▶ Net and teleseminars

MAKE THE MOST of what you have already created to publicize your book. Take content from your book, information that you have written, and repackage it as speeches, workshops, seminars, articles, columns, games, contests, and other promotional tools. Publishers call this slicing and dicing. Think of it this way: the content in your book is your raw material. It's the crude oil from which gasoline, kerosene, plastic, and thousands of other products are refined. It makes both financial and practical sense for you to try to squeeze every little drop out of your material because you will be creating more products that bear your name and the title of your book. Each new item or use that you create can get you and your book more visibility.

Take your content and dissect it. Carefully re-examine what you created in a new light, from a different perspective, and for different markets or applications. Think of promotional uses for your content—how you can tweak it, change it, or spice it up to attract new interest.

Timing is everything! Content that you slice and dice can be recycled and used over and over again for different seasons, holidays, or similar events such as birthdays, anniversaries, achievements, and special milestones. Also recast your existing content in light of what's hot, trendy, or in the news.

In this discussion of slicing and dicing, we can't point out every way that you could reuse your content. It's impossible for us to address them all. So the purpose of this chapter is to introduce you to the concept of slicing and dicing, to introduce you to the concept of making multiple uses of your content and to stimulate your mind and give you a taste of some of the promotional opportunities that your content can provide.

## Your Title

Great book titles have gigantic impact! Your book's title can be the most important element in your book's publicity campaign. A fabulous title, by itself, can generate tremendous interest in your book. Upon hearing it, others will react and want to know more about it.

Great titles practically sell books by themselves. Of course, books with great titles will do even better when the books' content is also fabulous, but the fact that they have outstanding titles certainly never hurts.

In your title and subtitle, explain the benefits your book will provide. For example: *Networking Magic: Find the Best—From Doctors, Lawyers, and Accountants to Homes, Schools, and Jobs* and *The GIFTionary: An A–Z Reference Guide for Solving Your Gift-Giving Dilemmas . . . Forever.* The media loves titles that tell it the benefits that the book will provide or the problems it will solve.

Analyze recent wonderful titles and the reasons for their successes. For example: *The One Minute Manager, Who Moved My Cheese?, Catch-22, Chicken Soup for the Soul, The Tipping Point, L.A. Confidential, Swim with the Sharks Without Being Eaten Alive,* and *Guerrilla Marketing.*

Write an extraordinary title for your book, one that people will immediately respond to and retain. Test it by running it past your friends, family, and associates and observe the reaction it evokes. Great titles get repeated and mentioned by the media. They alone can sell books.

Plaster the title of your book on everything and display it widely. Incorporate it in your Web site address, your e-mail signature, and your letterhead. Make T-shirts, postcards, bookmarks, calendars, and other products that can publicize your book. Wear them, carry them, and give them to your family and friends.

Have branded items created that relate to your book. For instance, if you wrote a gardening book, have items such as pots, tools, gloves, fertilizer packs, or plant markers made that bear your book's name, logo, and/or cover art.

## Speaking and Appearances

Speaking engagements, personal appearances, and workshops can help you get exposure and build your following because they put you face-to-face with people who may buy your book. And many authors earn more money giving speeches than they receive from the sales of their books. Speaking can build your following because people who are interested in you or your book frequently want to see who you are and hear what you have to say.

The easiest and often the most enjoyable personal appearances are book signings, readings, and book parties, and their advantages are clear. Audiences love to hear authors read from their soon-to-be-published novel, collection of short stories, or book of poems. They attend in order to meet authors—even if just briefly—buy their books, and get them signed. When an author meets people and/or signs their books, it creates a connection, and those people often become the authors' staunchest followers. These supporters spread the word about books, devote chat rooms and Web sites to them, and become unpaid, unofficial publicists. An army of these supporters can get a book on the bestseller list, and the top authors cultivate such armies.

Speeches and public appearances are usually on a larger scale than book signings and readings. More people generally attend, so you can receive greater exposure. Audiences will frequently buy your book. According to the experts, when authors' books are sold at their personal appearances, 25 percent of the audience usually buys a copy. For big, more established, and popular authors, they say the percentage is higher.

### Speaking engagements:

- Cement your status as an expert or personality.
- Enable you to meet others with similar interests.
- The more acknowledged you are as an expert or personality, the more books you can sell and the more it can boost your business.
- Being an acknowledged expert or personality can expand your network contacts and interest more successful and accomplished individuals in you. As an acknowledged expert or personality, you will be more attractive to businesses.

At speeches and public appearances, the questions and comments you receive from attendees can inform you about problems, issues, or developments that may increase your expertise. They can provide material for your future books, articles, presentations, and business. They can also alert you to new directions that you might want to check out and pursue. Since speaking engagements are often a part of larger events, they provide marvelous networking opportunities, and the media is frequently on hand. As a speaker, you will have celebrity status, so people, including the media, will be eager to meet and spend time with you. Everyone you meet could help your book sales and career.

### Your Topic

Okay, you're sold on the value of speaking and public appearances, but how do you get them? First, find a compelling topic.

Speeches and presentations must educate and entertain. The National Speakers Association (*www.nsaspeaker.org*) found that audiences primarily want education and skill building, so that's what 75 percent of speakers are hired to provide. Give your audiences realistic, practical information that will help them solve or avoid problems. Show them how to save time and money. Provide solutions to problems they can immediately implement, explain how others solved similar dilemmas, and explore new approaches. Always give audiences tangible benefits so they leave feeling that you gave them important information that they can really use.

Talk about what you excel at, what you've successfully done a thousand times, and what people pay you for. Make sure that your topic is not only relevant to your audience, but that it's important to them. Know the information you give inside out and present it in an entertaining and logical way. List the steps that should be followed: one, two, three. Give information besides that which is included in your book, and don't constantly refer to your book or dwell on complex material.

If you write fiction, talk about how you got the idea for your novel and how you researched it, wrote it, and went about getting it published. Discuss your experiences, observations, feelings, and views. Audiences love stories associated with your book and the writing and publishing process because they give them a closer connection to you

**Rick Says**

Before you book an engagement, find out who will be in the audience, because some audiences may not be right for your talk. For example, events at some local organizations may cater to retirees or segments of the business community that will not be interested in you or your book. However, appearing before these groups might help you get valuable experience.

Build a strong local base by speaking frequently. Local audiences are usually less intimidating and more supportive. Usually, you know some of the attendees, and seeing friendly faces can help you relax. Spice up your talks with comments or references to local events or personalities. Become a local favorite and then try to move up.

and the book. Such stories also provide aspiring writers with a blueprint that they could follow.

No matter how well you write or how brilliant your book is, if your presentations aren't entertaining, people will fall asleep and you won't be invited back. So tell spellbinding stories, give vivid anecdotes and clever quotes. Reveal secrets, expose hoaxes or myths, make your audience laugh, and create controversy. Learn the art of PowerPoint so you can illustrate your talks with graphics such as charts, lists, diagrams, and graphs. Sprinkle in some jokes and asides that will help your audience enjoy the process of learning. Show the media that you will be a lively, informative, and entertaining interview subject. Become a performer so audiences talk about you, spread the word, and look forward to attending your presentations. Remember that host organizations ask audiences to evaluate speakers, so make it your mission to be informative and entertaining so you are the first speaker they invite back.

### Venues

Start small and locally, in your own backyard. At first, volunteer and don't charge. Do it for the experience. Concentrate on gaining exposure, polishing your speaking skills, and learning from your

**Robyn Says**

When you accept speaking engagements, you often must travel, which can take lots of time. While you're in other cities, leverage your appearances by arranging for book signings or other media appearances. Frequently, the host organization or your publisher can help, so ask if their in-house publicity arms could help you get on some local morning shows.

When you speak at engagements, prepare messages that will help sell your book. In your presentations, provide strong, interesting content. Throw in interesting and provocative stories; explain ideas that your audience could explore further in your book. Be tactful; be an interesting, entertaining speaker; and don't dwell on your book!

mistakes. Select organizations where you can make good contacts and start building a following. Learning to be a good speaker takes practice, so start small and work your way up.

To get speaking engagements, use your contacts in civic, community, business, and charitable groups. Approach religious or social groups that you, your family, or your friends belong to or service clubs such as the Rotary Club, the Elks Club, and the Veterans of Foreign Wars. Contact your local chamber of commerce and local business, industry, and professional groups. Develop your speaking career by:

- Taping your presentations and then reviewing them.
- Asking your friends and associates for constructive critiques and working to improve your performances.
- Attending accomplished speakers' presentations, noting their strengths, and adapting those that could work for you.
- Taking media training (see Chapter 9 for more information on media training).
- Hiring a professional videographer to record your presentations as you grow more proficient. Professional videographers can capture your performances in the best light, suggest how

you can improve your performance, and recommend you to other groups that hire speakers.

- Assembling a reel that demonstrates the excellence of your performances. Work with your videographer and/or a designer to put the reel together. Then take it to booking agencies or larger, higher-profile organizations that use speakers.
- Promoting your appearance by contacting the local media:
  1. Send announcements or press releases to newspapers and radio and TV stations and ask them to post your upcoming appearance on their event calendars.
  2. Insert items in the host organization's newsletters or bulletins and ask them to post and send separate announcements of your speech.
  3. Place posters and fliers in busy, high-traffic areas and send postcards announcing the event to your media list, your network, and the host organization's list.

## Workshops

Use content from your book in workshops that you organize and produce and in those that are run by others but in which you participate as an instructor. The promotional benefits of leading workshops are similar to those derived from speeches and personal appearances, but the audiences at workshops and seminars are usually more tightly focused. Typically, everyone who attends is in the same industry, has the same interests, and wants to learn from you and the other instructors. Giving speeches may give you more exposure, but leading workshops can do more to build your following with the specific audience your book targets.

When you run your own workshop, part of your job will be to plan and/or oversee the publicity efforts. You can make great media contacts if you become the contact person for the media, because the media will have to go through you for all information and interviews. By running workshops, you can also raise your stature in your industry.

Since most experts enjoy instructing at workshops, they will be pleased and somewhat obligated to you for inviting them to speak at or help lead your workshop. Putting on a workshop can place you among the movers and shakers and in the inner core of your industry. It can bring you invitations to other prestigious events.

In the past few years, Internet workshops and telephone seminars have proliferated. Without leaving home, you can now reach people in far-flung places who want to learn from you.

## Writings

Reuse or adapt content you've written for your book in a free newsletter or e-zine that you publish. Incorporate the name of your book in the title, such as *Author 101 Newsletter*, and distribute it widely. Send it to only those who specifically request it or it could offend recipients and backfire on you.

Condense, edit, and rewrite portions of your book as articles or columns for your newsletter or other newsletters or publications. Send a short story or an excerpt from your novel to newspapers, journals, and magazines. Try to get your writing serialized. With nonfiction, each chapter of your book should contain enough material for several articles or columns.

Make your newsletter more interesting and relevant by tying its articles and columns to topical events, trends, and developments. Also conduct interviews; run surveys; give questions and answers, facts, quizzes, and contests. List announcements and provide a calendar of relevant events. Feature both your upcoming appearances and the appearances of others of interest to those in the industry. Provide ways for subscribers to contact you so that you can conduct interchanges with readers. Submit your writing to other publications and Web sites.

Prepare a list of subjects that you can turn into articles. Focus on problems that you can solve. Write provocative titles or list subjects such as "The Truth about Mortgage Fees," "How to Describe Intimacy," "Five

Fatal Flaws of Elective Surgery Exposed," or "Do Artificial Sweeteners Kill?" Contact newspapers and magazines; give them a list of the articles you can write and your credentials. Find outlets for your writing by:

- Approaching industry and trade associations in your field. Most have newsletters, Web sites, and other publications that can always use content. Appearing regularly in these publications can enhance your profile within your field. In exchange for your writing services, request a byline that gives the name of your book.

- Contacting local organizations such as the chamber of commerce; service clubs; and other community, business, or religious organizations. Volunteer to write columns or features that tie your book to events of concern in your community. Become the expert they can consult for questions, explanations, and insights in your area of expertise.

- Checking with your area newspapers. Focus first on free shopper newspapers or advertisers. Examine them, find out the type of content they provide, and determine if they might be interested in having you write a regular column based on information from your book.

- For fiction, submit your work to literary publications and to periodicals that appeal to readers who might be interested in your writing.

If your field constantly changes, revise your book annually or put out yearly supplements or updates. Create spin-offs for segments of your audience, such as men, women, seniors, and children. Write workbooks, books of forms, recipes, or directions.

## Net and Teleseminars

Create a Web site and use portions of your content on your site. See Chapter 10, "Web Sites and Blogs," for more detailed information.

Submit articles, games, quizzes, contests, and other materials to other Web sites or strategic partners. Post your fact sheets and questions and answers (FAQs) with discussion groups that allow them. See the Internet FAQ Archives at *www.faq.org*. However, be sure the groups permit the posting of the information you submit.

With the FAQs on your Web site and those you post, attach a form for readers to send you their questions and comments. Add their names and e-mail addresses to your names list.

Hold either online or telephone teleseminars. At each session, select a particular problem that you cover in your book and allow participants to ask or e-mail questions and comments. Invite guests who are experts in particular fields related to your book and who may be able to provide in-depth expertise on areas that you just touched on in your book.

At Planned Television Arts, Rick runs regular teleseminars that feature leading experts on many topics related to book publicity. Services are available to set up and handle all aspects of teleseminars, so all you have to do is line up your guests, show up, ask questions, and field calls. Rick works with Paul Cohen of Brainwave Communications (*www.bwccom.com*).

## *Products*

Examine the product potential of all the content in your book. In addition to recycling your writing, explore other possible uses for your photographs, illustrations, charts, diagrams, and to-do lists. Could any of them be published and marketed as stand-alone products? Could the illustrations be included in other books or articles that would give you credit and publicize your book?

Surveys and reports that you compiled for your book can also enjoy extended lives. They can be ideal additions to speeches, other books, articles, courses, and Web sites. Since the media is so fond of surveys and reports, send it copies of yours because it could help promote your book.

Determine if the logo for your book or your book's cover could be placed on products such as T-shirts, tote bags, notebooks, and coffee mugs. Look for opportunities to put your book's artwork and logo on lots of products because it can build your brand and publicize your book.

## Action Steps

1. Explain what the term *slicing and dicing* means.
2. List five ways that you can use the information in your book to get publicity.
3. Name the two essential benefits that your presentations must provide for your audiences.
4. What content should your newsletter or e-zine include?
5. Describe the benefits of a teleseminar.

### Remember

🔺 **Put a new shine on an old gem.** Take material from your book and repackage it in other forms; for example, as speeches, workshops, seminars, articles, columns, games, contests, and other promotional tools. Publishers call this slicing and dicing. Create a great title for your book and plaster it across everything.

🔺 **Attendance counts.** Get exposure from speaking engagements and public appearances where you can discuss information from your book. Conduct and participate in workshops and seminars.

**CHAPTER**
**6**

People everywhere confuse what they read in newspapers with news.

*A. J. Liebling*

# Build Bridges with the Media

**THIS CHAPTER COVERS:**

▶ Educate yourself
▶ It's about news
▶ Become a resource
▶ Finding who to contact
▶ The rules

THE SMARTEST, FASTEST, most efficient way to get your story told is through the media. You could spend endless hours on the phone calling all your contacts—and all your contacts' contacts—and you couldn't reach as many potential book buyers as could a single story in the *New York Times* or *People* magazine or on the *Oprah Winfrey Show;* you couldn't come close!

In our information-intensive society, the media controls the channels through which information circulates. Those channels include print publications, television, radio, and the Internet. The media finds, shapes, and disseminates what we read, see, and hear. Its handiwork is constantly beamed into our homes, cars, and computers. We're surrounded by news and everything we get is filtered through the media.

Telling stories and spreading the word are the media's job, and it's really good at it! Providing news is the media's profession; the news is the media's entire focus. When most authors try to get the media to publicize their books, they're entering foreign turf and are out of their element. They don't know the ground rules, how the media works and how to approach and deal with it. These authors are amateurs in a professional world, and although they may make valiant efforts, they usually don't get the desired results.

In this chapter, we're going to teach you about the media, how it operates, what it wants, and how to make it work for you. Then in Chapter 7, we will tell you how to get bookings and coverage, and in Chapter 8, we will cover interviews. In addition, we've included another chapter, Chapter 9, devoted to media training, which we feel is absolutely essential to make the best of the opportunities you get with the media.

## Educate Yourself

If you want to work with the media, learn about it and how it works. Study it; become a media junkie, a media expert! Start by reading everything; get a broad overview. Concentrate on national and local newspapers and magazines. Identify the trends and subjects the media is covering and which media outlets are providing that coverage. Then follow the breaking news and ongoing stories in your field.

Systematically monitor the media. Keep a list of the items each outlet reports and its favorite way of presenting them. Follow the patterns of individual journalists, editors, producers, and program hosts. When they cover books:

- Do they write reviews, news articles, or profiles of authors?
- Do they write features on groups of books or on subjects on which they quote books or authors?
- What approaches do particular radio or TV talk shows typically take?
- What types of books or authors do they feature and which do they avoid?
- What are their tendencies, preferences, and styles?

Media outlets have diverse styles; they handle different subjects and deal with them in varying ways. Just look at the differences among the styles of Oprah, Howard Stern, and Chris Matthews. Compare the approaches of the *New York Times*, the *New York Post*, and the *Wall Street Journal*. Magazines vary even more, especially those that are written for specific niche subject matters.

Identify the writers, publications, and programs that are most likely to cover your book. Before you contact them, read their articles, and tape and study their shows. Note what they're writing or producing, where they're working, and what interests them.

The media thinks in terms of story ideas. The first question it asks is, would you or your book make a good story? Therefore, present yourself to the media in terms of story ideas. Link yourself and your book to each media outlet's interests, and show how well you would fit.

### Sample Story Ideas

The following story ideas were created by Planned Television Arts to promote Dr. JoAnne Robbins's book *Easy-to-Swallow, Easy-to-Chew Cookbook: Over 150 Tasty and Nutritious Recipes for People Who Have Difficulty Swallowing* (Wiley, 2002).

**The size and diversity of the population that suffers from dysphagia**
Over 15,000,000 people suffer from a disability known as dysphagia—about the same number of people who suffer from diabetes—and the demographics vary wildly, from geriatrics to motor vehicle accident victims to those who have had a stroke or suffer from any one of numerous diseases such as multiple sclerosis, cerebral palsy, Alzheimer's disease, Parkinson's, muscular dystrophy, Lou Gehrig's disease, as well as victims of cancer of the throat or mouth. Those undergoing radiation of the head, neck, or chest or chemotherapy may also have dysphagia. Even those taking certain medications could suffer symptoms of a swallowing disorder. It's more common than people realize, and anyone can develop this

*continued*

*continued*

problem. The critical nature of dysphagia is emphasized by its causal relationship to pneumonia, dehydration, malnutrition, and even death. Dr. Robbins identifies the warning signs and suggests numerous treatments while placing a spotlight on this underreported malady.

### How to help others swallow with ease

A person challenged by swallowing and chewing problems need not suffer. Dr. Robbins identifies hundreds of tips for making the process of eating, drinking, and swallowing a smoother, less painful, and more enjoyable experience. She identifies over a dozen types of problems and provides solutions for them, including: choking, dry mouth, tongue thrust, mouth soreness, dysfunctional tongue, food getting stuck, coughing while eating, reflux, mucus buildup in mouth and throat, difficulty tasting foods, getting full fast, and constipation. While putting a feeding tube in the stomach to avoid eating by mouth is actually thought of as a solution to the problem, Dr. Robbins and her coauthors have many behavioral modifications that can retain quality of life as it relates to eating while minimizing, if not eliminating, the dysphagia.

### Identifying easy-to-chew, easy-to-swallow food

When you have difficulty swallowing, eating moves from a fun experience to a chore to a downright near impossibility. *Easy-to-Swallow, Easy-to-Chew Cookbook* is a breakthrough package of 150 tasty and nutritious recipes for people who have difficulty swallowing. Included are delicious desserts, entrees, appetizers, soups, vegetables, spreads, and beverages. Sound advice is provided by Dr. JoAnne Robbins on how to prepare easy-to-eat foods. The texture, size, and moistness of food play a key role in what can be consumed and how it can be eaten by individuals who need to think about every morsel of sustenance to pass through their mouth.

Contact magazines that regularly write profiles of authors and explain that you would make a fascinating subject because you can teach audiences how to be productive with just two hours of sleep. Tell radio and TV producers fascinating stories about your near–fatal experience in the Peace Corps, the secrets you learned at NASA or while working as a law clerk for Justice Sandra Day O'Connor. Inform the media how its audience can benefit from your groundbreaking invention, your successful parenting methods, or your huge investment profits from biotech.

Understand that people in the media are busy and vastly over-worked. They're under constant pressure to find new stories and meet deadlines. Media people are usually flooded with more submissions than they can use. So, they must constantly take time from their jammed schedules to sift through stacks of leads in the hope of uncovering gems that they can use. Basically, they quickly scan all submissions for flags, key words, or phrases that grab their attention, and if they don't imme-diately find them, they quickly jump to the next lead. So make your pitches short, clear, and convincing. Bait your hook with irresistible descriptions that will make them bite.

When you pitch them, people in the media will probably be work-ing on other stories. So, they may not answer, return your messages, or even glance at what you sent. Don't take it personally, don't let it dis-courage you; just understand that it's how the media works. So be persis-tent; follow up and keep trying to reach them. Plus, don't expect them to call you and even if they do mention your book, it's your job to follow up. While some media outlets might supply a copy, they are usually not in the habit or business of supplying tapes, tear sheets, or reviews.

In Chapter 4, "Your Book Publicity Tool Kit," we discussed media lists. As we mentioned, media lists are essential in dealing efficiently with the media and recording your contacts with specific individuals and outlets. Review that material because it will help you build bridges with the media.

## It's about News

The media is in the information business, and its product is news. Its mission is to furnish information to the public that has not been presented or to deliver what was previously covered in a different way. Basically, here's how the media operates:

1. It's constantly on the lookout for new information.
2. It finds new information that it can cover.
3. It shapes that information into print or Internet stories or radio or TV features.
4. It publishes or broadcasts the reshaped information as news.
5. When each item runs, the media needs another story to replace it. It has to fill the space in the paper, on the Web site, or on the air.

So, the media is caught in a perpetual cycle; it consumes gigantic amounts of information that it must continually replace. Since the media can't supply all of its needs, it looks to other sources. That's where you come in. You and your information about your book can become one of those sources if the media considers what you're pitching to be news. All the media cares about is news; it worships news. Sorry to say, it doesn't really care about you, but it will cover you, your book, or information in your book if it considers it newsworthy. Simply put, your job is to persuade the media that a significant segment of its audience will be interested in a story about your book or you. Here's what you should do.

## Become a Resource

Build relationships with people in the media by becoming a source that they value. Identify journalists and radio or TV producers or personalities who have covered items similar to those in your book and who might be interested in information about you and your book. Identify new, up-and-coming people with whom you can grow.

Learn what features the print media is planning by checking media calendars. Print publications prepare editorial calendars that list the features that are scheduled to appear in upcoming issues. Contact target publications to see if they have scheduled features that relate to

**Robyn Says**

With the media, it's whom you know and then, of course, what you know. Never underestimate the importance of knowing people in the media. Build a network of media contacts before you need them. Take every opportunity to get to know them. Attend functions and places where the media goes.

Instead of focusing on what the media can do for you, think more about what you can do for it. If you make the media's job easier by doing research, delivering great sound bites, and telling your media contacts about great people, those contacts will usually consider you when they could use information related to your message.

the subject of your book, or find this information in Bacon's Media Calendars, *www.mediacalendars.com*. Then see if you can link your book to the features that a publication is planning to run.

If so, contact the editor and pitch a story idea. Find interesting angles that will enhance the editor's stories, make them more interesting, and round them out.

Send media people items and information that could help them. For example, tips, leads, story ideas, facts, and the names of people they can contact. If you see an article in the paper about the rising popularity of hybrid cars, send it and mention how your mechanic friend built a device to give such cars more pep. Help media people in their areas of interest even if those areas are unrelated to you and your book.

Present information to the media in the style or format it usually follows. Whenever possible, connect the items you submit to well-known people or experts and state if you can arrange to make those personalities available.

Since you have written a book, you are an expert on the information covered in your book. The media needs quotes, explanations, and observations from experts, so let people in the media know that you're available. Send them your qualifications, your photograph, and a tape of your prior appearances. Increase your value to your media contacts by:

*Regularly asking them what they're working on.* Then, see if you have information or sources that could help them.

*Responding to their requests.* Try to furnish what they want even if it requires you to do research or check with your personal sources.

*Sharing your sources.* When you can't provide what media people request, refer them to others who could. Offer to make introductions.

## Finding Who to Contact

How do you get the media to tell the world about your book? You find media people and outlets that you can contact. The information is in:

Bacon's directories, available in annual print and online versions (*www.bacons.com*). The print versions are out-of-date as soon as they're published, whereas online editions are continuously updated and are searchable by areas, media, outlets, and more. The newspaper/magazine directory includes contact information for editors and outlets, Web site addresses, editor contact profiles, and types of press materials accepted. The radio, TV, and cable editions include personnel rosters, formats, guest and press material acceptance policies, target audience, and news and reporter contact profiles.

Alex Carroll's Radio Interview Database (*www.radiopublicity.com*) lists the names of hosts and producers of every prime-time talk show on every major U.S. talk station having at least 100,000 listeners. It describes and categorizes 1,206 prime-time talk shows on the top 153 stations and gives bios for most hosts.

*Broadcasting & Cable Yearbook* (*www.bowker.com/catalog/000061.htm*) lists every TV and cable station in America.

Editor and Publisher (*www.editorandpublisher.com*) lists information about every newspaper in America.

Other media lists can be purchased at book marketing sites such as *www.bookmarket.com*, *www.radiopublicity.com*, *www.partylinepublishing.com*, and other resources. For onetime book launches, it might be more cost-effective to purchase a targeted list from one of these sources, with preprinted labels and a disk.

When you're ready to contact a media outlet, identify the decision makers. All outlets have a hierarchy of decision makers, so speak with the person who makes or contributes to the decision to cover you or your book. Get their names by networking with other authors and your media contacts. Read the credits at the end of shows.

## The Rules

To build strong relationships with the media, be flexible and constantly remind yourself that your goal is to get the media to publicize you and your book. So stay focused, be patient, persistent, and understanding because the road may be bumpy and long.

Since your relationship isn't equal, the media makes the rules and they differ from industry to industry, outlet to outlet, and person to person. When it wishes, the media can change the rules, and it will change them arbitrarily, when it suits its purposes. Suddenly, after all your hard work, your story or appearance may be cut, rewritten, or canceled.

- Even though you're fuming inside, be professional, which in this case means act like you understand, because frankly, in most cases, there's nothing you can do about it.
- Salvage something that will benefit you. Instead of wasting time and energy arguing, complaining, and raising your blood pressure, act understanding; be a team player. Ask if he or she can recommend anyone else whom you could contact.
- Never show anger or threaten. Instead, immediately focus on finding bargaining chips to position yourself for the future. Don't say, "Okay, you owe me one"; just let it go. During subsequent contacts, plant subtle reminders by asking how the matter turned out.

Call media outlets and ask, "Who is in charge of bookings for the noon news and can you give me his or her telephone number or e-mail address?" Find out how he or she prefers to be contacted, by e-mail or by phone. Then, enter the name and contact information in your media list.

The media has gatekeepers whom you usually have to go through to get your book covered. For print, they're editors, and for radio and TV, they're producers; so contact them first. Normally, it's a waste of time to pitch reporters and hosts and better to work top-down because reporters generally cover stories assigned to them by their editors. Usually, hosts are not involved in the booking process. On rare occasions, it can work in reverse, but your chances are usually stronger when an editor or producer wants to feature your book.

■ When you communicate with the media, nothing is off the record. Don't say anything that you might regret or that you would not want to read in a news headline or story.

## Action

1. List the factors you should note on how media outlets cover books.
2. What information should be collected in your media list?
3. Describe the three levels of a media list.
4. Explain how you can become a media resource.
5. How do you find what features print outlets are planning?

### Remember

⚠ **The best way to get publicity for your book is through the media.** So before you approach the media, study it and know how it works. Get to know the types of items various media outlets and people prefer, and link your pitches accordingly. Build large media lists, databases that contain the names of media contacts who can promote your book, and fill them with information about those contacts.

⚠ **Become a media resource.** Learn what media outlets are working on and feed them information and the names of sources that can help them. Offer your services as an expert in your specialty area. Understand that the media is busy and probably won't be responsive to your pitches. Expect it to take you at least seven tries before you connect.

**CHAPTER 7**

To solve a problem or to reach a goal, you ... don't need to know all the answers in advance. But you must have a clear idea of the problem or the goal you want to reach.

*W. Clement Stone*

# How to Get Bookings and Coverage

**THIS CHAPTER COVERS:**

▶ What the media wants
▶ Initial contacts
▶ Following up
▶ Press releases
▶ Contests
▶ Parties and events

SO NOW YOU HAVE a basic understanding of the media, how it works and why it's so important to establish close media relationships. But writers and producers aren't calling you. How do you get them to call? How do you get on *Oprah* or get covered by the *New York Times, People* magazine, or even the local press?

Usually, you get bookings and coverage because of numerous, cumulative efforts. Media coverage is generally the product of many individual efforts that when lumped together create groundswells, grassroots movements that build over time. It also results from building strong media relationships, campaign planning, implementation, and coordination.

When you hire publicists, they already have media connections. Knowing who to contact is their business. They have worked, often for years, to get to know journalists, editors, and producers. Frequently, they have built long-standing relationships, so they know exactly who to call, what to say, and how to play the game.

## What the Media Wants

When you approach the media, it's essential to know what it wants. When you know what it wants, you can develop hooks to capture its interest. Although each media person and outlet will have his or her own favorites, most usually want the following:

*News.* As we've indicated, the media wants items connected to the news that interpret, analyze, and give insights and tie in to it. So, if you want coverage for your book, tie your pitch to items and events in the news. If a high-profile trial is dominating the news, try to connect with it. In your pitches, show how your book relates to the latest diets, sports stories, or business scandals.

*Specificity.* For example, if you wrote a book about ethical business practices, most media outlets won't be interested if you pitch it in the abstract. However, if you tie your book to a particular scandal or story that's currently getting lots of play, the media will sit up and listen. With regard to scandals, good hooks might be, "What Business Scandals Cost You," "Three Fitting Punishments for Enron Perpetrators," and "How Scandal Victims Can Strike Back."

*Experts.* Offer to make yourself available to the media as an expert who can comment and be quoted as an expert on your topic, even if you did not specifically address it in your book. Write a list of the subjects that you can expertly cover, and identify the media outlets that you could approach to offer your expertise. Be willing to comment on subjects that everyone else is discussing and questioning.

*Timeliness.* Link the subject of your book to current and upcoming events. If your book is about love, vigorously promote it around Valentine's Day or prior to National Romance Awareness Month, which takes place every August. If it's about tax savings, promote it before April 15. Find events with which you can connect in *Chase's Annual*

*Events* (Contemporary Publishing, 1993), which can be found in many libraries. List how your book is newsworthy and some upcoming events you could use to promote it.

*Story ideas.* The media looks at everything in terms of its story potential: could it make a good story for its publication or show? So pitch story ideas! Jess Todtfeld, associate producer for *Fox & Friends* and media trainer with Success in Media, Inc. (*www.successinmedia.com*), teaches his clients to, "Send the media a very short e-mail or letter with a few bullet points that are story ideas. The story ideas should read like newspaper headlines. The media doesn't want long stories about people's lives; they want story ideas that they can pitch in a meeting. They don't want an explanation of someone's book, everything they've done in their life; they want story ideas."

*Problem solving.* To get the media's attention, identify a problem or problems that affects a large number of people and offer solutions that actually work. Better yet, state how to solve the problem in three to five steps. The media looks for stories that provide real benefits to its audiences.

"The best types of stories are those that solve a problem, that have 'take away,'" Jess Todtfeld explains. "That means the audience will take something tangible from the story; that it will learn something, and get information it can put to use." List specific problems that information in your book solves.

*Exploding myths.* "If you can take a conventionally held notion, something that is widely believed, and turn it on its ear, you will have media liftoff," Joel D. Roberts, media trainer and former Los Angeles talk-show host explains. Dr. Robert Atkins, who taught that lowering carbohydrate intake, not decreasing fat, was the key to weight loss, was a great myth buster and it got him enormous publicity. When John Gray wrote that men and women differed, it went against the accepted thinking for that time. In *The Tipping Point* (Little, Brown and Company, 2000), Malcolm Gladwell re-examined why change occurs.

Myth busting will get the media's attention. It may not believe what you claim, but it will certainly listen. List the myths your book debunks.

*Showing opportunity.* If you can appeal to people's dreams and show them new opportunities, the media will pay attention. Showing opportunity is more than telling the public "how to"; it's explaining how they can change, improve, and better their lives. For example, how they can get rich, beat illnesses, and be happier. The media considers itself a central part of the community and part of its job is to improve the lot of its audience. Great and inspirational stories provide terrific hooks. Storytelling is a deep-rooted part of our culture; it's an entertaining way in which we learn. The public and the media are drawn to personal success and inspirational stories because they create hope and blueprints for success.

*Radio-TV Interview Report* publisher Steve Harrison had no acting training but had always loved Shakespeare and wanted to play Hamlet. When a local church group decided to mount the play, Steve trained, took lessons, and landed the role. He also agreed to help promote the production. To do so, he pitched a story to the local media on how "a local businessman fulfilled his dream of playing Hamlet," which it was happy to run. Identify possible opportunities that your book can provide.

*Celebrities.* Since the public is obsessed with celebrities, the media loves stories about or connected with celebrities. So involve famous people in your book and use their celebrity to get it publicity. Go beyond the usual endorsements by asking celebrities to contribute information to your book, answer surveys, write chapters, or even coauthor it with you.

After he obtained local coverage for his church group's production of *Hamlet*, Steve Harrison wrote to famous actors, asking each of them for one piece of advice on how he should tackle the role. Responses poured in from famous leading men such as John Gielgud, Anthony Hopkins, Patrick Stewart, Mel Gibson, and a host of others, which

Harrison sent to the area's premier arts publication. The publication wrote a story about the advice that these stars gave a fledgling, local actor, and every performance of Harrison's *Hamlet* sold out.

For their book, *Everybody Loves Pizza* (Emmis Books, 2005), Penny Pollack and Jeff Ruby compiled a directory of over 500 great American pizzerias. They solicited suggestions from food writers across the country; featured recipes from famous chefs such as Wolfgang Puck and Mario Batali; and conducted interviews with pizza chain operators, the pizza acrobatic champ, and the nation's oldest delivery boy. Everyone they included became a publicist for their book.

Similarly, Douglas M. Isenberg asked experts to write and contribute material on their areas of expertise to his book *The GigaLaw Guide to Internet Law* (Random House, 2002). Their input not only helped Isenberg produce a better book, but his contributors became champions of Isenberg's book. List how you could connect information in your book to celebrities.

*List formats.* The media loves and pays attention to pitches that are structured as lists. For example, "5 Ways to Better Health Now" or "5 Secrets to Getting Unlimited Credit." The media also loves pitches that reveal secrets as well as shocking and controversial information.

Alex Carroll knows what the media wants. He's a bestselling author who's been a guest on 1,264 radio shows over the past ten years and sold $1.5 million worth of books in the process. He maintains a database of the top 1,364 radio shows in America (100,000 listeners or more) and also has an audio course on how to pitch radio producers, in which you get to listen to actual phone calls Alex made to producers while booking seventy-seven radio interviews. Visit his Web site at *www.RadioPublicity .com* for a free list of the Top 20 Nationally Syndicated Radio Shows.

Carroll notes that the media wants to interview people who can:

1. Save people time or money.
2. Make them rich.
3. Tell an amazing story.

4. Make them laugh.
5. Share little-known tips or secrets or teach something.
6. Get them arguing.

Identify information in your book that can be compiled into lists.

## Initial Contacts

When professional publicists want bookings and coverage, they generally operate as follows: They write a killer press release in the format we've previously detailed. They find the perfect hook—the book's benefits, story ideas, or timely angles—and catapult themselves into the media universe. Some create media kits that include the items that we described.

"Most authors don't know the difference between their messages and their hooks," media trainer Joel Roberts points out. "The message is what you want to share with humanity, and your hooks are the strategies that get you on shows so that you can share your message." We will discuss messages and hooks in greater detail in Chapter 9, "Media Training."

After they write press releases, the professionals usually e-mail or call contacts on their media lists to inquire if they would be interested in receiving the release or information about the book and/or the author. When they have established relationships with contacts, they usually add a personal comment to personalize the pitch. As we've mentioned, people in the media differ on how they want you to contact them. So find out if they prefer you to phone, e-mail, fax, or contact them by postal mail. Add their preference to your media list. Most media people now prefer e-mail because it's quick and direct. However, be sure to keep your messages brief. Limit most e-mails to a single screen.

If you don't have a publicist, prepare a press release or information that you can send to the media. Then, contact each by e-mail or by phone. You can also hire services that will send your releases to tens of thousands of outlets. These services include: PR Newswire (*www.prnewswire.com*), BusinessWire (*http://home.businesswire.com*), Imediafax (*www.imediafax.com*), and many others. If you don't use a service and decide to contact media outlets yourself:

- Contact specific individuals at your target outlets.
- Find out who to contact by calling the media outlet and asking, "Who is the editor for the business section?" or "Who is the producer for the morning show?" Journalists' e-mail addresses are often included with or after their byline credits.
- Ask for the person's name and contact information.
- Make sure to double-check how all names are spelled.
- Find out how he or she prefers to be contacted, by phone or e-mail.
- Send e-mails with return receipts to make sure they received them.
- Add a signature line that automatically appears on your e-mail messages.

For radio and TV, call producers, not hosts. Call them after their shows have run because that's when they usually have time. Prior to their shows, they're usually totally occupied by details required to put on their programs. When you call, chances are you won't get through. At that point, you can leave a message or ask to have them paged. In all contacts—by e-mail or phone messages or when speaking with the media—give or recite your silver bullet. Say, "This is Robyn Freedman Spizman. My book *Make It Memorable* tells you how to give the most meaningful and memorable gifts on earth." Then add, "I'd like to send you a press release telling you all about it." It often pays to ask the operator to page a producer. Frequently, producers will answer pages and you can make your pitch. When they take paged calls, they probably won't be at their desks. Usually, they will be in the middle of something else, so you may not get their full attention.

Authors often send the media packages that include the book, a press release, and other information. Producers want book covers to explain the story idea, which they rarely do. They want a title that says,

"Five Ways to Get a Husband," not "Kiss a Frog," which doesn't explain what the book is about.

If you send your book or a press kit, be sure it includes a one-sheet with bulleted story ideas. Write your story ideas like newspaper headlines or TV teasers. For example, "The Truth about Second Marriages," "What Innocence Means to Teenagers Today," "Three Secrets That Wives Always Hide." Don't write, "Tax Code Explained"; instead, say, "Five Ways to Save $1,000 on Your Taxes Now." To get story ideas, pay attention to headlines in entertainment magazines and the teasers for TV shows like *Access Hollywood* and *Entertainment Tonight*. TV entertainment programs are loaded with teasers.

If a particular contact responds to your call or e-mail by saying, "Sure, send me more," immediately verify the address. In bold letters, write on the envelope, "REQUESTED MATERIAL ENCLOSED." Then send your information right away—don't wait. If a contact declines, pleasantly express your thanks.

Alex Carroll uses a red envelope to send information to the media. "Any color but manila or white!" he stresses. He also addresses each envelope by hand and pastes a copy of his book cover on it. When media contacts give him the okay to send his material, he tells them, "Look for a red envelope with an illustration of a cop writing a ticket on it."

### Expect Rejection

Rejection is a basic part of the business. When you're rejected, ask the contact, "Do you know anyone else who might be interested?" If he or she does, get permission to use that contact's name because it could make a difference in how your next pitch is received.

After you are rejected, finish on a positive note. Don't burn your bridges with that contact, because you may need to contact him or her again. Lay the groundwork for building a relationship by politely thanking him or her for his or her time, courtesy, and consideration. Don't gush; just be polite, grateful, and brief.

**Robyn Says**

If you call the media directly:

- Leave a clear message.
- Begin by clearly stating your name and phone number.
- Then, repeat your phone number—slowly.
- Briefly state your expertise: "I'm a gift-giving expert," "I'm a nationally known cardiologist," or "I'm a coupon-clipping, money-saving, stay-at-home mom."
- When you call back, don't assume that media contacts will remember who you are or why you contacted them. Don't repeat your entire message, but identify yourself by saying, "This is Rick Frishman of Rick's Cheap Domains."

Voice mail is an audition; every media contact is an audition. When you leave a message, remember that it's going to be evaluated and judged. While you ramble, someone could be deciding whether you might be a good interview or guest. So be brief and to the point. Media people are busy, so don't monopolize their time.

On those rare occasions when media contacts enter into a dialogue with you, find out what else they're looking into or in the process of writing. When you know what they're up to, you will have a better shot at attracting their attention by linking your book to their interests. You can also build your relationship by providing names and information that could help them with their projects.

When you make contact, you have, at most, only thirty seconds to interest them in your initial pitch. Don't send unsolicited press releases, because they will get lost. If an editor or producer is interested, he or she will ask you to send a one-sheet, a press release with the key points bulleted. Then, if he or she is still interested, send your press kit and your book.

How do you get the media to answer your calls? According to Willy Spizman of Atlanta's Spizman Agency, which specializes in publicizing books, "Media usually prefers to be pitched via e-mail, but each media personality and outlet has its own individual preferences. If you have a track record and a relationship with a media outlet, it's acceptable to call, but it's critical to understand and respect their time. They're super busy people multitasking and managing breaking news and endless details. The majority of media people prefer e-mail, which allows them to review the information you have sent them at their leisure and leaves the decision to follow up or not in their hands."

"If you decide to call, avoid charging forward with your spiel. First, ask if the journalist is on deadline or has a moment to talk with you. If they are on deadline, ask for a good time to call back. If he or she is available, make your point in thirty seconds or less. Know your message inside and out, and be able to deliver it quickly."

As we've noted, people in the media are extremely busy. So, when you contact the media, be:

- Brief
- Direct
- Polite
- Professional
- Clear

When, and if, you speak with media contacts:

1. Call them by name. Make it personal and establish a quick connection.
2. Don't waste their time. Get right to the point.
3. Ask if they received your information.
4. If they did, ask, "Is there anything you didn't understand?" "Is there anything else you want to know?" "Would you like to arrange an interview?" If they didn't, ask if you can resend it.

When the people in the media you contact are abrupt or unresponsive, don't take it personally or be discouraged. Chalk it up to their being under the gun. Most of them are terrific people who will help you if they can, but they also may reflect the unrelenting pressures of their jobs.

## Following Up

Most of the time, media contacts don't respond, but don't give up or become discouraged. Don't stop; just regroup and try and try again. Follow up promptly. Following up is essential in getting publicity!

Professional publicists follow up their initial appeals by e-mail or phone to inquire about the contact's interest. Following up is what distinguishes professional publicists from amateurs. Following up is the repetitive and unglamorous aspect of getting publicity that many authors don't want to or won't do. However, professionals will. If you want to get the media to publicize your book, learn to follow up!

Call a day or so after they should have received your initial contact. Then follow up every day or two. Leave your silver bullet, your initial message, only once, but give your name, identify yourself, and state how you can be contacted. For example, say, "This is Jim Brady. Call me about the latest handgun death."

After you contact people in the media a number of times, they begin to recognize your name. They start connecting it with your area of expertise and your book, which is the way that you start building relationships.

Be persistent; continue following up until you make contact or are convinced that it's hopeless. Some media contacts will appreciate the fact that you follow up because it may alert them to items they missed or remind them of others that they might want to revisit.

Publicity is a business with lots of rejections and few responses. It can take a dozen phone calls to get an interview with a major-market media outlet. Remember the Rule of Seven—it takes at least seven tries before you make contact. But one response, one yes, may be all you need to get your story told. Look at each no or lack of response not as a defeat or a setback, but as a small victory that puts you closer to the yes that will land you a feature or a booking.

Remember, timing is everything with the media! In the course of a week or two, everything can change. A contact who was totally disinterested last week may now want lots of information on a subject that he or she virtually ignored before.

When Robyn began pitching her books, she thought a no was just the word *on* backward. "So when a contact said no, I began to passionately pitch because I knew it was do or die," Robyn explains. "I listened to the media and in a few moments, I'd know if I was shooting blanks or connecting. I always knew what I wanted to convey and was ready to rocket. Sometimes it helped to ask, 'Thank you for your feedback. Do you know anyone working on any topics that relate to my focus?'"

To follow up without being a pest and to get the media to lower its guard, say something like, "I'm sorry to bother you so much, I know how busy you are. But I thought my new book would really be up your alley and you'd like to know about it." Usually, your apology and understanding of how busy they are will loosen them up.

When you don't have something to pitch, stay on their radar screens. Periodically call, e-mail, and send information. Put them on your Christmas card list. Send copies of your promotional materials and newsletters. When they cover you or your book, send thank-you notes. Convey your congratulations when they get awards, promotions, or new jobs. Send them birthday cards; consider it a part of following up, but sincerity is key. Send items in order to connect with people in the media, to get to know them and enable them to become more familiar with you.

## Press Releases

Publicity expert Paul Hartunian believes that conducting a press release campaign is the most effective way to get bookings and coverage. So he instructs his clients to:

- Start early, as soon as they think about writing a book and even before they write or try to shop it.

- Every week, send a different press release. If you can't send one every week, send one at least every other week. Distributing press releases at longer intervals is not as productive.
- In each press release, give solutions to specific problems. Think of the most common and troubling problems in your area of expertise and provide solutions for them. When the media continually receives your solutions, it will recognize your name and think of you as an expert in your field.
- Continue sending press releases well after your book is published in order to continue your media presence long after the buzz on your book has faded.

Although writing and sending so many press releases sounds like a ton of work, Hartunian feels it isn't difficult. First, he recommends that authors develop a template that they can easily follow, which will become routine after a while. An effective approach is to first identify the problem. Then, explain why it occurs, its implications, and its impact. Finally, offer solutions.

Hartunian notes that after about six months, old press releases can be recycled. "The reporter you may have pitched may have moved to a different paper or might not have read your release the first time around," he explains. "Audiences change and those who read a release today may be different than those who read it before. Set up a stable of press releases, update them, tweak them, link them to current news and developments, and recycle them," Hartunian advises.

Anticipate and capitalize on events. Hartunian knows that in every field, certain events will eventually occur, so he prepares to use them to get publicity. When he represented a client who marketed a golf putter, he realized that sooner or later, some high-profile professional golfer would miss a putt that would cost him a tournament. So, he dashed out a press release with the headline, "Did You See _____ _____ Just Miss That Putt?" and left the name blank. Under the headline, he added the subhead, "Call me. I can tell you why _____ _____ missed that putt and how it could have been prevented."

Then, Hartunian filed the press release and waited. Sure enough, before long, a major golfer missed a critical putt to lose a major tournament. Seconds after the miss, Hartunian pulled out the prewritten release, filled in the golfer's name, and faxed the press release to his distribution services, which in turn forwarded it to tens of thousands of media outlets. The media was floored by Hartunian's lightning-quick action and overwhelmed him with interview requests.

## Radio-TV Interview Report

Attract the attention of radio and TV producers by advertising in *Radio-TV Interview Report: The Magazine Producers Read to Find Guests* (*RTIR*). *RTIR* is a magazine that is read by over 4,000 producers throughout the United States, and Canada. The interactive version can be visited at *www.rtir.com*. It makes sense to advertise in *RTIR* because producers receive the magazine and read it to find authors and experts who could appear as guests on their shows.

*RTIR* is published twice a month and each issue features 100 to 150 authors and spokespersons. Ads in *RTIR* include a headline; photos of the author and the book cover; and information about the book, which is often bulleted. The ads also give the author's credentials, availability, and how he or she can be contacted.

At no additional charge, *RTIR*'s copywriters will work with you to write your ad and find hooks that will attract the media. Most interviews will be from radio stations and will be conducted via telephone from your home or office. However, ads in *RTIR* have led to bookings on *Oprah, Good Morning America, Larry King Live*, and more.

## Contests

Everyone loves contests, so the media is usually delighted to cover them. Contests generate wonderful publicity for sponsors, especially when they involve great prizes; benefit special people, organizations, or interests; and are creative and unusual. Since contests run for extended periods of time, they can provide their sponsors with continuous publicity opportunities. Contests can get coverage when they are announced; as they progress; when awards are made; and in subsequent stories, follow-ups, and events.

We like contests so much that our publisher and we held a contest to promote the first book published in the Author 101 series, *Bestselling Book Proposals*. Our publisher, Adams Media, gave the person who submitted the best book proposal a contract to publish his or her book. We gave that individual a package to professionally publicize his or her book, which is worth $20,000.

Run your own contest related to the subject of your book. If you wrote a how-to book on making cookies, furniture, or flower arrangements, award the reader who made the tastiest, sturdiest, and most aromatic. Follow Paul Hartunian's advice by ratcheting up your press release machine. Bombard the media with press releases that spread the word about your contest and your book.

Karen Quinn, the author of *The Ivy Chronicles* (Viking Adult, 2005), used an inventive approach to build her book sales. She sent a letter to her friends, family, and network contacts asking them to help promote her book. Those who did were entered in a drawing to win a $1,000 gift certificate to Karen's family's jewelry store. Karen classified helpers into three categories—Friends, Cheerleaders, and Cult Members—depending on the extent of the effort they made, and the more they helped, the more chances they received in the drawing.

## Parties and Events

Parties and events can be the ideal way to introduce your book. Launch parties are wonderful rewards for all your hard work and marvelous celebrations to share with family and friends. They can also be exceptional promotion opportunities. Think beyond the usual book-launch party. Do more than invite all your friends and contacts to a bookstore where you sit, sign away, and have little chance to talk. Be inventive; create an event or a series of events that will not only attract the media, but that will wow it. Make it memorable by thinking bigger, bolder, and brassier.

- If you wrote a book on baking, hold your party at a bakery. Overwhelm your guests with food. Serve each of the pastries featured in your book. Put on cooking demonstrations, give out recipes, and teach.
- Promote your gardening book by holding a series of events in underprivileged neighborhoods. Put on demonstrations and give away seedlings, plants, containers, and potting soil. Serve some of the food featured in your book. Invite the mayor, local officials, and notables.

Connect your parties to newsworthy events. Penny Pollack and Jeff Ruby decided to launch their book, *Everybody Loves Pizza* (Emmis Books, 2005), in October, which is national pizza month and the 100th anniversary of the oldest pizza parlor in the country. Their launch party featured lots of slicing and dicing and drew gobs of media attention.

Host events for charities and worthy causes. Find sponsors, companies that make or sell items that are related to your book. Ask them to donate their goods or services, financial support, or the help of their employees. Give them full sponsorship credit. Ask them to invite their media contacts as well as their customers, clients, and associates.

When Robyn launched her book *Make It Memorable*, the owner of the top restaurant in Atlanta hosted an extravaganza honoring her as an author and the leading holiday-gift expert. Since they knew that the best route to the media is through its stomach, they provided an abundance of incredible food. So the media poured out for Robyn's bash even though it was held on the rainiest night in Georgia!

At Robyn's party, she gave out interactive door prizes. Robyn demonstrated ideas from her book and gave a copy of it to each attendee. Attendees also received a festive gift pack filled with a variety of Robyn's favorite goodies and party favors. A magnificent necklace that was created by a local artist was draped around the neck of a marble sculpture that dominated the entrance to the restaurant. The necklace was encrusted with hundreds of gorgeous gems and a contest was held in which the guests tried to guess the exact number.

## Networking

Writers are a uniquely supportive group. They know the effort it takes to write a book and will usually be more than willing to help fellow writers succeed. Many writers are journalists and have fabulous contacts. They've interviewed many important people and made great contacts over the years. Usually, they will be happy to help you tell others about the wonders of your book.

Prepare a one-sheet for writers that describes your book. It should contain everything someone needs to know about your book. Cover the basics, and if you have the space, add details like key endorsements, book review comments, and anything that will make it an appealing sales sheet with pizzazz.

Also provide all of the usual information, such as the title, your name, the benefits it will provide to readers, and your contact information. Hand these sheets out liberally. Distribute them at writers' groups and organizations, bookstores, and libraries. Ask your agent and publisher to send them to their authors. Speak with them and explain how much you would appreciate their help in publicizing your book. Ask noted writers, agents, and others for endorsements that you could use to promote your book.

Speak with people who work at bookstores and libraries. Often, they are writers and are involved in writers' circles or communities. Tell them about your book, give them written information about it, and ask them to talk it up with their friends. Consider giving key people a signed copy of your book in which you thank them for their help.

Earlier in this chapter, we told you about Karen Quinn's letter in which she asked her family, friends, and network to help support her book. Well, here is part of her request letter to them.

- Send an e-mail recommendation to your buddy list (and ask them to pass it on to their list).
- Personally tell people about the book.
- Send a note of recommendation to friends and family (I have postcards if you need them—just call or e-mail).
- Give copies as birthday, Valentine's or Groundhog's Day gifts to people you know who like this type of novel.
- Post a (glowing!) review to Amazon.com, Barnes & Noble .com, Booksense.com, or BooksAMillion.com. *Hint:* You can post the same review on all sites.
- Arrange for a book club to read the book (I'd be happy to call in on discussion night, or even stop by if it's close).
- Go to *www.urbanbaby.com*, *www.ivillage*, or other sites that attract parents. Recommend the book on a bulletin board or chat room.
- If you know anyone who writes for a magazine, newspaper, TV, or newsletter, tell them that we can get them a review copy of the book if they'll write a review or do a story.

## Action Steps

1. List the steps you should follow to contact people in the media.
2. If you don't reach the media directly, list what you should include in your message.
3. State what you should say when you speak with the media.
4. Name the steps you should take in a press release campaign.
5. List five ways in which your network members can help you promote your book.

*Remember*

⚠ **It usually takes numerous, cumulative efforts to get media bookings and coverage for your book.** The best way to start is usually by writing a killer press release and then e-mailing or calling media contacts to see if they would be interested in it. If they don't respond to you, continue to follow up. If they reject your pitch, be polite, pleasant, and try to salvage something. See if they will refer you to someone else.

⚠ **To attract the media's attention, consider conducting a press release campaign.** Send weekly releases that provide answers to problems that are faced by the audience for your book. Also advertise in *Radio-TV Interview Report*, hold contests, put on parties and events, and get the word out through your network contacts.

**CHAPTER 8**

Keep your face to the sunshine and you cannot see the shadow.
*Helen Keller*

# Interviewing

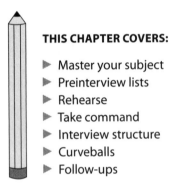

**THIS CHAPTER COVERS:**

▶ Master your subject
▶ Preinterview lists
▶ Rehearse
▶ Take command
▶ Interview structure
▶ Curveballs
▶ Follow-ups

AN INTERVIEW is a performance; it places you on center stage, directly in the spotlight, where you're the headliner, the featured attraction. During interviews, all eyes and ears are focused directly on you, and everyone's waiting eagerly for your words of wisdom. You're expected to perform and to perform brilliantly; the success of your book or your career may depend on it.

Interviews are the epicenter of book publicity campaigns; they're where you send out shock waves and make big impressions. If you consistently give lively, entertaining, and informative interviews, it will endear you to the media's heart and you will become one of its favorites. Suddenly, your name will pop up everywhere, and your fame will spread.

Interviews can be your best friends because they give you unparalleled opportunities to tell your story and build your legend. If your interviews are compelling, informative, and inspirational, you will be in demand. You will become a media star and attract interest in your book.

For some, the thought of giving interviews strikes fear in their hearts and makes them want to take off on the run. If this happens to you, don't worry—you've come to the right place. We know the secrets of giving fabulous interviews and overcoming your fears, and we're going to teach them to you now.

## Master Your Subject

The most important element in giving interviews is having complete mastery of your subject matter, knowing it cold. Before you expose yourself to the media, learn your topic inside out so you will be able to promptly answer any question about it.

Most problems with interviews arise because interview subjects don't really know their material. When they're questioned, they can't give the right answers so they try to bluff, which rarely works.

Don't be afraid of interviews. It's natural to feel apprehensive and uneasy, especially when you're not used to being interviewed. However, when you know your stuff, the butterflies will vanish the moment you speak. As soon as you utter your first words, your brain, and the storehouse of knowledge it holds, will kick in. The power of knowledge is awesome; let it work for you. It will moisten your throat, engage your mind, loosen your tongue, and pull the words from within you. Soon, you'll be speaking as fluidly as if you were on autopilot.

The secrets are practice and concentration. Write out the key questions you expect to be asked and great answers to them. Ask your friends and family to grill you until you can recite them flawlessly. Have them ask you their own, unscripted questions and critique your responses.

Concentrate on each question as it's asked and your answers will flow. In no time, you'll forget your fear and be totally involved in the interview. As you speak, your spirit will lift; you'll feed off the interest and reactions of the interviewer and audience as well as your own clarity and expressiveness. You'll find that you're having fun.

Rick requires all his clients to undergo training before they give interviews. "No director would send an untrained, unrehearsed actor onstage," Rick says. "And in PR, we're the directors and our clients are the actors. Our clients must know their lines and how to deliver them or the audience will get up and leave." Willy Spizman of the Spizman Agency agrees: "It's important to rehearse your content and prepare for the unexpected. Getting your message down to a few succinct points that you can give the producer beforehand also can help keep the segment on target. When visuals or props are used, they also can help get your message across, so evaluate your options and whenever possible, incorporate examples."

Never hold an interview without having first answered each of the following questions.

1. What am I an expert on?
2. What specific problems can I solve?
3. What precise solution can I recommend?

Robyn suggests, "The most important thing an author can provide is a solution to some problem or everyday situation that people experience. While you want to give a fabulous interview, you also must inspire

---

### *You Have the Knowledge*

It takes extensive knowledge to write a book. First, you had to acquire all that knowledge. Then you had to understand it thoroughly enough to clearly explain it to others so that they would immediately understand it. Those are huge accomplishments and represent the hardest work.

Compared with writing a book, giving an interview is a snap, especially when you get a few under your belt. Think of each interview as a showcase for your knowledge, as an occasion where you can tell others about your expertise. Speaking about topics on which you're an authority is both rewarding and exhilarating, especially when others are receptive to it, impressed by it, and it can really help them.

readers to buy your book without sounding like you're giving a commercial. If you share a few ideas that really work, your readers will want more. Test your content and determine which tips are of most interest. Ask the station to post your cover and information on their Web site and post a link to your site. Add some helpful information and perhaps a list of resources to your site, so you capture people's interest. Leave a business card that gives your book title and Web site plus a copy of your book with the receptionist at the station since he or she is the gatekeeper who will get calls inquiring about the book.

"Most authors do a great job telling audiences about their topic, but they don't always do as well in selling their book. Be listener friendly by sharing three time-saving tips for getting organized, five fabulous ways to fight fat, or four ways to get your kids to go to bed without you're having to yell and scream. Structure your content to make it easy for the media to stick to your agenda and to articulate your topic in a succinct way."

"The most important piece of advice I give authors is know what you want to say, know exactly how you want to say it, be committed to getting it across and under no circumstances let anything stop you—including the interviewer's questions, which can take you down roads that are sometimes murky, confused, and have nothing to do with your book," Barbara De Angelis reveals. "You can't control the questions, the questioners, and where they're coming from. You can't let yourself sink to the level of their awareness or intelligence and answer their questions on the level of the questions. If you do, you can be pulled down the questioner's road, with his or her map to his or her destination, which may not be where you want to go. You have to know how to take any question and turn it into something that allows you to give your answer."

## Preinterview List

Know the media outlet that will be covering you. Read the writers' articles and watch or listen to their programs. Look for patterns and similarities; find out their styles. Understand the questions, slants, and approaches they usually take and plan your responses.

Before each interview, write a list of exactly what you want to say. Prepare a new list for every interview so you can review your information and make adjustments that freshen it. In making your preinterview list, here's how to proceed:

*Write five main points that you want to include in the interview.* These points should be similar, if not identical, to the main points in your press release. Place each point in the order of its importance, with the first item being the one you wish to stress most.

*Under each point, write three or four subpoints that you could cover if the interview runs long.* Also prioritize the subpoints. For each of your main points, have at least one joke, story, statistic, or other device that will make you more entertaining, interesting, and memorable. Decide if you're going to give away copies of your book, and if so, to whom and how many.

*For every interview you give, try to add something new, even if it's just a slight twist.* Tie it to something topical by drawing on events in the news, occasions such as upcoming holidays, the seasons, or developments in your field. Whatever you add doesn't have to be earth shaking or a major point or subpoint. It can be a new story, statistic, observation, theory, or quote. Besides providing a spark to each interview, new additions can revive your own enthusiasm and help keep you fully engaged.

## Rehearse

Few people are born performers who can immediately give great interviews. For most of us, it takes practice, lots of repetition, and understanding what you should do.

In interviews, you want to appear to be natural, spontaneous, and unrehearsed, which takes lots of practice. You also want to deliver your points clearly, convincingly, and with authority. Make clarity your top priority because an interview is worthless if no one understands what you said! Before each interview:

1. **Find the audience demographic.** What group or groups will the interview target? Be as specific as possible. Will it be high school teachers, automobile salespeople, or security analysts?

2. **Determine which of your points would be most likely to grab the target audience's attention and hold their interest.** Anticipate the problems they have, the questions you can answer, and the tangible benefits you can give them.

   "It's important for authors to realize that there are many different versions of the same exact question," Jess Todtfeld points out. "The very first question is always going to be some variation of 'Tell me about your book.' They can be framed as, 'Explain the _____ story,' 'How did you get to this point in your life?' 'What made you write this book?' However, they're all basically the same question, and ironically, it's always the question that stumps authors the most."

3. **Make a list of industry-specific language or analogies to which each particular audience will relate.** For instance, for accountants, sprinkle in terms such as *bottom line, in the red,* and *balance sheet.* In analogies, refer to the *plus side of the ledger, net gains,* or *long-term yields.*

4. **Study the interviewer's prior interviews.** Most interviewers tend to have favorite questions and approaches. Observe their questioning style: They may be confrontational, probing, sarcastic, or supportive to interviewees. Anticipate the questions they might ask and plan how to present your main points in your answers.

5. **Draft questions for your friends, family, and associates to ask you.** Have them toss in questions of their own. Videotape your performance and have your friends, family, and associates honestly critique it so you can improve your weaknesses.

6. **Prepare stories that vividly illustrate your message.** Audiences relate to stories, and they will set the tone for the entire interview. If possible, change stories from interview to interview so people in your audiences don't constantly hear the same old story.

7. **Rehearse when you're alone, at home and in your car.** When you're home, observe yourself in the mirror and pay particular attention to your posture, facial expressions, and gestures. Correct what doesn't look or sound great.

Rehearse to make interview responses seem more spontaneous. When you answer questions, speak directly to the audience. Don't give speeches or lectures. When you notice that you're giving canned replies, change the wording or stories and examples accompanying them to give them new verve.

## Take Command

Arrive at interviews early. Check that they have your name and the name of your book right. Make sure that they spell your name and title correctly and that they know how to pronounce your name and any difficult words in your book's title. As soon as you arrive, ask to see exactly what will be shown on the screen because mistakes frequently occur. Fortunately, they can easily be corrected.

If you have any special agendas, discuss how they should be handled. Clarify who will give contact or other information. For example, ask, "Will you be giving my Web site address or should I?" "Will you give the phone number to order my book or should I?" "Will you give the address of the charity so viewers can donate?"

Plan exactly what you want to say and how you plan to say it. Submit a list of questions that you want to answer. More often than not, the media will ask you those exact questions. Be prepared to make your key points in response to each of those questions.

## Sample Questions

The following questions were prepared by Planned Television Arts to promote Dr. Kevin Leman's book *Making Children Mind Without Losing Yours* (Revell, 2005).

- What are the pitfalls parents face today in trying to raise healthy, happy, and successful children? What aspects of the modern world pose challenges and particular difficulty to raising good kids now?
- Has the art of parenting changed greatly in the past twenty to thirty years? Is it possible to bring up good children in an era of selfishness, day care, the Internet, busy schedules?
- You have raised five kids, been with the same loving wife for thirty-five years—what would you do differently with what you know now?
- How far have we grown, as a nation, in raising kids since Dr. Spock came onto the scene?
- Are you a believer in time-outs or corporal punishment—or both? Do you recall the number of spankings you've given out over the years? What are the proper guidelines for spanking?
- You say parenting with a system of rewards and punishment is not an effective style—why?
- To run a strong household, parents wield power and authority. You suggest this must be done without becoming authoritarian. How does one take control without being controlling?
- Some parents seek to be the child's friend or to act more like a sibling than a parent. Is this healthy for child and parent?
- Are parents too selfish and less committed to parenting than they used to be?
- Tell us about the approach you call "reality discipline."
- What are the common mistakes a new parent is likely to make, and what can be done to help him or her avoid such errors in judgment or action?
- Does a permissive style of parenting work, and if not, why?

- What role does birth order play in child development, and how does it impact upon a parent's style of raising children?
- Do parents still serve as the primary role model for children, especially young teens—or have they given way to entertainment celebrities, pro athletes, and faces in the news media?
- What should a parent do when a kid is lying, swearing, talking back, tattling, acting selfishly, or acting up to seek attention?

Usually, producers, hosts, and interviewers will be supportive. Most of them simply want entertaining interviews. They really don't care why you wrote your book or what direction you want to take in the interview as long as it pleases their audience. Assume the attitude that it's your interview and take charge, but don't upstage the interviewer. Be direct and assertive, but polite. Most interviewers want you to look good and will usually help by asking the questions you submitted or other easy stuff. In response to interview questions:

- Answer the question that was asked, even if it doesn't let you state any of your main points. Answer the question directly, but briefly. Then, slide into one of your main points. Try to make a smooth transition by moving into the point that fits most closely. If you're abrupt or reach too far, your response will sound contrived and you will come off as just a promoter. Slide by prefacing your remarks with, "That reminds me of a story," "When I was _____," or "I heard about a _____." Sliding is an art that takes subtlety and practice, so work on it in conversations with your friends.
- "Master the art of 'clever segues,'" Barbara De Angelis suggests. "No matter what anyone asks you, say what you want to say. Comment on the question that's asked in one quick sentence, but then move on to the point you want to make. Practice until you learn to move gracefully from the question asked to the answer you want to give. To do so, you must really know your own material so you can quickly decide which point to make."

- If you get stuck and don't know an answer, say, "Thank you, that's an excellent question. But what I want to share with your listeners is . . ." and then go straight to your message. Study politicians; they use this technique all the time. Watch how they deflect questions to always get their messages across, regardless of what they're asked.

- If, as the interview continues, you have not had a chance to address your main points, do so, but don't be rude. Remember that you're there to make your points. So answer the questions you're asked briefly and then state, "But I'd really like to point out that _____" or "I think it's important for you to know (or understand) that _____" and then make your point. Speak directly, calmly, and pleasantly. Never let built-up frustration or anger seep through.

Be professional and totally prepared. Don't leave anything to chance. Look your best. Be neat, well groomed, and dress to sell. Even dress for radio and print interviews. Although the audience won't see you, the interviewer will—so make a great impression. Notice how often in print, writers describe the subject and what he or she was wearing or how he or she acted or looked.

Prior to TV appearances, watch the show to see how the host and guests dress and conduct themselves. It's usually safe to dress in the same manner as the host. If, after watching, you're still not sure what to wear, ask the producer.

Keep excellent records of everyone's telephone numbers, including the producer's cell phone numbers in case an emergency arises. Know how to check into the reception area at the station because some stations' doors are locked early in the morning or they have tight security and require photo identification. Also, be aware that when important news breaks, your segment can be postponed or cancelled. Whenever possible, watch or listen to the station on which you will be appearing.

- Keep your answers short and simple. Don't lecture or preach. If interviewers want more information, they will ask for it.
- Give your interview for the audience, listener, or reader, not just the host or interviewer. "Ninety percent of the people who interview you are not listening to what you say. They're thinking about the next question, the next interview, lunch, or their own problems," De Angelis points out. So focus on the audience.
- That said, make the host or interviewer look good. Say, "What a great question" or "No one has ever asked me that before." But do it only once or it will seem insincere. Act as if every question is insightful even as you change the subject to stress one of your main points.
- Listen closely so you can respond appropriately and gracefully tie your answers to your main points. If an audience is present, listen, watch, and speak directly to them. Treat the audience as your conversation partner: Smile, pay attention to it, and observe its reactions.
- When possible, try to work the title of your book into your answer. For example, Barbara De Angelis will say, "It looks like she was having a *How Did I Get Here?* moment." However, sometimes the title of your book won't work or it will sound too forced. Also, don't state your title constantly.
- Be yourself. Don't put on airs or try to be someone else. Avoid language, expressions, and gestures that you don't ordinarily use or that the audience might not understand.
- Be polite, respectful, and likable. Laugh at the host's or interviewer's jokes, but not hysterically. Smile and call him or her by name: "Well, yes, Phil" or "Thank you, Jane." Never steal the limelight from the interviewer or host or be pushy. Remember that it's the host or interviewer's show.
- Smile and act as if you're enjoying yourself. Don't paste a big, goofy grin across your face or laugh loudly. Be humble. Wear a pleasant look on your face and don't act like you're going through an inquisition.

**Rick Says**

Avoid coffee before an interview; it dries your mouth. Instead, drink water—even when the camera is on you, it's acceptable. If you're not dry, still drink water during interviews because it prevents dryness and will enable you to keep speaking smoothly.

Use water as a prop. For example, if you need time to decide how to an answer a tough question, stop and take a sip of water. As you do, think about what would be best to say. After you finish your drink, put down the water, smile softly, and give your response.

Publicist, speaker, and bestselling author Jill Lublin offers the following interviewing advice:

1. **Remember that interviewers have a job and their job is to entertain and give their audiences information, so help them.** If you make them look good, they will usually reciprocate by making you look good.

   Robyn concurs: "Overprepare for your interview. Keep in mind that your job is to share your information and deliver an entertaining and informative interview. To begin, it's important, even if you only have a minute, to successfully interact with the host. When you greet him or her, be sure to pronounce your name. Say, 'Hello, I am Robyn Spizman, which rhymes with 'wise-man.' I'm the co-author of the Author 101 series.'" This will increase the odds that your name is pronounced correctly and that the host knows that you wrote your book.

   Immediately thank the host for having you on and if you watch the show regularly, say so. "Jill. You're a credit to television. I have been your fan since you started." Create a connection.

2. **Never give interviews from a cell phone.** Landlines are clearer and provide better recording quality. Cell phones go down, and

incur interference—usually at the most critical time and you frequently won't sound your best. Once an interview opportunity is lost, it may never come again. Find a quiet place and use a landline for the best possible results. "Also, be sure to get the studio back line in case you are disconnected," Robyn advises.

3. **When you book an interview, don't cancel it unless you're actually dying or dead, and even then try to keep it.** Cancelled interviews are murder to reschedule because something newer, sexier, more immediate always seems to pop up. "If you are a hassle to work with or hard to schedule," Robyn notes, "they'll remember that. Also, know when a show airs, if it is live or taped, and listen to it ahead of time, which will give you an edge."

4. **Before every interview, study the local media.** Check out the top stories and, when possible, work them into your answers. Don't refer to your book. Don't say, "As I said in Chapter 12" or "In Chapter 5, I wrote. . . ." It should never be about the book, but it should always be about the readers and the value they will get from your knowledge. Instead of saying, "In *Guerrilla Publicity* we recommend _____," rephrase it as, "A great guerrilla publicity tactic is to _____." Or "A wonderful Author 101 rule is _____." Weave the title of your book into the interview by referring to it as a method, tactic, secret, or tip.

   The key is to not sound so overly promotional that you turn off the media. Also, be aware of what's going on in the news that day. Consider making reference to topical items that tie in to your topic because it will increase your chances of being kept on longer and invited back!

5. **Stand up for every interview, even if you're on the phone at home; it will help you sound more energized and alert.** Smile. Listeners can hear your smile over the phone and the airwaves. "When giving an interview on the phone or even on television," Robyn suggests, "watch your posture and hold your head up slightly, lifting your neck so that you are not slumping. This will

allow the air to move through your vocal cords more efficiently and your voice will sound clearer and stronger.

6. **Match the interviewer's energy and pace.** Everyone operates at a different speed, so know your interviewer's style beforehand. If she's a fast-talking morning DJ, be upbeat and lively. If it's an academic who wants in-depth answers, go that route. Joel Roberts advises, "Feel the beat; get the rhythm. Think of it like a Ping-Pong game in which you have to step up to the pace of the match and jump in."

"Reflect the tonal quality of your interview, but still be yourself," Rick notes. "News formats have a more serious tone, so give statistics and references to current news events when you get the chance. Morning and afternoon DJs are usually energetic. They generally want great topics and a steady stream of talk and lively guests. Reflect the show's tone, but be yourself. Never compromise your message even if the host goes down a different path or becomes silly or adversarial."

7. **Part of being a great guest is being who you are, but be yourself in a way that complements interviewers and hosts and helps them do their jobs.** "Remember, at all times," Robyn warns, "that you are a guest and they can cut you off as easily as they booked you. Connect with the host, follow the producers requests, and fully understand the show's format. Listen carefully to the questions asked, but don't be afraid to bring up topics and your message. Say, 'That's a great question, but it may be even more relevant to ask, what authors should do if they don't hear back from publishers after they submitted their book proposals?'"

## Interview Structure

Interviews usually follow a three-tiered structure that consists of (1) questions, (2) answers, and (3) solutions.

### Questions

As we've previously stated, the media frequently relies on the questions you send it. So prepare both great questions and riveting answers because you will probably repeat them often and they can really make you look good. Study the interviewer's prior interviews to see what types of questions you can expect. Then, practice working your main points into the answers you prepared for those questions.

"Every opportunity is defined by the person you're talking to: the interviewer, host, whomever," Barbara De Angelis told us. "You may go into an interview thinking that you're there to promote your book, get certain points across, or share information, but may end up colliding with the interviewer's consciousness; you collide with his or her day, relationship, background, career—with everything. What you think will be a purely professional interchange often is not. It's naïve to believe that people who interview you will have the same agenda as you."

When you truly know your information, you can usually overcome obstacles that interviewers might erect.

### Answers

In your answers, be explicit and graphic. Explain the depth of the problem you can solve and how serious it is. Describe how it affected you and the specific damage it caused. Use colorful descriptive words and examples that will enable the audience to picture what you say. Customize your answers for each particular audience and draw them in by asking, "Have you ever had this happen?" or "Don't we all know someone who _____?" Ask them to raise their hands or to say yes or no. Hold their attention by asking them questions.

Don't be afraid to make strong claims or promises, but make sure that you can deliver on them because your credibility will be on the line. When you're sure of your position, be bold and create controversy and disbelief, which hosts and producers love.

If you don't know the answer to a question, never bluff. Look directly at the interviewer and say, "Sorry, Mary, but I really don't

know the answer. But let me look into it and get back to you shortly."
Then, find the answer as soon as you can and get it to the interviewer.
If you can't come up with the answer, inform the interviewer that
you're still trying, haven't had any luck, but will contact him or her
when you do.

### Solutions

Solutions are your closer. They're the payoff that you give the audience as a reward for sitting through or reading your interview. Providing solutions will distinguish you from other interview subjects because
most are big on entertainment and short on answers.

Focus on giving solutions because they're what everyone ultimately
wants. Tell your audiences exactly what to do, step-by-step. Break it
down in ways that they can easily understand and apply. Provide lists:
five ways to get the best home loans, seven places to find vintage floor-
ing, or how to lose twenty pounds week by week.

Always provide solid, meaningful information that works. Make it
your goal to have every audience believe that you taught them something of real and lasting value. And if they like you and find you entertaining, you will become a popular guest.

When possible and practical, give guarantees. Offer to refund the
price of your book if it doesn't help readers. While guarantees are helpful, giving results is even better! When you deliver as promised, both the
media and its audiences will remember you, support you, and sing your
praises to their friends and associates.

## Curveballs

Most interviewers don't have bad or mean-spirited motives. Most only
want to get a good story, and they're usually happy to help make you
look good. Usually, the word gets out about sneaky, controversial interviewers, so you can avoid them. And sometimes, their interviews are
worth enduring because they provide such great exposure.

Certain shows require special preparation because they're taped and heavily edited. You may feel that you gave a great interview, but you may be shocked when you see how it was chopped. If you know your material thoroughly, it usually protects you from looking bad.

Many shows, especially radio talk shows that feature authors, can be wildly unpredictable. If a guest who is scheduled for four minutes is boring, they may rush him or her off after a minute or two. However, if a guest who was scheduled for three minutes is great and all of the phone lines light up, they will extend the interview. When shows take calls from listeners, you never know what you will be asked; that's when you get the trickiest curveballs.

Some interviewers have thrived by helping writers. The legendary New York City talk show host Long John Nebel boosted authors' book sales by starting his interviews with indignant statements such as, "How could you write what you wrote on page 157? That's absolutely scandalous! So shameful in fact that I can't even talk about it on the radio."

Although Long John would refer to "scandalous page 157" a few more times, for the balance of the interview, he would feed creampuff questions to the authors he interviewed. Naturally, the books flew off the shelves because everyone wanted to read the scandalous writing on page 157.

Since you can't control interviewers, be prepared. Know your book's weak points and anticipate criticisms and objections it might receive. Write responsive answers to counter them. Admit where you may be wrong; acknowledge opposing theories and positions, but stand tall and don't be intimidated when you believe you're correct. Never be contentious or argumentative, no matter how tempting it may be. Always remain poised, calm, and under control.

Remember that the reason you give interviews is to sell your book. So respond with direct answers and with dignity under fire. Don't get drawn into battles or roll in the dirt. Control your emotions and never be rude. Don't expect fairness, reasonableness, or even politeness. Often, the only victory over hostile interviewers is achieved by not stooping to their level.

## Following Up

After each interview, thank the interviewer, host, producer, other guests, and anyone else who may have been of help. Have copies of your book to hand out and personally sign. Since publicity is built on creating close relationships, give them pleasant parting thoughts of you.

Ask how you can get copies or tapes of your interview or appearance and obtain them. Explain that you're new to interviewing and solicit suggestions that can help you improve your performance from interviewers, hosts, and producers. If they seem too busy or preoccupied, ask if you could speak with them later regarding their opinions. If they agree, be sure to do so soon. Also ask for a letter, on the station's official stationery, stating how good a guest you were.

Send a thank-you note to the producer and ask him or her to contact you if a last-minute replacement is needed. About a month after your appearance, call the producer and ask if he or she would be interested in booking you again. Pitch story ideas linked to the news and subjects that the show covers.

Conduct your own postmortem by:

- Reviewing copies or tapes of the interview.
- Grading your answer to each question asked.
- Checking whether you covered all your main points.
- Evaluating how well you handled each of your main points.
- Identifying how you could improve each main point.
- Determining where you could have worked in main points that you didn't cover.
- Identifying other information that you could have provided and where it could have fit.
- Asking your friends and colleagues to objectively critique your performance.

## Action Steps

1. Determine what the most important element in giving interviews is and describe why it is so important.
2. Tell how items on a preinterview list should be structured.
3. List the three tiers of an interview.
4. Explain what you should say when you don't know the answer to an interview question.
5. Name an effective way to provide solutions in your answers to interview questions.

### Remember

⚠ **Interviews can be authors' best friends because they give them great opportunities to tell their stories in the most favorable light.** The most important element in giving interviews is knowing your subject cold so that you are able to answer any question about it. Before each interview, write a list of exactly what you want to say.

⚠ **Review the interviewer's prior interviews.** In answering questions, make clarity your top priority. In your answers to questions, give solutions that will help the audience and really work. Don't get sucked into arguments or fights with contentious interviewers or hosts.

**CHAPTER 9**

Act as if what you do makes a difference. It does.
*William James*

# Media Training

**THIS CHAPTER COVERS:**

► Why media training?
► The media lens
► What trainers do
► What training entails
► Essential rules
► Biggest mistakes

IT'S RECKLESS TO SLIP behind the wheel of a car for the very first time, turn on the ignition, and take a spin on the highway. The potential for injuring others or yourself is too great. So, most sane people learn to drive; they take driving lessons, and practice with their folks in safe, controlled, low-traffic areas. Before long, they get the hang of it and drive safely for the rest of their lives.

Dealing with the media can be equally dangerous. Making your media debut on a major-city drive-time talk show can also be suicidal—at least, to your book promotional campaign and even your career. But authors constantly do it.

The fact is that most people are simply not natural-born communicators—although many may delude themselves into thinking they are. Presenting themselves favorably to the press, producers, hosts, and large audiences is not their forte. So when they deal with the media, they may not know what to say, how to say it, and how to capitalize on golden opportunities. Many authors are shy or they get nervous, lose focus, and freeze. In front of a microphone, camera, or interviewer, they blank out on information that they know as well as their own names. Despite their complete mastery of complex subjects, they're simply not witty, captivating, or even accomplished communicators. Instead, they're more apt to hem, haw, and wander off message. They come off as stiff, wooden, and just plain boring. So, they don't get their messages across, which defeats the entire purpose of their appearance.

Authors need media training even when publicists represent them. Few authors have publicists forever; most publicists are hired for limited periods, say three to six months. Hopefully, your media opportunities will extend beyond the terms of your publicist's contract, so you must know how to fend for yourself.

Even when publicists represent them, authors may be asked to do preinterviews, where producers gauge whether they would make good guests. Preinterviews are part audition and part pitch and most untrained authors don't know what to do. Media training teaches them how to talk to producers, understand the factors that influence producers' decisions, link their books to current news, and broaden their audiences.

In addition, media opportunities can be spontaneous. They can occur at unexpected times and places—when your publicist isn't around.

**Rick Says**

Every author who wants to promote a book needs training before he or she deals with the media. I won't allow any of my clients to be in contact with the media unless they've had training; it's a firm rule.

Even if you think that you're good with the media, media training can make you better—much better. Media opportunities don't always arise, so when they do, make the most of them or they can quickly vanish because the media can't waste time with authors who are not great interview subjects or guests. To successfully promote your book, learn how to make the most of every shot you get; get media training!

When media opportunities pop up, you must be able to be your best. To pull it off, you need media training.

*Warning:* Many people call themselves media trainers. Be wary of those who have not held high-level media positions; they may not have the knowledge, experience, and understanding to properly train and advise you. As media guru and former Los Angeles talk-show host Joel Roberts, founder of Joel Roberts Associates (*www.joelroberts.com*), warns, "Make sure they've flown the plane."

Some former actors, publicists, and media people call themselves media trainers. While they may have experience or strengths in certain areas, they may not be as proficient as trainers who have spent years in front of microphones and cameras and in production meetings. Plus, not everyone can teach or teach well! Protect yourself by:

- Starting with solid, firsthand recommendations.
- Reviewing their client lists.
- Speaking with those they have trained.
- Specifically asking about:
  1. Their backgrounds;
  2. Their experience;
  3. Precisely what they will provide; and
  4. The benefits you will receive.

Media training will broaden your perspective by showing you what the media wants. If you begin your training during the writing process, it can help you write a better book. Media training can expand your vision and awaken you to new worlds, which can help you with future books and virtually all other areas of your life. It can also heighten your sensitivity so you can more easily tell how others, not just the media, perceive you, and when you're not making yourself sufficiently clear, interesting, or likable.

Since media training is about communication, it can improve your ability to make and maintain close relationships because you will be more aware of how you come across. Many of the lessons you learn from media training will remain with you permanently and can dramatically enhance your life.

## The Media Lens

As present or former card-carrying members of the media, trainers will teach you to see yourself and your book from the media's perspective, from the other side of the fence. As a result, you can create pitches that will deliver what the media wants. In other words, you can make yourself more appealing.

Media trainers teach you how to play the game. They will lay out the rules and explain that the quickest way for you to receive coverage is to tap into the media's needs. As you recall, we previously advised you to become a media resource—to build relationships with the media by supplying your contacts with tips, information, and expertise they need and by being available to them. Media trainers will concur and expand on that advice.

Trainers will stress that when you're working with people in the media, it's about them, not you. Yes, your job is to deliver your message, to get your story across, and to sell books, but the bigger, more critical objective is to give the media what it needs, to make it look good. Your main goal should be to build solid, long-term relationships, not just to get occasional, isolated coverage of your book. Often, you must take a backseat, a secondary position, and help the media accomplish its mission, which is to provide news and entertainment.

## What Trainers Do

According to Joel Roberts, authors need media training in two areas:

- Getting media coverage.
- Making the most of the coverage they receive.

As both an author and a member of the media, I've seen how a book can attract media attention. Be respectful and ask beforehand if the host or interviewer will mention your book and introduce you as its author. As a guest or interview subject, your goals are to serve the media and do a great job, but that doesn't mean that you shouldn't refer to your book when it's appropriate.

When you are booked on a show or an interview, request that you would like your book mentioned and the cover shown—if possible when they introduce you. Send them an e-mail attachment of your book's cover and make sure they received it. The media is usually accommodating, and if you're up front, your book will usually get the attention it deserves.

In Chapter 7, we discussed how to get bookings and coverage, and in Chapter 8, we covered how you should handle interviews. Much of the information that media trainers teach can be found in those chapters. Therefore, in this chapter, we will focus on giving you a general overview of media training—what it is and what it entails. Keep in mind that every media trainer operates differently and that the intention of this chapter is not to tell you everything about media training, but to alert you to its existence, its importance, and what it can provide.

Most media trainers concentrate on interview training. They sharpen their clients' interviewing skills, teaching them how to make their major points, answer questions, and impress interviewers and audiences. Many also help their clients to define their messages and hooks, but interviewing is usually their main focus.

Joel Roberts and Associates varies from the norm by giving equal weight to teaching authors both how to get media coverage and how to develop their interviewing skills. Roberts believes that in today's market, interview training is only half the battle, and he does not feel that teaching clients how to pitch and position themselves is the job of publicists.

So Roberts starts by teaching authors to distinguish between their messages and their bona fide media hooks. According to Roberts, your message is what you want to share with humanity, while your media hooks are what will get you on the air—the strategies that get you the interviews, coverage, and appearances that you need to convey your message. Roberts, who is hired by publishers as well as authors, is a renowned "hook-meister" who comes up with strategies that help authors get on the air.

As experienced media veterans, trainers know what the media wants and can quickly spot bona fide media hooks that authors miss. They will show you how to recognize hooks that the media will latch on to and how to frame them in the most concise, compelling, and sexy ways. They also advise clients how to present their hooks in various formats, including pitch letters, press releases, and e-mails.

Trainers also help authors define their messages. According to Jess Todtfeld, associate producer of *Fox & Friends* and media trainer with Success in Media, Inc. (*www.successinmedia.com*), "The hardest thing for 99 percent of authors is figuring out their message. It's difficult because they have an entire book that they can pull from, an entire body of knowledge, so it's hard for them to boil it down into one sentence."

Other lessons that media trainers teach clients include how to:

- Show the media that problems exist that they can tell audiences how to solve. Joel Roberts teaches authors how to see issues through a problem and an opportunity lens. He emphasizes that every author who deals with the media must be able to address compellingly and concisely:
  *What problem he or she can solve.*
  *Who has that problem.*
  *What benefits the author can provide.*
  *What it will cost not doing it the author's way.*
- Debunk myths. The best media strategy is exploding a myth; taking an accepted notion and proving that it's invalid. If you can expose the falseness of a significant belief, you will get media coverage. Trainers show their clients which beliefs to examine

and challenge. Other good hooks include offering people opportunities, inspiring them, and generating controversy.

■ Offer the media tangible items that provide benefits and will interest its audiences. The media isn't interested in vague or conceptual ideas. For example, the media wants to know that you can tell its audience how to save money on taxes, how to get a first date, or how to avoid identity theft. As Jess Todtfeld puts it, they want guests who give their audiences "take away."

■ Connect their pitches to current news items. "The best hooks are topical," Joel Roberts explains. "Everyone needs to tie in to news stories whenever possible." As an example, Roberts cites the book *The Moral Intelligence of Children: How to Raise a Moral Child* by Robert Coles (Plume, 1998). "If you tried to pitch it in the abstract, it would be a hard sell even though we all want a world inhabited by moral children. But if Coles could comment to the media on the motivation behind a recent, grisly murder, it would be a great avenue for him to get on shows."

What is topical can also be relative. "In radio and television, there's a huge turnover and a lot of the radio producers are twenty-two, twenty-three, or twenty-four years old," publicist David Thalberg explains. "So, something that happened five years ago may be ancient history to them. They may never have heard of authors who were big five or ten years ago and be reluctant to put them on the air. However, if those authors connect their books to current news stories, they stand a better chance of getting bookings."

■ Broaden the audience for their books. The media wants to reach large audiences, so it's wise to expand your hooks to address problems shared by larger audiences. Expand the appeal and stature of your book by referring to news events in broader or elevated terms such as *syndrome, disorder, epidemic, outbreak, phenomenon, condition, influence,* and *technique*, which indicate greater importance and scale, not just single, isolated events. If the media is focusing on stories about violent crimes committed by teenage girls, present your parenting book as providing answers and insights into VIGS, "the violent girls syndrome."

■ Broaden their audience. If your book addresses women, media trainers will teach you how to broaden your audience by also reaching men. For example, if you have a book on mothers' advice to their daughters, interest men by asking, "Men, have you ever wondered what women are thinking?"

■ Improve their performances. Media trainers can be expert evaluators. Within five minutes, experienced pros like Roberts can usually spot an author's strengths and weaknesses and explain precisely what he or she must do to improve and how to do it. Many trainers are also terrific coaches who excel at motivating and teaching their clients how to improve.

■ Dress, sit, stand, gesture, speak, and respond during appearances. Trainers also teach protocol, courtesy, posture and grooming.

■ Create new spins, angles, or approaches. Although little is new and virtually everything has been said, every message can be delivered differently and, perhaps, better. The media is enamored with new names and angles. It treats them as rediscoveries.

■ Come up with names that will become catchwords or phrases that can be great media hooks. They will also explain how to tap into emotional outlets by giving strong, controversial opinions in order to generate dialogues and exchanges, which can become ongoing stories that the media can milk.

## What Training Entails

Media training can be conducted in many different ways and will generally vary with every trainer. Although numerous approaches exist, let's review some basic precepts.

■ Traditionally, media training for authors wasn't considered advisable until the book had been written. The conventional wisdom was that authors would probably forget information that was not fresh in their minds. However, many publishers and trainers have changed their tune. They believe that training should begin during the writing process because authors will turn out more successful books if they have a fuller understanding of the media and publicity. To guard against authors forgetting their lessons, they can receive brush-up or refresher sessions, just before the book is published or appearances take place.

■ Although media training can take many formats, many trainers begin with a tutorial that gives authors an overview of what they will be taught. Usually, this covers messages, hooks, interviewing, the media, and publicity. Trainers explain how interviews can differ depending on whether they are for print, radio, or TV, and what clients can expect in each and how they should act with media contacts face-to-face, via telephone, in a studio, and in other places. Trainers will also go into how authors should dress, be groomed, sit, stand, gesture, and respond.

■ Media trainers will help you find your message hooks. In your 300-page book, you may have twenty messages, but only one will be a major hook. For example, when Jose Canseco first shopped his book *Juiced* (Regan Books, 2005), it didn't generate much interest. However, somewhere down the line, they came up with the idea that the author should name well-known athletes who used steroids. Suddenly, everyone wanted to interview Canseco and his book's sales soared.

■ Frequently, authors are unable to pinpoint the issues that will generate the greatest public interest. Good trainers will help them identify their most important messages. "We boil the message down and in that process come up with some sound bites as well," Jess Todtfeld explains.

■ To hone their messages, authors should think:

● How can I explain my book in one sentence?
● How will my book help readers? "Figure out what your mission statement is, what's the ultimate mission of your book,"

Todtfeld suggests. "When you realize how your book will help readers, it will help you connect better with the people at home. Think in terms of 'take away,' what readers will receive from the book or your appearance."

- Trainers will teach you how to form your thoughts in interviews so that you can express yourself clearly and succinctly. Since you have only a little time to make your points, trainers will teach you how to be concise and compelling. They will show you how to identify the five most important message points that you must make in every interview. Deliver those five messages in every interview because when they're constantly repeated, they become embedded in people's minds.

- To help authors master interviewing, media trainers conduct mock interview sessions. Trainers frequently record or videotape mock interviews, critique their clients' performances, and offer constructive suggestions. Mock interviews are a major part of most media training.

- After conducting training, many media trainers will be available to give authors short telephone refreshers a day or so before they're scheduled for major interviews or appearances. Most are also willing to answer e-mail questions at any time.

Steve and Bill Harrison, the publishers of *Radio-TV Interview Report*, have taken media training a step further. Every year, they run a four-day event in New York City called the National Publicity Summit (*www.nationalpublicitysummit.com*), an event that they limit to 100 attendees. At the summit, the attendees receive media training on how to pitch and package themselves and how to handle interviews. But what makes the summit special is that over 100 producers, journalists, and editors—including those from the largest, most well-known media outlets—are present and available to meet face-to-face with attendees. So trainees get to make invaluable media contacts and interact with them while the information they learned is still fresh in their minds.

# Essential Rules

Despite the differences among media trainers, all seem to stress certain basic points to their clients. Those points include:

- Be prepared so that you're totally in command of your topic. "You must have a thorough command of your key message points," Joel Roberts stresses. "Although you're there to impart certain central ideas, it should not be at the expense of clumsily going wherever you're going no matter what they say. It's really a dance, but the reward for people who can learn can be enormous." So trainers teach clients to master their subjects, to know exactly what they want to say and precisely how they want to say it.

  Be spontaneous, which can be difficult. Audiences can sense canned responses and they hate them. Ironically, making your answers sound unplanned takes training, work, and lots of practice. If you know your information cold and have thoroughly rehearsed, your responses will appear to be more natural and spontaneous. Both audiences and the media will find you more likable and believable.

- Be human. "Your power as a communicator is a balance between your humanity and expertise," Roberts explains. "Authors are often so focused on their subjects, that they come off as dry, detached, and academic, which turns everyone off! We bring them into their humanity, into their hearts. We get them to loosen up, tell personal stories, express their feelings, paint vivid pictures, smile and laugh." Since you're an expert, also be human—someone the audience will identify with and like.

  Roberts concentrated on humanity when he coached doctors who were charged with heralding the breakthrough of a new cancer-fighting drug. Instead of just describing the technical aspects of the drug in lay terms, he encouraged the doctors to relate what it feels like "to give hope to patients in the same sentence that I give the diagnosis."

- Eliminate jargon. Authorities who have great expertise often make poor guests because their responses are laced with terminology that the general public doesn't understand. Their language makes their answers unnecessarily complex and loses their audiences. Media trainers show their clients how to translate that terminology into terms that audiences comprehend.

- Be alert for opportunities to share your message. Don't force your message, but jump on openings when they arise. Author and trainer Barbara De Angelis advises, "Learn the art of the graceful segue" and smoothly transition into your main points. If you're patient, your opportunity will probably come, because most media people usually want to make you look good.

- Respect the direction and needs of each individual show you're on. All shows have different cultures. Try to work within the context of the shows you're on even when they're not your style.

- Match the energy of the show. If it's fast and up-tempo, dance to that beat. Don't try to waltz to the cha-cha. Remember, you're the guest on the show and the subject of the interview. So be flexible and accommodating.

## Biggest Mistakes

According to media trainers, the biggest mistakes that authors make are:

1. **Not serving the show.** Joel Roberts believes that, "The biggest mistake authors make is not serving the needs of the show they're on. A lot of authors get nervous; they want to mention their book as many times as possible and at all costs, which is not the way to go. The way to get bookings and to be kept on the air is to be in the moment with the host. Respond sincerely and credibly to whatever you're asked at the time. If you're on for four minutes with Katie Couric, Diane Sawyer, Charlie Gibson, or Matt Lauer, you don't

want to sound like a machine; you don't want to sound like a robot. You want to really interact and be in the moment with them."

2. **Saying too much.** They try to include their entire body of knowledge in answers. They want to show the interviewer that they know a lot, so they jump around from topic to topic and put too many messages out there. In print interviews, journalists can go and pick whatever message or messages they want. When authors give too many messages, interviewers can pick less important messages, which can take away from the results that the interview could have produced. So, it's important to know your most important points and work them into your answers quickly.

3. **Giving interviewers too much control.** An interview is an exchange of questions and answers; it's an opportunity to deliver your message. Hosts or interviewers often stray; they may ask about points that have nothing to do with your message or your book. When this occurs, authors must know how to turn questions to make their points; they must bring the interview back to their message and keep it on track. When you know the essential message points you must make in every interview, it becomes easier to work them gracefully into your answers.

   Joel Roberts suggests that guests control interviews by judiciously asking questions. For example, after replying to a question regarding what he or she did, the guest can ask, "Can I tell you how I did it?" The host can't say no, and the guest has opened the door to give information that he or she wants to emphasize.

4. **Not distinguishing between messages and hooks.** Most authors and many publicists don't understand and overlook this critical distinction. Although your message and your hooks are related, in most cases, they're not the same. Your message is what you want to share with humanity, but your media hooks are the strategies that get you the interviews, coverage, and appearances that you need to convey your message.

5. **Not realizing the need for media training.** You have a lot riding on the success of your book. Writing and getting it published

took an enormous amount of hard work. So don't stop now; don't take the chance of becoming a media flop and squandering the time and effort you invested. Remember the analogy to driving lessons that we made in the beginning of this chapter; protect your investment, all your hard work. Get media training before you start promoting your book.

## Action Steps

1. Name the two basic areas in which authors need media training.
2. Explain the difference between an author's message hooks and an author's message.
3. Explain when you should start media training.
4. Describe generally what media training involves.
5. What are the biggest mistakes authors make during interviews?

### Remember

⚠ **Every author should have media training before embarking on a publicity campaign.** Media training can teach authors how to get media coverage and how to make the most of the coverage they receive. It can instruct them on the difference between their message hooks and their messages.

⚠ **Media training will help authors develop message hooks that will grab the media's attention.** It will teach them to tie their hooks to current news stories, frame their pitches as story ideas, and expand their messages to reach broader audiences. Media training will show authors how to perform during interviews in order to promote their books and become coveted guests.

**CHAPTER 10**

I would hurl words into the darkness and wait for an echo. If an echo sounded, no matter how faintly, I would send other words to tell, to march, to fight.

*Richard Wright*

# Web Sites and Blogs

**THIS CHAPTER COVERS:**

▶ Why you need a site
▶ Your mission
▶ Site design
▶ Site sections
▶ Blogs

WHEN MEMBERS OF THE MEDIA hear about books and authors, one of their first moves is to find out more about them on the Internet. It's become standard procedure. Since journalists and producers are always looking for stories, they want to learn about authors: who they are, what they've accomplished, what others have said about them, whether they're interesting and unique, and how they present themselves.

So, reporters, editors, and producers search the authors' names and their book titles using their favorite search engine and on the sites of online booksellers. They read everything that's posted about them and visit their Web sites. From that, they start forming impressions. Usually they're trying to determine if this author or book would be of interest to their readers, listeners, or viewers.

In today's media world, you must have a great Web site; it's the sign that you are a professional, someone who should be taken seriously. Like it or not, your Web site can play a major role in how you're initially perceived. For many, the fact that you don't have a Web site will raise questions that you must overcome. So, do both the media and yourself a big favor and put up a great Web site.

## Your Mission

A Web site is a tool, and its main purpose is to support your mission. Some sites can be dazzling; they can have all the new and most exciting technology, all the bells and whistles, but most visitors—especially the media—won't go there again if the sites don't provide the information they want. Visitors won't waste time with sites that are all style and no substance, are not clear about their purpose, and don't deliver what visitors need.

Before you even consider creating a Web site, clarify its purpose—what you want it to achieve. Know exactly what you want your site to do. If it has several purposes, prioritize them and then apply your efforts and resources to those that matter most.

Authors often have multiple objectives: They may want their Web sites to help build or maintain their careers, promote their books, and sell their products or business services. Experienced Web site designers know how to build sites that will accomplish all of your objectives. They know and can advise you on all of the elements that should be included and how they should be structured and work.

Think of your Web site as a storehouse of information about you, a one-stop place where the media can go to find out about you and your book: who you are, your background, your platform, what you've written, and what has been written about you. In this chapter, we will discuss the specific elements that your Web site should contain.

## Site Design

The quality of your site—how it looks and works and the content it provides—is crucial. It can attract and interest visitors or turn them off.

And since your site will be targeting the media and publishing professionals, who are experienced Internet users and will be looking for specific information, it must be great! It must quickly give them access to what they want or they might lose patience and turn elsewhere.

Before you design your Web site:

- Visit many other sites.
- Examine:

  *How they're laid out.*
  *The type of content they provide.*
  *How they're organized.*
  *If they're easy to use.*
  *How they work.*

- Ask:

  *Do they look good?*
  *Are they easy to navigate?*
  *Do they have a focus?*
  *Do they provide good information?*
  *Do they have lots of links and do all those links work?*
  *Are they trying to give you information or sell you something?*

When you find sites you like, list the features that most appeal to you and that you could include on your site. Also list the features that you would want to avoid. If you hire a Web site designer, give him or her a copy of each of those lists.

Come up with a great URL, which is also called a domain name or Web site address, and register it. For your address, use your book title or a variation of it that people can easily remember. For example, the URL for our site for this book series is *www.author101.com*. Consider registering common misspellings of your domain so that browsers can visit your site even when they misspell its address. Check the availability of and register your URL at *www.rickscheapdomains.com*.

Identify the target audience for your Web site, the group or groups you most want to impress. For the purposes of this book, let's say that the media is your primary target and build your Web site with that in mind.

Go back to Chapter 4, "Your Book Publicity Tool Kit," and review the list of tools we discussed. Think about each item and determine which of them should be included on your Web site. As you may recall, we divided those items into two groups: primary and secondary tools. Some of the primary tools are your press release, biography, photograph, newsletter, promotional materials, and questions and answers. The secondary tools include articles, brochures, contests, endorsements, fact

**Robyn Says**

A Web site must make an instant impression. The media is extremely busy and needs to make an immediate decision if you're right for its show, article, etc. When it visits your site, it wants to get a quick understanding of your book, see where you've appeared, and examine your credentials.

As a media personality who researches loads of Web sites daily, the first thing I look for is a link to the press link or press contact. If I can immediately connect, it helps me do my job. Instant connectivity is very important because the media is also working on time-sensitive topics.

File and save all your passwords and your content and webmaster information, unless you built your own site, because webmasters move and go out of business. Also, copyright your site.

sheets, graphics, lists of topics for the media, quotations, reviews, and stories about the book. All of those tools could work well on your site.

Register your Web site with search engines, including Google, Yahoo, and MSN. Register it under the subject of your book as well as every subtopic included in it and all related subjects. Think of every possible category that you could include because the more categories you provide, the more hits you may receive. Register each of your products and/or services. Create links with other sites and strategic partners.

## Site Sections

Your Web site should include a home page and at least a few other sections. Every page of each section should provide:

- Links to all the sections of your site.
- A copyright notice.
- The cover image of your book.
- Your contact information.
- A link for visitors to subscribe to your newsletter or e-zine if you have one.

Visitors should be able to access each section by clicking on that section name, and you should consider making certain content downloadable. Many sections can be included on your site; too many for us to describe them all here. However, at the least, you should consider including the following sections to best promote your book.

### Home Page

Think of your home page as the place where you welcome visitors and set the overall tone of your site. Your home page should have a clean, uncluttered look. It must be inviting, not densely packed and intimidating. Your home page should welcome visitors and tell them about your book generally. Prominently reproduce your book cover and incorporate your book's logo and design features on your home page. Then carry that theme throughout your site.

Provide links for visitors to access the other sections of your site. You can also include endorsements for your book as well as your photographs. Your photograph can be helpful if you look good and are interested in promoting your business or nonwriting career.

### About the Authors

In this section, tell visitors about yourself and especially why you're so uniquely qualified to have written this book. Focus on your experience and accomplishments, not on listing every degree you ever received or school you attended. Write no more than two or three paragraphs.

Write your biography in a light, breezy style. Include your photograph. If you have a personal Web site, you may want to create a link to your site under your photograph.

### Parts of Your Book

Post parts of your book on your Web site to give visitors a fuller understanding of what it's about and the quality of your writing. You can tempt readers by giving them juicy, provocative, or scandalous teasers to read. You can also post selected excerpts or quotes. Clear it first with your publisher. Posting parts of your book will also help you get feedback that could be helpful for future books, revisions, or versions.

Post your book's table of contents to show what the book covers; how it's organized; the length of the chapters; the length of the book; and any additional materials such as forewords, afterwords, appendixes, reference materials, and forms.

### Endorsements

Include a page or two containing a representative sampling of the wonderful compliments well-known people gave you and your book. Use the blurbs that your publisher included on the front and back covers of your book and those inside. Pull words, phrases, or short sentences

**Rick Says**

Your home page should be like the living room where you live; someplace that is welcoming and that visitors will want to visit. Remember, it's the first thing they will see when they arrive and you want them to stick around and visit other parts of your site.

The amount of content that you can include on your home page is a matter of personal style. It should be enough to adequately describe your book and tell visitors the benefits you can provide. Keep the content light and breezy. Think in terms of headlines and try to convey basic information rather than teach, go into detail, or try to sell.

of praise from reviews and post them. Follow the format of blurbs used in motion-picture advertisements.

If you have authored more than one book, give endorsements for all of them. Place the endorsements for your current book first and then add some additional blurbs praising each of your earlier titles in reverse chronological order. Concentrate on plugging your latest title by posting more blurbs about it and fewer praising your earlier works.

### Tips, Q&A, or Facts

Give visitors a sense of the content in your book by providing tips, questions and answers, or facts. In these materials, address real problems that interest visitors, and provide solutions. Don't tease them by giving incomplete answers that will force them to read your book, newsletter, or other sources. Again, furnish information rather than try to sell.

Keep your answers to questions brief. If, in order to provide complete answers, you need to give longer explanations, summarize your answer in a sentence or two and then provide a link to a fuller, more detailed response.

As an alternative to tips and Q&As, provide the text of an interview that you gave. Use the interview to give visitors an understanding of your book and to answer common problems.

### Press or Media Room

Create a section that the media can access to get information about you and your book. At the top of the section, identify it as the "Media Center," "News Room," "Press Room," or "Press Page." Divide the section into categories for press releases, articles, and reviews. Identify each item in each category by its headline, give the date and source, and link it to the full text of that item. Arrange all items in reverse chronological order, with the most current piece listed first. Make all files downloadable and printer-friendly.

For some books, including fiction, poetry, and business books, it might be worthwhile to create a separate section for reviews. In the event that you do, list book reviews by headline in reverse chronological order. You can also include quotes or blurbs from the reviews and sprinkle them throughout the site.

### Calendar and Appearances

Post your calendar with all your speaking engagements and personal appearances for at least the next several months. Give the exact time when you will appear, the address, cost if applicable, and contact information so your visitors can arrange to attend. Also, create links to the host organizations' Web sites where your visitors can find further information about the event.

On your calendar, include entries for all major events in your industry, even those that you may not participate in or attend. Also provide links to the host organizations' sites.

### Products

If you have other books or products that you sell, set forth information about them in this section. Give the name of each book or product, describe it in a short paragraph, and provide a photograph of it. State the price of the item and create a link for visitors to order the product that says something to the effect of "To Order." These links can be connected directly to online booksellers or other vendors.

### Book Ordering Information

For most authors, it usually makes more sense to work with online booksellers than to take and fulfill book orders themselves. Create a link directly to online booksellers that will receive the orders, handle payment, and fulfill them. Contact online booksellers to get information on how to establish these links.

### Newsletter Link

If you publish a newsletter or e-zine, provide a link for visitors to order it on each page of your Web site. Post the statement, "To subscribe to the free Author 101 Newsletter, click here," and place it in a box. Visitors can then click on the newsletter name or link to receive it.

Newsletter and e-zine links will help you capture names and e-mail addresses to build your lists. These lists can be valuable for future promotions and communications. It's tempting to create sign-up forms that request lots of detailed information, but they usually turn off visitors. Resist the temptation and include only enough information for visitors to get your e-zine.

### Contact

Provide a form that visitors can use to contact you. The form should request each individual's name, e-mail address, business name, and enough space for him or her to ask questions or submit comments. Request people's phone numbers and position titles, but try to keep your form brief. Include a box that visitors can check to subscribe to your newsletter or e-zine. Your contact section is also helpful in capturing names and e-mail addresses.

### Additional Sections

■ **Resources.** Provide a list of links to resources that you believe will be helpful to visitors as well as to your strategic partners' sites. Resources can include books, services, directories, organizations, and other links that your visitors might want.

- **Your business information.** Information about services that you provide may also be included. In a few short paragraphs, describe the goods and services you offer and the benefits you provide. It's often helpful to bullet the benefits. Create a link to your business Web site.
- **Interactive or chat rooms.** In this section, you can create a forum in which visitors can conduct dialogs or exchanges with you. Chat rooms can help you build your platform, your expertise, and support for your book. Create a form that gives you information about chat-room visitors, such as their names and e-mail addresses, which will also help you build your lists.
- **Privacy policy.** Privacy is a major concern of many visitors. Listing your privacy policy can make them more willing to give you their names and e-mail addresses, especially when they know exactly how you will and will not use them.

## Web Site Hints

To make your Web site more productive, our Web designer, Steve Lillo (*www.planetlink.com*), has offered the following tips:

- **Make your site easy to use and clear.** Web sites must be easy and intuitive to use. Most visitors aren't engineers and they don't have the time or inclination to have to figure out how to navigate your site. Keep it simple and make sure all links work. Constantly check to make sure that all your links work.
- **Make sure your site looks good.** The first thing visitors notice is your site's look and feel; it's the first impression of you and your book that visitors receive. Your site may have the best content and the most valuable information, but if visitors don't like the way it looks and feels, they may leave.
- **Be consistent.** Since your Web site is only a part of your arsenal, make it look consistent with your other marketing

materials. Create a coordinated visual front because people find inconsistency confusing. Periodically, make minor design changes in colors, typefaces, layout, and other aspects to show that your site is always evolving and to keep it looking fresh.

- **Stay current.** Commit to keeping all your content current and to ensuring that all your content is always correct. Visitors to your site will depend on the accuracy of your content; they will rely on it. Consider putting the current date on your home page or saying "Updated September 15, 2006."
- **Announce changes.** When you make significant updates and changes to your site, tell the world. Post a notice on your home page informing visitors and send e-mails to those whose addresses you have collected. Let them know that you're constantly working to update and improve your site.

## Blogs

The blogosphere, the wonderful world of blogs, is now upon us. Blogs, which are online diaries, journals, or logs, are one of the hottest and most influential new book promotion techniques. The word *blog* is a contraction of the term *Web log*, and blogs are written on an endless array of subjects in an equally endless number of styles, formats, approaches, and viewpoints. As we go to press, some 9 million blogs are estimated to exist.

In comparison with other publicity vehicles, blogs can be a great bargain. They cost little or nothing to create, produce, and distribute; you don't have to pay printing or mailing charges or need any special technical skills. All you have to do is sit at your computer, type your content into a template, and when you're finished, send it to everyone on your list. Templates are available from a number of services, including *www.blogger.com*, *www.myblogsite.com*, and *www.typepad.com*.

Most blogs are commentaries that are written in a personal, conversational tone. Since they don't have to be balanced, like many other publications do, their content generally reflects each blogger's feelings, opinions, or observations. Many are passionate about their subjects, positions, or points of view. Overall, blogs are less formal than Web sites or other online publications like newsletters and e-zines.

Blogs can be written in virtually any format. They can follow any publishing schedule or no discernable schedule. They can come out each day, weekday, week, or whenever—it's totally up to the blogger. Since blogs can be updated at any time, they are often most topical.

Blogs can be powerful promotional tools for books because they enable writers to:

- *Establish expertise.* Writers can show and impress others with their expertise. In a relatively short time, writers can build impressive bodies of published work in their specialty areas. They can also establish themselves as specialists more quickly by writing blogs than through other, more traditional routes.
- *Build followings.* Blogs attract groups of devoted readers and supporters. Reading their favorite blog is often the highlight of their day. Blog readers frequently subscribe to the blogger's positions, outlooks, or points of view, so they buy and help promote the blogger's books and products.
- *Provide information.* Writers can inform readers about news and developments relating to their books and topics. In addition to text, blogs can contain graphics, including photographs, and links to other sources. They can also publicize speaking engagements and list when they're scheduled. If fact, blogs can contain anything that you find in other publications or on Web sites.
- *Expound passionately.* The writing in blogs is personal, so writers can express the full depths of their feelings. They can speak directly to others who share their passions and intensity. And, they don't have to give equal time to others who may not agree with their positions.
- *Receive feedback.* Writers can get comments, suggestions, and information from their readers, which they may or may not

decide to post. The feedback they receive may be of invaluable help for their future writing projects.

- *Encourage dialogues.* The conversational style of blogs and their eagerness for feedback can encourage exchanges with readers. These conversations can be fertile sources of information for future projects. They can also send up trial balloons and test concepts being developed for upcoming work.

- *Break the isolation.* Through blogs, writers can be in contact with the outside world, which they often miss out on in their work. Besides giving them new ideas and information, contact with others can break their myopia and help them gain newer and broader perspectives.

- *Publicize future books.* Through blogs, writers can publicize their future book projects and build solid readership bases that will be first in line to buy their books as soon as they're published.

Since the success of most books depends on word-of-mouth recommendations, blogs can work for writers because they usually love to write. Search engines will automatically index your blog, but for more details, contact Google Support (*www.google.com/support*). To find links to blogs, go to *www.google.com/blogsearch, www.technorati.com, www.feedster .com, www.icerocket.com,* or *www.blogpulse.com.* Links to literary blogs can be accessed through *www.complete-review.com/links/bloglink.htm.*

A number of great blogs about books and publishing exist.

Buzz Girl
*http://bookpagebuzz.blogspot.com/*

Everyone Who's Anyone in Adult Trade Publishing and Tinseltown Too
*www.everyonewhosanyone.com*

Seth Godin
*http://feeds.feedburner.com/typepad/sethsmainblog*

The Literary Salon
*http://www.complete-review.com/saloon/index.htm*

## *Action Steps*

1. Explain why it's important for your site to support your mission.
2. List five sections that can be included in your Web site.
3. How would you set up a Media Room?
4. Explain what blogs are.
5. List five ways that blogs can help promote your book.

### *Remember*

⚠ **When the media hears about books and authors, it checks them out on the Internet.** So, it's essential for authors to establish a strong Web presence. Make sure that your site supports your mission, which can be to publicize your book. Find a great domain name that is easy to remember, and register that name with all the major search engines. Create a site that looks great and is easy and intuitive to use and understand.

⚠ **Blogs are online diaries, journals, or logs.** As publicity vehicles, they can be great bargains because they cost little or nothing to create, produce, and distribute. You don't have to pay printing or mailing charges or need any special technical skills. All you have to do is sit at your computer, type your content into a template, and when you're finished, send it to everyone on your list. Blogs are great for establishing your expertise, providing information, getting feedback, creating dialogues, making contacts, and getting the word out about your book and future books or endeavors.

**CHAPTER 11**

When I have an idea, I turn down the flame, as if it were a little alcohol stove, as low as it will go. Then it explodes and that is my idea.
*Ernest Hemingway*

# E-Mail Blasts

**THIS CHAPTER WILL COVER:**

▶ What is a blast?
▶ Know your market
▶ Partnering
▶ Incentives for partners
▶ Outcomes
▶ Sales letters
▶ Bonus gifts

TO PROMOTE *Networking Magic* (Adams Media, 2004), Rick and Jill Lublin ran a promotion known as an e-mail blast, which catapulted the book to number one on the Barnes & Noble.com bestseller list. Their blast was so successful that *Networking Magic* held the top position for the better part of a week and stayed in the top twenty-five for several weeks. Two years earlier, Rick, Jill, and Jay Conrad Levinson employed the same technique to lift their book *Guerrilla Publicity* (Adams Media, 2002) to number eight on *www.amazon.com*.

So what is an e-mail blast? Randy Gilbert (Dr. Proactive), a leading authority on e-mail blasts and the author of the bestselling book *Success Bound: Breaking Free of Mediocrity* (Bargain Publishers Co., Inc., 2001), defines it as, "A powerful direct marketing approach that uses endorsements. Basically, it's a technique that brings direct marketing online and uses endorsements to get people to open e-mail promotions. E-mails are opened because they are sent only to opt-ins who want to receive e-mail from the sender." E-mail blasts are known by a host of other names, including Internet blasts and Amazon blasts.

Randy Gilbert and Peggy McColl, authors of *On Being a Dog with a Bone* (Destinies Publishing, 2003), have created a remarkable, in-depth online course, *Best Seller Mentoring*, which goes into great depth on how authors can create e-mail blasts. Their course provides everything you should know about e-mail blasts and even includes an extensive variety of forms that you can follow.

The information in this chapter was compiled in collaboration with Gilbert and McColl, whom we thank for their expertise and generosity. For more detailed information and to find out about Gilbert and McColl's course, visit *http://bestsellermentoring.com*.

## What Is a Blast?

Essentially, a blast is a coordinated effort in which authors or their publicists enlist partners to make a book a bestseller with one of the big online booksellers. Briefly, here's how it works:

1. The author or his or her publicist makes strategic alliances with partners who have lists of e-mail addresses. They also use names from their own lists and their publisher's and network partners' lists, and they can buy addresses from list brokers. Partners agree to give authors access to the names on their lists and contribute incentives that will sweeten recipients' interest in buying the book.
2. The author or publicist composes a sales letter that will be e-mailed by the author and the author's strategic partners to individuals on all of the lists.
3. The sales letter offers recipients free incentives to purchase the book provided that they buy it (a) from a particular online bookseller and (b) on a certain date or time.
4. The sales letters contain links to the bookseller's Web site, on which recipients can purchase the book.

5. After the book has been purchased, buyers are e-mailed instructions on how they can get their bonus gifts.

E-mail blasts are effective because every hour, the big online booksellers calculate the sales rankings for their top 10,000 bestselling books. So, if you generate a flurry of sales within a certain window of time, it can propel a book onto an online bookseller's bestseller list. Once the book makes the list, even if it's just for an hour, the book can legitimately be promoted as a national bestseller.

When your book makes it to the bestseller list, influential members of the book world take notice. The media notices, as do industry insiders such as literary agents, book editors, and foreign rights buyers. "Instead of me having to hound the media to get coverage, the tables turned and they began calling me to be on their shows," Gilbert reports. "The credential of being a bestselling author holds a huge amount of weight. The media loves to use that credential; it gets attached to your name—'bestselling author Randy Gilbert.'" On the basis of the success of a blast that Gilbert ran for Jenna Glatzer's book *Outwitting Writer's Block* (The Lyons Press, 2003), she was able to command a substantially higher advance for her next book. The publisher upped the ante because it knew that Glatzer had a mechanism to sell lots of books right away.

Interestingly, blasts have an unexpected secondary benefit—brick-and-mortar sales can increase during blast periods. In addition, hundreds of thousands of people hear about the book through blasts, which helps it gain name recognition and can prove helpful down the line.

**Robyn Says**

When your book is a national bestseller, it dramatically increases your promotion quotient. It invariably generates more interest in your book and boosts its sales. And once a book is a national bestseller, it can always use that designation. In addition, the author, even if he or she never writes another word, can always be called a bestselling author or the author of a national bestselling book.

## Know Your Market

The first step in the blast process is to know your market. Identify your audience, the people most likely to buy your book, down to the smallest detail. Ask what group or groups is most likely to purchase your title. Will it be men, single men, married men, women, single women, married women, parents, grandparents, sports enthusiasts, music lovers, and so on? The more sharply you define your potential buyers' profiles, characteristics, likes, dislikes, etc., the more tightly you can promote your book. Knowing your market will also help you select the best partners for your blast, which can make the difference in how well it succeeds. To define your potential market, specifically answer the following questions:

- What do potential buyers of your book have in common?
- What specific behavior do your potential buyers commonly display?
- What are your potential buyers' interests?
- What do your potential buyers read?
- What radio and television programs do your potential buyers listen to and watch?
- What entertainment do your potential buyers like?
- How do your potential buyers spend their money?

Zero in on specific groups. If you wrote a book for parents of young children, research the behavior of the parents who would be most likely to buy your book. What books and magazines do they read? What Web sites do they visit? What words do they use for Internet searches? What newsletters, e-zines, or blogs do they subscribe to? Where do they shop and what do they buy?

Gilbert believes that the best way to learn about people's behavior is by sitting in on online forums. Since forums exist for virtually every subject, Gilbert visits those on his areas of interest. After he gets to know the people in the group, he asks them what their favorite newsletters, e-zines, and blogs are. He asks them where they shop and what they buy.

Do some detective work. Go to search engines such as *www.google* *.com* or *www.yahoo.com* to find the sites that your potential buyers browse and visit. If you wrote a science fiction book, enter the phrase *fans of science fiction* or *science fiction readers*; check sites for fan clubs devoted to sci-fi movies, TV shows, or books. Visit those sites and look for common interests, advertisements, and links; note what they have in common. If they indicate that science fiction fans like video games, identify video game newsletters, e-zines, and lists that have lots of names. Then contact them to inquire if they might want to become one of your blast partners.

## Partnering

To run e-mail blasts, you don't have to have your own e-mail list, because large list owners will endorse your books and send your offers to people on their lists. Gilbert and McColl suggest that you look for partners who will support you by:

- Sending your offer to their contacts, subscribers, and those on their lists.
- Providing bonus gifts that will make your offer more attractive.

To enlist partners, you must convince them that partnering with you will benefit them. Usually, your offer will help your partners by:

- Giving people on their lists high-value bonuses if they buy your book.
- Making them a part of high-value or quality packages.
- Making them partners with your other partners, which can increase their networks and prestige.
- Spreading their names and the bonus items they contribute to new markets, which consist of your people and your other partners' people.
- Giving them your and your other partners' endorsements.

Identify potential strategic partners by:

1. **Making a list of everyone you know personally and those on whom you have collected information.** On your list, include their Web site addresses; their contact information; their newsletter, e-zine, or blog names and number of subscribers; bonus gifts they can contribute; and their ranking on *www.alexa.com*, which tracks Web sites' traffic. Adding personal information also could come in handy—especially if you encounter any initial resistance.

2. **Compiling a list of your colleagues and associates.** Include people in your genre, such as other authors on your subject, experts in your field, industry movers and shakers, and power brokers. List all of the information that you included for your potential strategic partners (see item 1).

3. **Listing all your customers or clients.** Give special emphasis to your larger customers, but include all of your customers or clients. Again, list the same information that you entered for your potential strategic partners (see item 1).

4. **Identifying all your vendors and suppliers and those who would be interested in getting some of your business.** Visit their Web sites, get their contact information, and include the information that you listed for your potential strategic partners (see item 1).

5. **Including your competitors.** List all relevant information about them that you can find. Often, you can get great information on your competitors from your vendors and business brokers. Also check out your competitors' Web sites.

6. **Networking with everyone on your lists to see if they would qualify as or be interested in being your strategic blast partners,** or ask if they know anyone who might be a partner for you.

7. **Running keyword searches by entering words or phrases that identify your audience, the subject of your book, your publisher, and all related topics.** When you find more Web sites, add them to your list. Keep building. It may take you some time, but

When you look for partners, concentrate on sites that have lots of traffic. Check newsletters, e-zines, and blogs because they tend to have the biggest address lists. Dig deeply into listings to find the best potential partners. Don't simply visit the first ten sites you come up with. Take your time, check links, and continue to dig. Take the attitude that you're looking for life-long business partners.

Finding the right partners can take a number of steps. Some people you approach will not want or be able to help you. With each rejection, ask if they can refer you to someone else who could. They may know others who would be ideal partners who could play a major role in making your blast more successful.

it will be worth the investment. Visit the sites and see which ones could be strategic partners. Look for partners that are in related businesses and that could help you on this, and future, promotions.

### Incentives for Partners

Make your partnership more beneficial by designating potential partners as "sponsors" of the bonuses you offer. To be a sponsor, they must donate a gift to everyone who buys your book as a result of the blast. Bonuses have "bounce back" because in return for their contributions, sponsors get (1) publicity, because new people on your list and on your other partners' lists learn about them, their goods, and their services, and (2) they build their lists. Their lists expand because in exchange for their contribution, they receive the names and e-mail addresses of people who purchase your book and claim bonuses.

Consider offering your partners bonuses for helping you. If people on their lists buy a certain number of books, that partner would receive a bonus. You can offer them tickets to concerts, performances, and sporting events or evenings out if people on their lists buy a stated number of copies of your book. Other options could be participating in their workshops or in their teleseminars and conferences.

Chapter 11 ■ E-Mail Blasts

Additional incentives that might attract list owners include:

- Giving them business referrals.
- Directing traffic to their Web sites from your site, newsletter, e-zine, or blog.
- Giving them your expertise.
- Giving their subscribers special discounts.
- Offering them affiliate commission on your other products.
- Providing them with ad space in your newsletter, e-zine, blog, or Web site.

If your campaign directs buyers to *www.barnesandnoble.com,* tell your partners about Barnes & Noble's affiliate program. Under this program, your partners can make money when their people buy your book. This information may also help them reap rewards for other books that they recommend in the future, which can increase the benefits they can receive by partnering with you.

## Outcomes

Before you begin your blast, identify the outcome you hope to achieve; know exactly what you want to accomplish by partnering with others. Quantify it by setting specific goals such as sending your offer letter to 300,000 people, enlisting five partners that each has at least a 50,000-name list, or partnering with three bestselling authors whose contributions will be their participation in free workshops or teleseminars.

Ask your friends and colleagues about other blasts:

- Have they received blast solicitations?
- Did they buy? If so, what?
- If they didn't buy, find out why.
- What were they offered?
- How was it presented?

- What impact did the offer produce?
- What did they like/dislike about the offer?
- What convinced them to buy?
- What turned them off?

Often, your blast can produce more than just book sales. It can help you get a distributor for your self-published book or increase the number of people who sign up for your coaching program; your consulting services; or your newsletter, e-zine, or workshop. Some authors who run blasts are more interested in generating other lucrative benefits than they are in selling copies of their books.

Randy Gilbert believes that, "The most important reason to know what you want is so that you proactively attract people who want to help you. It solidifies what you want, who you need, and how you can make it happen. Find the right people, partners whose lists, networks, and contacts you can tap into to sell your book and yourself."

## Special Tools

The Web site *www.Alexa.com* gives traffic statistics and links to sites that are operated by those who could make great blast partners. This gold mine of information directs you to the most popular sites and then lets you drill down to other or secondary sites that are linked to them. Alexa might send you to a site that would be impossible for you to partner with because it's so big or because of its privacy policies. However, secondary sites that are linked to that site could be terrific blast partners. Often, they will be smaller outfits that would love to partner with you.

Find newsletter, e-zine, and blog owners that serve your target market; forums in which people share information on particular subjects; and newsletter and e-zine directories at *www.Groups.Yahoo.com*. It provides lists of active forums.

To learn more about your target market, join forums and subscribe to newsletters, e-zines, or blogs that target it. At *www.2BPOP.com*, you can download a free program to help you find contact information for Web site owners.

Since spam can be a problem, check your subject line for spam content at *www.lyris.com/resources/antispam/index/html* or *www.marketing-register.com/top_tools/Free_Spam_Checker/index.shtml*. Remove all spam or your e-mail will be blocked.

## Sales Letters

It's reasonable to assume that your prime targets, the ideal audience for your book, are inundated with e-mail. Chances are that they're hit with all sorts of e-mails every day, the bulk of which are unsolicited and probably are never even opened. If your sales letter is going to be opened, it must have a great, intriguing subject line. As we said, it also must be sent by a sender recipients recognize and from whom they want to hear. If you want people to buy your book, your sales letter better be great. If you want them to buy on a particular date from a specific Web site, your sales letter must be perfectly clear, well written, and direct. It must also offer them a package that makes them willing to comply with your request.

Set the date for your promotion and then inform the online supplier of that date. Make sure that you have a sufficient supply of books to send your supplier because it may not want to purchase copies of your books in advance. However, the supplier will want to have copies of your book on hand before orders for it pour in.

If you sell your books through your Web site, make sure that those who fulfill orders are ready and know exactly what to do. If you hire a fulfillment company, inform them in advance exactly when you will be sending your blast so it can be prepared for the influx of orders it may receive. Create an expiration date for your offer. Usually, twenty-four to forty-eight hours works best because it forces people to buy within that period. It also helps generate the number of sales you need to make the online bookseller's bestseller list.

Send your sales letter a day or two before the date you want buyers to purchase your book. If you send it too early, many recipients will forget about it. By sending it a day or two before the target date, they will be less likely to forget.

E-mail recipients are spam sensitive. If they don't recognize your name, your subject line may be the only way to convince them to open your e-mail. Think of your subject line as a headline: Make it short, snappy, and something that will arouse recipients' curiosity. Here are some sample subject lines that could work for you:

- $500 Worth of Gifts for Buying a Fabulous Book
- What Every Author Must Know to Sell Books
- Announcing—A Gold Mine of Publicity Secrets

Since the wording of the sales letter is so important, take your time. Begin it with an attention-getting headline or sentence. If you have a large following, include your name. For example:

** An Urgent Message Just for You from Rick Frishman **
(Please read this now! I don't want you to miss out on an
irresistible offer that expires at midnight EST Thursday, July 25)

Or

** A Time-Sensitive Message from Robyn Freedman Spizman **
Do Just One Thing Today to Get a Staggering Number of Amazing Freebies

In your sales letter:

- *Create urgency.* Give potential buyers a compelling reason to want the benefits you offer sooner rather than later. Make them feel the need to immediately buy.
- *Show value.* Tell potential buyers, up front, the value of your offer. Hit the benefits hard. State their value in dollar amounts, savings, time, or improvements.

■ *Stress it's one of a kind.* Be clear that your offer is short-term and unique. Emphasize that they can get the benefits you're offering only from you and not elsewhere. Point out that your offer is for just twenty-four hours or that only 318 are available.

Be straightforward and make your pitch quickly. People are pressed for time, so they tend to be impatient with long introductions.

In the body of your sales letter, continually emphasize the benefits you're offering. If you find that you're saying the same basic thing repeatedly, try to word it differently. Don't forget that your sales letter is intended to inform potential buyers of the benefits they will reap by accepting your offer. So, keep your letter focused on them and the benefits; use the word *you*, not *I*.

Make sure that all instructions you give are clear and easy to follow. Test them out on your twelve-year-old nephew. In your sales letter, tell potential buyers what you want them to do and exactly how to do it. Tell them often. Make it easy for potential buyers by including links, and make sure that they work. If your blast will be with *www.amazon.com* or *www.barnesand noble.com*, run a link to the appropriate site.

Keep it simple, not complex. Ask potential buyers to take just one action, such as buying the book, and make it as easy as possible for them. If you want them to take more than one action, list the steps they should take by numbers or bullets. Explain that once they place their orders, they will receive e-mail with easy instructions on how to get their bonus gifts.

## Sample Sales Letters

The following are two sales letters that were sent for Rick and Jill Lublin's book *Networking Magic*, which, as we said, rocketed the book to the top of the Barnes & Noble.com bestseller list. The first letter was sent by Rick and Jill to people on their lists, and the second was sent by their blast partners.

Dear Networking Friend,

This is urgent, important, and an absolutely amazing opportunity. Please take a minute from your busy schedule and read this letter . . .

We promise you will not regret it.

And, here's why . . .

During the next twenty-four hours, you can get some of the world's greatest networking secrets, tips, and strategies AND receive additional networking and success secrets valued at over $2,145.00 as free bonus gifts, but only for today!

After two months of long hours, late nights, and weekends preparing, our networking friends and we have created the biggest and most mind-blowing free bonus gift offer you'll ever get your hands on.

Why are we doing this?

Quite simply, to draw your attention to something that is really important—how you can finally achieve a truly strong and healthy network of friends and business colleagues who will help you achieve anything you set out to do.

And . . . we also have a deep desire to create a bestseller today with this life-changing masterpiece, *Networking Magic.*

What is *Networking Magic?*

It's a complete toolbox that is filled with proven techniques to build a super-strong network of relationships that will benefit you.

Using these easy-to-follow strategies, you'll experience dramatic results, which will begin immediately and continue for the rest of your life.

*continued*

Chapter 11 ■ E-Mail Blasts

*continued*

(And, you'll get to see a massive list of additional benefits when you read more of this e-mail below!)

Just how vital and important could *Networking Magic* be for your life and business success?

None other than Jim McCann, CEO of 800-Flowers.com, declared, "You have to build relationships to be successful today, and *Networking Magic* will show you how to do just that."

And Dr. Denis Waitley, author of the prestigious book *Seeds of Greatness*, says, "*Networking Magic* transforms the invisible ingredients for success into visible, viable, and practical action steps. Nobody does it better than Rick and Jill. They have taught me 'unless you are networking, you soon will be not working'!"

Life is short and none of us has time to just throw away—don't you owe it to yourself to get your own copy of this networking bible, so you can immediately begin building an incredible network using these proven secrets?

How can you get this powerful new book and over $2,145.00 in bonus gifts right now?

Easy! By following the next two steps:

Step 1. Get a copy of *Networking Magic* from Barnes & Noble by going to: *http://Networking-Magic.com/buyNM*

Step 2. Once you receive your sale confirmation, please follow this link and enter your Barnes & Noble receipt info and you'll be directed to the bonus page: *http://www.Networking-Magic.com/bonuses*

(Just in case you're wondering, the "free bonus gifts" are not deliverable or affiliated with Barnes & Noble.)

*continued*

*continued*

∧∧∧∧∧∧∧∧∧∧∧∧∧∧∧∧∧∧∧∧∧∧∧∧∧∧∧∧∧∧∧∧∧∧∧∧∧∧∧∧∧∧∧∧∧∧∧∧∧∧∧∧∧∧

That's the incredible deal we're offering you today!

================================================

NOW is the time to go for it! Make your decision right now because by tomorrow, this deal will disappear.

You're about to get more value than anyone could ever pack into a deal plus a whole lot more with *Networking Magic*.

How can you get all of these items right now?

Easy! By following the next two steps:

Step 1. Buy your copy of *Networking Magic* from Barnes & Noble by going to: *http://www.Networking-Magic.com/buyNM*

Step 2. Once you receive your sale confirmation, please follow this link and enter your Barnes & Noble receipt info and you'll be directed to the bonus page: *http://www.Networking-Magic.com/bonuses*

We're going to go out on a limb and ask you to trust us on this. There is no value you can place on the importance of creating a strong and healthy network. Whatever it is, your success is flat-out worth it!

Maybe all you needed is some basic knowledge and a willingness to follow through. We've made it really easy for you to do that—starting today!

And, you'll be rewarded with an immense amount of support and valuable products and resources from our own network of friends.

The only way you'll lose on this is if you don't take any action. When will you ever be able to learn everything you need to know about networking for only $11.65 (with your online discount)?

When you follow through on this unique opportunity and you get your copy of *Networking Magic*, you'll soon know why these networking success strategies work and others sometimes fail miserably.

*continued*

*continued*

And, you don't need other expensive coaching or consulting. You'll begin seeing a huge difference just by applying the strategies of Chapter One.

Mark LeBlanc, author of *Growing Your Business* and one of the top business strategists, tells you, "Make this book your desk bible on how to make positive connections every time you step out of your office and into the marketplace. Your networking strategy will come alive!"

"Come Alive" is precisely what will happen when you get *Networking Magic: Find the Best—from Doctors, Lawyers, and Accountants to Homes, Schools, and Jobs.*

Refuse to cave in to negative thoughts. Make one of the wisest decisions you'll ever make right now—and get *Networking Magic* and all of the other bonus gifts worth over $2,145.

The final fact is:

. . . no matter who you are or what your background is or what culture you come from, whether you are young or old, rich or poor, *Networking Magic* will show you, by demonstration, how to create a super-strong network of friends, completely and easily, and you can begin right away.

The time to sharpen your networking skills is right now—not next week or maybe in a month or sometime next year. As the saying goes, "It's now or never."

Grab a hold of this opportunity. It's rare, it's unique, it's jammed full of great value and you'll be rewarded immediately.

One more time!

You can get all of these bonuses and networking benefits by following these next two magical steps:

Step 1. Buy your copy of *Networking Magic* from Barnes & Noble by going to: *http://www.Networking-Magic.com/buyNM*

*continued*

*continued*

Step 2. Once you receive your sale confirmation, please follow this link and enter your Barnes & Noble receipt info and you'll be directed to the bonus page: *http://www.Networking-Magic.com/bonuses*

Trust us, if you have the desire to live a successful life and have a profitable and satisfying business, networking is the way to do it.

Warmly,

Rick Frishman and Jill Lublin

P.S. There are likely plenty of people who are trying to waste your time with things you don't really want or need. We're not those people. This is a real offer, carefully created for you by us and our network of friends. There is no such thing as a coincidence. You're reading this today for a reason. Don't let this opportunity slip through your fingers.

P.P.S. Just think! You're going to save yourself years of trying to find the best products and services, and the hassle of trying to figure out who has the best strategies to help you. Now, you can get everything, all made simple and easy for you, practically handed to you on a silver platter, wrapped up with $2,145.00 worth of f-r-e-e bonus gifts.

You simply place your order using the steps we outlined above . . . and you're on your way to owning the greatest networking secrets, tips, and strategies on the planet—within one minute—flat!

## PARTNERS' SALES LETTER

Subj: [Subscriber Name], Read today! *Networking Magic* special 150x bonus offer

Please read this e-mail now because there's a time-sensitive $2,145 (and climbing) bonus offer below.

*continued*

Dear [Subscriber],

I just got a copy of Rick Frishman and Jill Lublin's latest book, *Networking Magic*, and believe me when I say it's their best yet!

Rick and Jill expertly lay out the basics of effective networking so you never have to worry about getting the best of what you want or need. I face huge demands every day and quite frankly, I cannot afford to waste any of my time, so the type of networking they teach is perfect for my business and lifestyle.

Take my word for it—I've experienced it. Effective networking IS like magic and it will open the right doors for your success and happiness.

Rick and Jill have created a special promotion for their book that is out of this world.

When you buy *Networking Magic* today online at *www.barnesandnoble. com*, you're going to need a magician's-size bag just to carry away the over $2,145 of free bonus gifts that Rick and Jill's networking friends have put together for you.

Read their letter, and then I recommend you grab at least one copy of *Networking Magic* while the bonus gifts are available. Trust me, you'll be glad you did.

[YOUR SIGNATURE BLOCK]

## Bonus Gifts

People often decide to buy because of the bonus gifts that are offered. So, how you describe these bonuses can be a major selling point in your sales letter. It's usually best to describe the bonus gifts directly, without hype or exaggeration. Tell people exactly what they will be receiving so there will be no misunderstandings or subsequent resentment. Some good examples are the following.

- **The Goal Achieving eGuidebook.** Peggy McColl's masterwork; it's the single source for goal-setting and goal-achieving templates. If you're serious about achieving your goals, this is the tool! With it, you'll rediscover your innermost desires and dreams, which you may have completely forgotten about. This powerful resource will put all your goal-achieving resources right at your fingertips. Retail value: $12.97.
- **A Coaching Session with William E. Bailey.** Get a free, one-on-one, 30-minute telephone session with William Bailey, a legend in personal development, business building, team building, and more. Join the ranks of industry giants that Bailey has mentored and trained, many of whom now bring in six- and seven-figure incomes. Retail value: $200.

Explain why you are willing to give potential buyers so many valuable bonus gifts if they buy your book on the designated day. You could say:

We put together this amazing package to help Rick and Robyn reach the #1 position on *www.amazon.com*. But we have to do it tomorrow, September 27, and we really need your help! For helping us, we're going to reward you in a big, no, make that HUGE, way!

*Or*

Tomorrow, Wednesday, November 20, 2006, I will be selling my book to raise money for the Ronald McDonald Children's Charities. Every dollar that is received for books sold tomorrow will be matched by a private foundation. But it will only match what we receive tomorrow. To benefit this worthy charity, please buy my book tomorrow. Thanks for your help!

*Or*

If you're wondering how we can make this offer, here's why. This series has been so wildly successful that our publisher specifically printed nearly 3,000 extra books that we have earmarked for this promotion. It's our way of thanking you for your support. In just two days, we will run a second edition, so this offer will never be available again. To get your hands on this limited first edition, buy now because it won't be around next week.

## Action Steps

1. Explain the steps in conducting an e-mail blast.
2. List five benefits that your potential blast partners can receive from partnering with you.
3. State five questions that you should ask others about e-mail blasts.
4. Describe the information your sales letter should include.
5. Write three headlines for your sales letter.

### Remember

⚠ **E-mail blasts can make your book a bestseller with an online bookseller.** Here's how they work: Accumulate e-mail addresses by forming alliances with partners who have big lists and buy addresses from list brokers. Convince your partners to give you access to names on their lists and to contribute incentives to those who buy your book. Compose a sales letter that you and your partners e-mail to people, offering them free bonuses if they purchase your book from a particular online bookseller on a certain day or time.

⚠ **If a blast makes your book a bestseller, it will generate more interest in it and boost its sales.** When you're a bestselling author, the entire book industry takes notice. Instead of your having to fight for media coverage, the media will suddenly become interested in you.

**CHAPTER 12**

Without push pull is useless.
*Malcolm S. Forbes*

# Special Areas

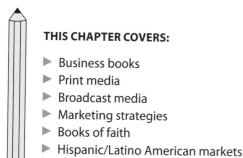

**THIS CHAPTER COVERS:**

▶ Business books
▶ Print media
▶ Broadcast media
▶ Marketing strategies
▶ Books of faith
▶ Hispanic/Latino American markets

BOOKS ARE CLASSIFIED in many different categories and those categories determine where they sit on bookstore shelves. On soft-cover books, the category or categories are frequently printed in the upper portion of the back cover.

Although it's impossible to address the promotion of all categories, in this chapter, we would like to focus on three types of books: business books, books of faith, and Hispanic/Latino books. We've decided to call particular attention to these books because they represent large, power-ful, and emerging markets.

*We would like to thank and acknowledge David Hahn, senior vice president of New York City's Planned Television Arts, for his great help in writing and consulting with us on the business books portion of this chapter.*

## Business Books

Lets start with business books. The term *business books* covers lots of territory: They are written on a wide variety of topics, including management, leadership, entrepreneurship, strategy, sales, marketing, workplace issues, career building and development, business narrative, motivation, and success. Personal finance is a popular major subcategory that includes books on taxes, financial planning, consumer issues, investing, real estate, retirement, and debt reduction. In addition, many general motivation, self-improvement, and how-to books include information about careers and the workplace and some of it may be extensive.

For publishers, business books are a most lucrative niche. According to estimates compiled by Simba Information, over 5,600 new business books were published in 2004 and took in over $828 million. The importance of business books is clear from the fact that most booksellers give them so much shelf space and their constant presence on national bestseller lists. Business books even have their own bestseller lists.

Before you begin to promote a business book, factor in that the nature of your campaign will vary according to your book's subject area. Consider the following:

- Your core market. Clearly identify the main market for your title because business books are not always aimed at all businesses or businesspeople. Your book may target groups such as young professionals, women in the workplace, senior-level management, or specialized niche audiences like financial officers or human resources executives. Focus getting your book covered by the media that best reaches your core market.
- Long-range planning. In promoting business books, you often have more opportunities to work a business audience, and many of these opportunities take longer to secure. For example, you may need six months or a year to:
  - Identify companies that could buy bulk copies of your book directly from the publisher. Usually, your best targets will be

businesses with which you have established relationships and great contacts. Making volume purchase deals is generally an involved process that takes time. First, you must identify companies that might be interested in your book and the precise people to contact in each organization. Then, you must speak with those people and get them an advanced reading copy of your book before you're passed up the line.

- Work out the terms, if they like the idea. Finalizing deals with large corporations to buy in bulk and dealing with their legal and purchasing departments takes time.

- Which industry and related groups or associations reach your core market? For example, research trade, industry, professional, or nonprofit associations such as the National Association of Corporate Directors, the Global Association of Risk Professionals or the American Hospital Association, Young Presidents' Organization (YPO), chambers of commerce, and business school alumni clubs. Identify them, find out whom to approach, and then speak to them. Do they hold monthly luncheons or is a conference coming up? If you would like to speak at those events, you may have to set it up months or even a year ahead. Dealing with industry associations and nonprofits can be notoriously slow because frequently, many individuals must sign off on decisions and they can be exceptionally protective.

- Do third-party groups exist that might support your book? To publicize Harvey Mackay's book *Pushing the Envelope: All the Way to the Top* (Ballantine Books, 1999), David Hahn, senior vice president of New York City's Planned TV Arts, wanted to reach the business-traveler market. So he contacted the marketing director for the Admiral Clubs at American Airlines, which agreed to place in the front of ten Admiral Clubs across the country a poster of Mackay with his new book. Below the poster sat a fishbowl in which business travelers dropped their cards. Each week, a winner was selected who received a copy of *Pushing the Envelope*. At the end of the promotion, a grand-prize winner was selected who was flown to Minneapolis on an all-expenses-paid trip where he spent the day with Mackay, did the town, met celebrities, and attended sporting events. This award-winning promotion helped launch *Pushing the Envelope* onto the bestseller lists for the *New York Times, USA Today, Business Week*, and the *Wall Street Journal*, where it stayed for four months.

■ Who can endorse your book? In business books, endorsements take on added importance because of the credibility factor. Businesspeople tend to have heroes, authors whom they follow, trust, and respect. They are often influenced by their heroes' recommendations and may be more prone to buying the books they suggest. Try to get the right mix of endorsers for your book: big names who have different specialties, experiences, backgrounds, talents, and levels of achievements. Getting the right mix and great endorsements takes planning and time.

■ How to present your credentials. An author's credentials are of utmost importance for business books. For some other books, they are not as critical. However, neither the market nor the media will pay much attention to business books unless their authors have outstanding track records in their areas of interest. If you, like many authors, have extensive and far-ranging credentials, carefully decide which of them you want to stress to best promote your book.

### Authors

Most authors write business books to establish or solidify their status as experts and deliver their message. They may have a deep commitment to inspire the next generation, give them the benefit of their experience, and enhance the state of the art in their field. Some may want to gain greater visibility for themselves and their businesses. They know that successful books can boost their businesses, advance their careers, launch them as celebrities, and help them earn more money.

The authors of business books can be CEOs, top executives, entrepreneurs, business journalists, management consultants, academics, and theorists. Many business books attract devoted corps of loyal readers, so authors such as Ken Blanchard, Tom Peters, and Steven Covey turn out additional books that become franchises. These authors often become highly paid speakers, consultants, and media personalities.

If you expect to earn big royalties from writing your book, think again—it probably won't happen. Only a handful of business-book authors make big bucks from their book sales, for instance, celebrity authors like Donald Trump and Jack Welch. The average business book sells only 3,000 copies. However, authors can make tons as a result of their books and the prominence, visibility, and celebrity they bring. Once business-book authors become well established, book buyers admire them. They want to play golf with them and do business with them and will loyally support them. So, these authors get more speaking engagements and consulting jobs for higher fees.

Occasionally, a book comes along, such as *The Tipping Point* (Little, Brown and Company, 2000) by Malcolm Gladwell, which grabbed everyone's attention and has sold millions of copies. Even if the sales of your book are only moderate, authors often find that the publicity surrounding their books enhances their careers, visibility, and business.

## Print Media

The foundation for business-book publicity campaigns centers around the print media. For most, print is the bedrock, the one basic on which their campaigns are built. When you start developing your campaign, plan the print publicity component first. Make print your priority and concentrate your resources on it.

Print publicity is essential because it reaches the primary audience for business books. Placement in small but targeted business press can produce huge returns. Unlike information presented on radio and TV, print items can be easily torn out, copied, saved, and e-mailed. E-mail has become a highly popular distribution source. With little effort, you can e-mail a print item to your boss, clients, customers, associates or pals, and other media—and they can read the actual text. As a result, an item about your book can have staying power and be more than just a quick buzz in listeners' ears.

Items can be placed with the business media in various formats, including the following.

### Reviews

Reviews of business books carry great weight because reviewers are selective and usually cover only top books or books by top names. Busy business-book readers look to reviewers for information and tend to follow their recommendations. Book reviews usually stick to a consistent length and regularly appear in the same place and issues. For example, on each Thursday, reviews will appear on page 2 of the business section. Good book reviews make fabulous promotional blurbs that are especially useful for future marketing efforts.

A strong review in the *New York Times, Fortune, USA Today,* or *Inc.* can send your book right to the top of the bestseller lists. Two weeks before *Authentic Leadership,* by Bill George (Jossey-Bass, 2003), was in the stores, the *New York Times* Sunday Business Section gave it a rave review. In a matter of days, the book rose to the ninth bestselling book

Another advantage of print publications is that the business media is sharply focused and highly respected by readers. Readers don't have to search all over the place to find items of interest, and they tend to believe what they read. Print publications are considered required reading for serious business types, so early in their careers, they form the habit of regularly reading the business media to get news and information. On the whole, business writers, especially those employed by respected publications, have a strong reputation for honest reporting, good information, and valuable insights.

position on Amazon.com, based on that review alone. And, supported by a strong media campaign, the book remained in the top 100 for some six months.

### Feature Articles

Articles can be longer and provide more depth, information, and explanations than book reviews. Features vary in length. Articles frequently go beyond a book's content and give information that can make you and your book more enticing. They can also cover some parts of your book, but also go into related material that may make it even more interesting to potential buyers.

### Author-Bylined Articles

Writing your own articles is an excellent way to promote your book and inform the public about it. Business books lend themselves to byline articles that can be placed in key publications relating to your core market. They can be placed as editorials, features, or op-ed pieces in newspapers, magazines, and trade publications and on influential Web sites such as *www.cbsmarketwatch.com*, *www.msn.com*, *www.forbes.com*, and *www.careerbuilder.com*. When bylined articles are placed in publications with targeted readership, it can increase your book sales and convince companies to call you for consulting jobs. Although bylined articles are not about your book per se, they often feature ideas from your book, so they will generate excellent publicity.

For bylined articles, it may be tempting to submit little more than an excerpt or summary of material from your book, which can be dry and less than effective when read in isolation or out of context. So redraft your article to suit the publication in which it will run.

### Profiles

In profile articles, you are the centerpiece. In a feature article, you may be only a part of the story; just two paragraphs of a three-page article may highlight your thoughts. In a profile, the entire article is about you. Good profiles are tightly focused and provide lots of interesting information. They also tend to go into more depth, run longer, and include your photograph; profile writers often spend considerable time with you. They can create great interest in both you and your book. After reading them, readers usually feel that they know you better, more personally, which can increase their interest in your book.

### Questions and Answers

These are articles written in the question and answer format. Interviews are frequently presented this way. Q&As position you as an authority and inform others about important or breakthrough information in your book. Readers may use that information and credit you. Q&As work best in a supportive role and make outstanding sidebars or fillers. If you can't get fuller, more comprehensive coverage, be happy with Q&As, which can produce good publicity. On complex subjects, give the gist of the story without getting hung up on details.

### Source Quotes

When you are an expert that the media comes to for explanations, opinions, or quotes, we call what they write source quotes. Although your words may appear in only a short paragraph or two of a twenty-paragraph article, source quotes give you great exposure and they usually include mention of your book. The media constantly needs explanations and quotes from experts on any number of subjects. If you always make yourself available, you will become a valuable, ongoing resource for the media. As a resource for the media, you can get into lots of media outlets and get terrific exposure. In the process, you will be building strong relationships with the media that can help you in the future. For instance, if you have a book coming out, the media could write a profile on you and your new title in response to the help you've provided.

### Media Outlets

Business books can be promoted in numerous print outlets, and when items about a book are published in the right publication, it can launch the book and help make it a success. However, placing a book in

**Robyn Says**

Learn to make the best matches by reading publications that could print items about your book. Before you pitch them, study them; find out their styles, preferences, tendencies, likes, and dislikes. Check their Web sites and request copies of their submission requirements before you approach them. Then, zero in on those outlets that would make the best fit for your book and frame your submissions in accordance with their styles.

the right outlet isn't easy! Creating great placements is an art, a skill that takes planning and can't be handled on a hit-or-miss basis.

Your book will be of interest to the general business media, but it will also be attractive to the subset of the business media that concentrates on specific business areas. With the general business media, it's hard to go wrong. But if you pitch inappropriate media outlets or submit items that don't fit, your credibility can be damaged and they may be less open to your overtures in the future. In contrast, when you bring them items that fit, they will remember and be more receptive to items you want placed.

"In choosing print outlets, match the subject matter of your book to publications that cover that subject matter," David Hahn suggests. "For example, if your book is on marketing or advertising, consider *Ad Age*, *Brand Week*, and *Sales & Marketing Management*. If it's on risk, try for *CFO* magazine. If you're writing on corporate strategy, contact *Harvard Business Review*, *Across the Board*, *Strategy & Business*, and *Chief Executive*. If you're writing on careers, try *www.Monster.com* or *www.careerjournal.com*."

The following are some of the categories of print outlets that publicize business books. Examples of publications in each category are also provided. They include:

### National business magazines

*Fortune, BusinessWeek, Fast Company, Entrepreneur, Inc., Forbes, Business 2.0.* As general business publications, these magazines cover many different business topics. So your topic might be of interest to all of them. You want to be very broad when dealing with the general business press because they are so inclusive. But when you drill down to publications with more specific focuses, you must offer a tighter fit.

### National daily business newspapers
*Wall Street Journal, USA Today, Investor's Business Daily, Financial Times.*

### Major daily newspapers
*New York Times, Washington Post, Chicago Tribune, LA Times, Miami Herald, Boston Globe, Dallas Morning News.*

### Newswires
Associated Press, Reuters, Gannett, Knight Ridder, Scripps Howard.

### City business journals
American City Business Journals own publications in forty markets that deal with local business authors and topics. Crain's Business Journals are published in Chicago, Cleveland, New York City, and Detroit. These local publications deal with local business, local topics, and local authors.

### Web sites
*www.cbsmarketwatch.com; www.fortune.com; www.businessweek.com.*

### Syndicated writers
Joyce Lain Kennedy, Jim Pawlak, Paul Tulenko, Bob Rosner, Tim McGuire, and Carol Kleiman. They tend to be tightly focused on what they write about. If you have a career book, you want a syndicated writer who specializes in writing about careers.

### Industry trade publications
*Jewelry Today, National Real Estate Investor, Automotive News, Air Transport World, Chain Store Age, Modern Healthcare, Restaurant Business, Network World, Supermarket News.*

### Airline magazines

*American Way, Continental, Spirit, Attaché, Hemispheres, Sky.*

### Freelance writers

Freelancers contribute features that appear in influential business publications such as *Investor's Business Daily*, *Continental*, *Wall Street Journal*, *Brandweek* magazine, the *Boston Globe*, and 800-CEO-READ. An article by a freelance writer about you or your book can provide invaluable publicity for your book. Freelancers will often cite authors and their books as sources in their stories, and they write book reviews.

Familiarize yourself with the freelancers who write about your area of interest by reading business publications and visiting business Web sites. Find names of freelance writers from search engines, Profnet, and Bacon's Business Directory.

## Broadcast Media

The broadcast media can reach millions of potential book buyers, who can get information about your book without making any major effort. They can receive this information in the comfort of their homes, in their cars, or while they're jogging. And, since all broadcast outlets now have Web sites, it's easy for viewers and listeners to visit these sites to get more precise information or check on items they may have missed.

The national morning programs such as *Today*, *CBS Morning Show*, and *Good Morning America* feature high-profile business leaders. They are also interested in authors who have written on workplace topics such as negotiating raises, getting along with difficult coworkers, and how to find jobs.

Business news programs may not attract as many viewers or listeners as big, general interest shows. However, they boast loyal viewers who are focused exclusively on business and are more apt to buy business books. The top broadcast outlets for publicizing business books include CNBC, Bloomberg, Fox News, CNN, First Business,

The following print publications wield the greatest influence in promoting business books. Although they cover books in various ways, the following generally describes their book review policies:

*New York Times*—Usually reviews business books in the Sunday Money section, not in the Sunday Book Review section. Covers a variety of business topics and writes in-depth reviews of single, high-profile titles and thematic reviews that incorporate examples from three or four books in one article.

*Fortune* magazine—Publishes some book reviews but primarily runs features of CEOs and business thought leaders.

*BusinessWeek*—Tends to write highly analytical book reviews. Concentrates on titles by CEOs, business journalists, and academics.

*Wall Street Journal*—Occasionally publishes reviews but does not review business books in a regular column. Reviews books of interest to businesspeople on topics including politics, sports, travel, and entertainment.

*Harvard Business Review*—This highly prestigious publication regularly runs reviews and in-depth, bylined articles by thought leaders.

*USA Today Book Review*—Publishes reviews in the Money section, usually on Mondays, on a variety of business books.

*Fast Company*—Asks readers each month which of five books should be reviewed and reviews the winner the following month. Being selected is an honor.

Airline magazines—Most don't run reviews, but publish articles on business topics by business-book authors. Have cut down on business articles.

Marketplace, *Today*, *Good Morning America*, the CBS *Early Show*, local business radio, and *Sound Money*.

In addition, a number of local TV and radio outlets target a business audience. They will feature business–book authors. Their shows tend to be financially oriented and concentrate on topics such as real estate and investment strategies.

The business news media tends to provide topical programming. So, when you approach the business news media, you will be of greater interest to them if you tie your book to current news stories or trends.

## Marketing Strategies

While you don't need to have every detail of your marketing strategies mapped out when you begin writing your book, the earlier you get started on crafting this part of your platform, the better.

### Speaking Events

When you appear at events, you can spread the gospel about your book, and sell copies of it. When people see and meet you, they frequently buy your book. If you give speeches, you're almost guaranteed to sell your books because at most events, your books will be available for sale. However, when you try to publicize your book through the media, selling books is iffier.

Become an accomplished speaker because speaking is a major platform for selling books. Plan ahead, early in the book-writing process. Begin speaking at least six months to a year before your book is published, to drum up interest in it and to build your speaking ability and reputation.

If you're not an established speaker, take public-speaking classes or media training. Join speakers' organizations. Then speak for free for local organizations where you can polish your craft. Start small and work your way up; build a following and a reputation for being a dynamic, entertaining, and enlightening speaker.

Also speak to local branches of industry or professional groups. If you've written a sales or networking book, you could speak at meetings of Sales and Marketing Executives International or the American Marketing Association. Try to build your base where you live and work because members of the community where you started will become your staunchest supporters.

When you become an accomplished speaker, assemble video-tapes of your presentations, testimonials, a speech description, and your biography in a professional manner. Then, sign up with as many speaker bureaus as possible to get bookings. The top bureaus include the International Speakers Bureau (*www.internationalspeakers.com*), Leading Authorities, Inc. (*www.leadingauthorities.com*), the Leigh Bureau (*www.leighbureau.com*), and Washington Speaker Bureau (*www.washspkrs.com*).

Hook up with 800-CEO-READ (*www.ceoread.com*), an online business-book retailer that sells books to the corporate market. It will feature your book in its newsletter and on its Web site and will solicit bulk orders for your book from corporations. 800-CEO-READ will arrange for copies of your books to be available at your public appearances, events, and speaking engagements. All sales made by 800-CEO-READ are reported to many of the leading bestseller lists. Either go through or clear it with your publisher.

### E-Mail Blasts

As we discussed in detail in Chapter 11, e-mail blasts are campaigns intended to make books bestsellers with online booksellers. E-mail blasts work well with certain business books, especially motivational books. Incentives that can be a part of the package include free or discounted audiotapes, videos, books or chapters of books, resource lists, courses, newsletter subscriptions, or seminars.

A variation of the e-mail blast that works well for business books is what we call an awareness blast. This blast is intended to provide information and awareness, not free gifts. For example, if your marketing book is targeted to C-level executives (chief executive officers, chief information officers, and chief financial officers), you probably don't want to conduct giveaways, because they're too gimmicky for your audience. So, instead, you buy a list of C-level executives from *BusinessWeek* and then send a general sales e-mail or letter to inform them about your new book. You can include high-level endorsements, favorable reviews, and even excerpts. The cost of buying sharply targeted lists can be expensive, but it can enable you to reach a precise audience.

As we mentioned in our discussion of authors' Web sites, capturing names and e-mail addresses is a major objective of such sites. If you acquire enough names and addresses, you can hold your own e-mail blast and send other promotions to people who you know have some interest in you and your book.

### Contests

Some business books lend themselves to creative campaigns. One that was highly successful was the Best Boss/Worst Boss contest that Planned Television Arts developed to promote *The Corporate Coach: How to Build a Team of Loyal Customers and Happy Employees* by James B. Miller, the CEO of Miller Business Systems (HarperBusiness, 1994).

The contest, which was promoted during Miller's twenty-city tour, invited employees to submit essays describing their best and worst bosses. The grand-prize winner in each category received a trip to Hawaii. The contest generated many additional interviews for Miller during his tour as well as national placements, including three with the Associated Press. Both *Today* and *The Osgood File* featured the contest winners and Miller's book. Interestingly, the worst boss winner appeared in disguise.

Chapter 12 ■ Special Areas

Miller's contest was so popular that he ran similar contests for another two years. He also used material obtained from the contests to write another book, *Best Boss, Worst Boss: Lessons and Laughs from the International "Best Boss/Worst Boss" Contests* (Summit Publishing Group, 1996).

Any entrepreneurial author should strongly consider running a contest. With the Internet, it's not difficult.

### Top Bestseller Lists

To make weekly bestseller lists, you usually need to sell at least 3,000 copies a week, and for monthly lists, 10,000 copies a month.

Making the business bestseller list is a matter of velocity; it's a matter of how many books you sell in a particular week or month, not your cumulative sales. So, create your book campaign strategy to sell as many books in the shortest period of time to generate the maximum number of reported sales during that time. Orchestrate all your publicity efforts to come together during that window of time: your speaking engagements, op-ed piece, your e-mail blast, and your corporate orders. If your promotional efforts and your book sales are spread over a period of months, you will be less likely to make the bestseller lists.

The only sales figures used for bestseller lists are those that come from retail chains, online booksellers, and independent bookstores. So, if you make a bulk sale to a corporation or sell tons of books from the back of the room when you speak, those won't be counted unless they're made by one of the groups mentioned above.

### Special Opportunities

Business news is always breaking. In areas such as parenting, lifestyles, entertainment, food, and even sports, the news can be slow. Since the business news never stops, business authors must seize upon developments in their areas of expertise as soon as they occur.

Bill George's book, *Authentic Leadership* (Jossey-Bass, 2003), featured his expertise on good corporate governance and CEO pay. His publicity campaign focused on his high ethical standards and visionary ideas. When former New York Stock Exchange chief Richard Grasso came under fire, the media turned to George as an expert on ethical CEO behavior. George gave interviews that spawned more interviews, and he received great publicity, which boosted the sales of his book.

Business authors must also anticipate future news in order to time their books and publicity efforts around upcoming cycles that the media will cover. If you have a book on job searching or career advice, make sure that your book is released during April or May to tie it into the annual graduation cycle that follows. Every year, prior to graduation, the media churns out stories on finding jobs and establishing careers. By anticipating the media's patterns, authors of books on these subjects can make themselves available to the media as experts. They can get great publicity for themselves and their books by giving the media explanations, insights, and quotations on careers. The assistance they provide to the media can pay off at other times of the year when the media needs experts to help it with news items on jobs and careers.

### Hometowns

Capitalize on the special attention you can get from the media in your hometown. Develop strong ties to the business editors and reporters for local newspapers and business journals. It pays to build strong hometown bases because locals take pride in the success of other locals and help promote them.

When it comes to hometown coverage, business authors have the advantage of having more outlets where they can speak than other authors. They can speak at chambers of commerce; at service clubs such as Rotary, Kiwanis, and Elks Clubs; and to local business groups. Business authors should take advantage of these opportunities to build a strong local speaking base and solid grassroots support.

### Extra Credit

Write biographies and promotional materials that build your credibility. In bios, stress the accomplishments that relate most to your book. Readers and the media want to know that you have outstanding credentials. It will make the information and advice in your book more authoritative.

The press materials for Bill George's *Authentic Leadership* noted that George was a member of the National Association of Corporate Directors (NACD). However, it stressed that he had been named the Corporate Director of the Year by NACD. The media picked up on this point and frequently referred to George as the former NACD Corporate Director of the year.

Tweak bios to emphasize the author's expertise in areas in which individual media contacts are most interested. Conform news releases and other promotional materials so they also highlight authors' expertise in the same areas.

Business authors should also utilize their media contacts. Over the years, most business authors, especially those who are business leaders, make extensive media contacts. To promote their books, they should call on their media contacts. When members of the media cover stories, they have the power to determine the direction and tenor of the piece. So, using your personal connections can get you favorable coverage.

It's a good idea to cultivate media contacts well before your book comes out. As we've suggested, become a media resource: Feed the media stories, information, and sources; write byline articles; and volunteer your expertise. Then, when you need the help of those contacts, your relationship will have been established and you won't have to start from scratch.

## Books of Faith

In recent years, segments of society have become powerful new markets, with the two most notable being the Christian and the Hispanic/Latino markets. Substantial markets also exist for Catholic, Jewish, Islamic, Buddhist, New Age spirituality, and other groups. In addition, a number of other markets exist within these individual groups.

As the size and market clout of these groups has grown, a vital, dedicated, and sharply focused media has taken root around them. This media tends to differ from the mainstream media because it wants more than just a good, newsworthy story; it wants news that is consistent with the beliefs and objectives of the groups it covers. If you and your book qualify, these media groups can become your greatest ally.

Although dedicated media cover various cultural, ethnic, and religious groups, the largest in scope and influence is the Christian media. In this chapter, we will primarily address the Christian media and what it includes and cite outlets that can promote your book. Keep in mind that a similar framework exists for the media that covers other religions and groups, but on a smaller scale, so that you can work with it to publicize your book. This chapter illustrates how niche marketing can work in a particular sector and that it can also be applied to your own area of religious focus.

### The Christian Media

When we use the term *Christian media*, we are referring to the Evangelical Christian media, the largest and most powerful segment of the Christian media. Segments of the Christian media also concentrate on denominations that exist within Evangelical Christianity, which include Baptist, Southern Baptist, Pentecostal, Methodist, Reformed, Lutheran, and many more.

The Christian media will usually cover a book if the author has some evangelical background and the book has a Christian theme. An author doesn't have to be a church leader or even be an accomplished parishioner provided he or she subscribes to evangelical beliefs. The Christian media wants to know that authors are actually connected to

---

#### Author 101 Advice

In the book-publishing industry, books of faith have been the leading growth area for the past few years. According to *Book Industry Trends,* this market increased by 11 percent in 2004 to $1.9 billion, and the growth is expected to continue.

a Christian denomination, that they are a member of a recognized faith and believe in its teachings.

Books of faith must be inspirational, devotional, and involved with Christian teaching. They can be either fiction or nonfiction. Devotional books involve following, interpreting, or understanding the Bible and religious texts or doctrine. They can also provide reflective thoughts and practices.

The Christian media generally won't book those who don't follow its beliefs. It will cover authors who are members of Christian denominations who have not written books of faith, but it requires those titles to have some faith component. The fact that the author subscribes to its beliefs is usually helpful, but to be covered, books also must be interesting and relate to Christian readers. A large crossover market exists, which the Christian media will cover. Crossover authors are Christian authors whose books also address mainstream audiences. Many Christian publishers would like to expand their markets by reaching the mainstream audience through crossover books.

Recent successful crossover books that penetrated the mainstream market include Chuck Norris and Ken Abraham's book, *Against All Odds* (Broadman & Holman Publishers, 2004), and *Trust Me*, by Wayne A. Hastings and Ronald Potter (WaterBrook Press, 2004). *Against All Odds* appealed to both audiences because it is the story of the actor Chuck Norris. *Trust Me*, which was written by two Christian business authors on building trust within your business, found a wide audience in the wake of the many recent business scandals and unethical business dealings. TV evangelist Joel Osteen's book, *Your Best Life Now* (Warner Faith, 2004), has also enjoyed great crossover success.

The Christian media is drawn to inspirational stories, so it helps for authors to have compelling stories of how their relationship with God grew during difficult times. It is also big on stories of encouragement that help readers overcome problems and substantial odds. Books on prayer are also popular.

Like mainstream publishers, faith-book publishers tend to publish books that are similar to those that have had major success. So, the market has lots of copycat books that try to imitate or follow the formulas of prior popular books. "Find what's unique and relevant, what hasn't been talked about before in the media, and go with that," Sharon Farnell, managing director of the Faith Division of Planned Television Arts, advises.

According to Farnell, "It's also important to link books to topical stories or issues that are of concern to large audiences. If it's newsworthy and you can add an inspirational or devotional slant, it can be more attractive to Christian publishers and Christian media."

Only a few of the publicity firms that specialize in promoting books have publicists who exclusively handle books of faith, Planned Television Arts being one of them. Some consultants and agencies also specialize in placing items with the Christian media, but not necessarily just books.

### Media Outlets

The outlets for Christian media parallel the outlets for the mainstream media. They have a strong presence in television, radio, print, and the Internet. However, three major factors distinguish Christian media outlets from their mainstream counterparts:

1. The loyalty and devotion of their audiences.
2. Having content consistent with Christian principles and beliefs.
3. The promotional power of churches, mega churches, and church organizations.

### Television

Major Christian television shows include the *700 Club*, *Hour of Power*, and the *Old Time Gospel Hour*. The North American Mission Board of the Southern Baptist Convention operates a twenty-four-hour-a-day television network, Family Net, which telecasts a range of programs from those that are religious in nature to classic sitcoms. Family Net programming is also lifestyle oriented and features cooking and health segments and feature authors discussing their works. Christian television has devoted viewers and many of them watch Christian television programs every day. To them, it's a central part of their lives.

### Radio

Salem Radio Network is Christian radio's leading news network. It serves over 1,900 radio stations, is a full-service news outlet with newscasts at the top and bottom of each hour, and produces nine live daily and weekend talk shows. Salem Music Network provides three twenty-four-hour Christian music formats and SRN Weekend furnishes weekend music programs.

Christian radio also proliferates. Its many rock stations, which play music that sounds like top-forty music but with Christian-oriented words, appeal to a younger, freer-spending demographic.

The market for books of faith revolves around Christian publishers and bookstores. Publishers include Thomas Nelson, WaterBrook (a division of Random House), Tyndale House, Baker Books, Regal Books, Zondervan (a division of HarperCollins), and many more.

### Publishing

Readers of Christian books are also extremely loyal, so selling Christian books has become a big business. *The Purpose-Driven Life*, by Rick Warren (Zondervan, 2002), has sold more than 23 million copies and is the fastest-selling nonfiction book of all time. The *Left Behind* series by Tim LaHaye and Jerry B. Jenkins (Tyndale House Publishers) has reportedly sold more than 75 million copies since 1995.

Christian retail booksellers have an active and powerful centralized trade association, Christian Booksellers Association (CBA). CBA has nearly 2,300 member stores that sell Bibles, Christian books, curriculum, apparel, music, videos, gifts, and other materials. Like its mainstream counterpart, the American Booksellers Association (ABA), CBA hosts an annual trade show, which attracts tens of thousands of attendees.

Major Christian general-interest print publications include *Christianity Today*, *Guideposts*, *Today's Christian*, *World*, *Christian History*, *Christian Century*, and *Discipleship Journal*. Specific publications also exist for denominations such as the Southern Baptist Convention, which has a whole network of publications like the *On Mission* magazine. Examples

> ### Audience Statistics
>
> A nationwide survey conducted by the Barna Group (*www.barna.org*; March 14, 2005) found that in a typical month:
>
> - Nearly half of all adults, 46 percent, listen to Christian radio.
> - Forty-five percent of all adults tune in to a Christian TV program.
> - One-third of all adults read a Christian magazine.
> - One-third of all adults read a Christian book.
> - One of every six adults (16 %) spent time visiting faith-oriented Web sites.
> - Approximately 13 million "unchurched" adults read Christian magazines.
>
> On a daily basis:
> - One out of every six U.S. adults (16 %) listened to Christian radio.

of ministry or denominational publications are *Ministries Today* and *Outreach* magazine, *Presbyterian Today*, *Presbyterian Record*, *Today's Pentecostal Evangel*, and *Baptists Today*.

Within the Christian media, many subcategories exist. They include, *Today's Christian Woman* (women's lifestyle), *New Man* (men's lifestyle), *Sports Spectrum*, *Christian Music Planet*, *CCM* magazine (contemporary Christian music), *Marriage Partnership*, *Christian Parenting Today*, *Focus on the Family*, and *Business Reform*. Many Christian radio stations and pop artists are also emerging who appeal to the religious market. Publications for teens include *Campus Life*, *Brio* (magazine for girls), *Breakaway* (for guys), and *Guideposts for Teens*.

### Networks of Publications

Companies that produce a number of Christian publications also exist. Some of those companies are listed below, as are some of the magazines that they publish. They include the following.

Christianity Today International
(*www.ChristianityToday.com*)
*Books & Culture*
*Campus Life*
*Christian History & Biography*
*Christian Parenting Today*
*Christianity Today*
*Leadership Journal*
*Marriage Partnership*
*Men of Integrity*
*Today's Christian*
*Today's Christian Woman*

Focus on the Family Magazines
(*www.family.org/fofmag*)
*Christian Living*
*Marriage*
*Parenting and Family*
*Public Policy Issues*
*Sanctity of Life*
*Spiritual Heritage*

Lifeway Christian Resources
(*www.lifeway.com*)
*Christian Single*
*Deacon*
*HomeLife*
*Journey*
*La Familia Christiana de Hoy*
*LeaderLife*
*Living with Teenagers*
*Mature Living*
*ParentLife*
*Special Education Today*
*Stand Firm*

Strang Communications
(*www.strang.com*)
*Charisma*
*Christian Retailing*
*Ministries Today*
*New Man*
*SpiritLed Woman*
*Vida Cristiana*

### Religious Assemblies

Speaking at houses of worship is a productive way for authors to inform people about their books and build their followings. Audiences at services are usually attentive listeners who, if they believe what you say, can become ardent supporters. Speaking at religious gatherings can also give you instant credibility, and many congregations let authors sell their books after they speak.

Speaking to congregations can help you develop your presentations. Worshippers tend to be generous and forgiving; if your message resonates, they will overlook flaws in your delivery. If your message and delivery are both great, you will be a big hit. Start locally and make your mistakes close to home. Then, try to work your way up. If you build a solid local reputation, it will accelerate your rise.

When you reach the top, you can address huge congregations. According to *BusinessWeek*, 880 mega churches exist that attract at least 2,000 people each week. Houston's Lakewood Church, where Joel Osteen (*Your Best Life Now*, Warner Faith, 2004) is pastor, boasts weekly attendance of 28,000.

After the Crystal Cathedral Ministries telecasts the *Hour of Power*, book signings are frequently held. Places of worship also host special events such as Women's Weekends that feature guest authors who are often permitted to sell their books. The Christian women's group Women of Faith also enlists authors to speak and then lets them sell their books.

Events are great venues for promoting and selling books. The prolific author John C. Maxwell (*25 Ways to Win with People*, Nelson Business, 2005) and Joel Osteen sell out stadiums. Maxwell, Osteen, and other Christian speakers are charismatic speakers; they inspire audiences, who flock to buy their books.

In addition, houses of worship sponsor many weekend and special events for people of all ages where authors may appear. They also host special events for kids, teens, adults, women, men, and seniors and on particular subjects.

### Promotion Tips

Endorsements can play a critical role in the success of books of faith, especially for authors who are not well known. Christian authors and leaders have loyal followers, so their endorsements carry great weight.

Endorsements also can open doors to the Christian media, which is extremely selective in the books and authors it covers. The Christian media goes to great lengths to be sure that the views of authors it covers are in sync with its readers' beliefs. So when the media sees that someone it respects has endorsed your book, it may be more prone to interviewing you and covering your book.

"If you're not known, start small," Sharon Farnell suggests. "Start locally, with the local media, contact the local Christian and mainstream stations and schedule interviews. Contact your own church, other local churches and local Christian publications. Build a solid reputation in your community and then expand. Christian churches, publications, and radio and TV stations are often linked to a network or association through which authors can get bigger bookings and coverage. Local outlets may have connections with regional groups and get reviews, interviews, features, and other coverage through these outlets."

Post press releases for your book with Religion News Service (RNS; *www.religionnews.com*). Press releases are distributed through RNS to over 1,000 editors and writers whose publications and programs reach over 25 million people. Many Christian writers subscribe to RNS and can learn about your book through it. RNS also posts on its Web site the top ten religious book bestsellers for both hardcover and paperbacks.

As we have previously reported in Chapter 7, "How to Get Bookings and Coverage," authors can also take out ads in *Radio-TV Interview Report* (RTIR; *www.rtir.com*), the world's largest database of authors and experts who are available for live and telephone interviews. RTIR is published twice a month and reaches 4,000 hosts and producers.

Many religious centers house bookstores and some are huge operations. According to *BusinessWeek*, the bookstore at the Willow Creek Community Church in South Barrington, Illinois, is a $3.2 million annual business. Approach church bookstores about holding signings and events where you can sell your book and build interest in it. Once you've successfully done a few, you can use them to get bookings at other Christian bookstores.

To get speaking engagements, make a tape. Set up a staged interview, tape actual appearances, or both because some Christian stations simply run videotapes of interviews that authors submit. A tape will demonstrate that you are a wonderful guest and that you're articulate and have a great rapport with audiences.

Christian bookstores can be a difficult sell because they are very protective. They want assurances that the products they offer to their customers are in line with their beliefs. As a result, mainstream publishers have difficulty breaking into Christian bookstores.

To overcome this problem, more Christian and mainstream publishers are now partnering. For example, Strain Publications, a Christian publisher, is partnering with Putnam, a mainstream publisher.

## Hispanic/Latino American Markets

The Hispanic/Latino American population is unique, diverse, and growing rapidly. It accounts for approximately 15 percent of the total U.S. population, or 43.5 million people, according to the Magazine Publishers of America. Of these, 66.9 percent are of Mexican ancestry; 14.3 percent have roots in Central and South America, 8.6 percent in Puerto Rico, 3.7 percent in Cuba, and 6.5 percent in other areas.

Hispanics/Latino Americans are also an enormous domestic market. From 1990 to 2000, the Hispanic/Latino population grew nearly four times the rate of the U.S. population, about 58 percent, and from 2000 to 2003, it jumped another 13 percent. Its purchasing power in 2003 was $653 billion, and the Selig Center for Economic Growth at the University of Georgia expects it to exceed $927 billion by 2007, which is 80 percent greater than the rest of the U.S. population.

"Since many Hispanic/Latino cultures reside in the United States, variations in the language exist," Deborah Kohan, director of PTA en Español, points out. "For example, in Argentina, the word for an item may differ from the word for it in Mexico. So, when you're writing a press release for your book, you really must know which audience you're targeting and which words or phrases to use. If you want to reach the overall Hispanic/Latino American audience, avoid slang or street language, which is usually more regional than universal."

Another unique feature of the market is the population concentration. While over 40 percent of Hispanic/Latino Americans reside in Los Angeles, New York, Miami, Chicago, and the San Francisco Bay Area, many other areas have a high percentage of Hispanic/Latino residents.

They constitute more than 40 percent of the population in McAllen, Texas; Brownsville, Texas; El Paso, Texas; Bakersfield, California; Fresno, California; Albuquerque, New Mexico; and many other cities.

Hispanic/Latino Americans are a powerful market force. According to *http://www.trustedtranslations.com/hispanic_market.asp*, Hispanic/Latino network/national television advertising has increased nearly 74 percent since 2000. Spending is expected to hit $1.41 billion in 2005, more than twice the figure for 1999. Other media expenditures for newspapers, magazines, and local TV have also jumped.

Many media outlets target Hispanic/Latino American readers, including *People en Español*, *Vanidades*, *Cosmpolitan en Español*, *Cristina: La Revista*, *Latina*, and *Ser Padres*. Popular newspapers are *Hoy*, *La Opinion* (Los Angeles), *El Nuevo Herald*, *El Diario*, and Lawndale News (Chicago).

Top television networks include: Univision, Telemundo, the Hispanic Information and Telecommunications Network, and CNN en Español. Some of the favorite programs are *Despierta America*, *Primer Impacto*, *De Mañanita*, and Urban Latino TV. In Los Angeles, the third and fourth top radio stations are KLAX-FM and KLVE-FM, respectively. Other major radio outlets are WPAT-FM and WADO-AM in New York, WAMR-FM and WAQI-AM in Miami, KLTN-FM in Houston, and WGBT-FM in McAllen

A final interesting fact about Hispanic/Latino Americans is that they use the Internet more than the general population: an average of 9.2 hours a week as compared with 8.5 hours, according to an AOL/Roper U.S. Hispanic Cyberstudy. The survey found that the Internet is the most powerful information medium influencing the purchasing decisions of online Hispanic/Latino Americans, so consider using the Web to reach them.

## Action Steps

1. What three items should you factor in before you begin promoting your business book?

2. Why is print publicity so important for business books?
3. Explain which authors and books the Christian media will usually cover.
4. How many mega churches exist?
5. What is the increase in spending by Hispanic/Latino Americans since 2000?

### *Remember*

⚠ **Business is good for business.** Business books are written on many subjects, including management, leadership, entrepreneurship, strategy, sales, marketing, workplace issues, career building and development, business narrative, motivation, and success. Most authors write business books to establish or solidify their status as experts and deliver their message. Authors can be CEOs, top executives, entrepreneurs, business journalists, management consultants, academics, and theorists.

⚠ **Use your roots.** If you're a member of a religious, ethnic, or racial group, work through that group and the media connected to it to spread the word about your book. A number of segments of society have become powerful new markets, with the two most notable being the Christian and the Hispanic/Latino American markets. Substantial markets also exist for Catholic, Jewish, Islamic, Buddhist, New Age spirituality, and other groups.

**CHAPTER 13**

Celerity is never more admired / Than by the negligent.
*William Shakespeare*

# Campaign Timelines

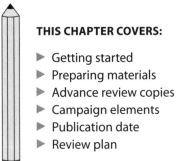

**THIS CHAPTER COVERS:**

► Getting started
► Preparing materials
► Advance review copies
► Campaign elements
► Publication date
► Review plan

BOOK PUBLICITY CAMPAIGNS are a lot like puzzles—in fact, they are puzzles; giant puzzles. To successfully complete them, numerous different pieces must be fitted together in a precise, sequential order. If all of the pieces don't fit just right, it simply won't work and you're still stuck with the bill.

Since book campaigns run for extended periods of time, they can't just be slapped together. Each piece must be carefully selected, shaped, and then coordinated to work with all of the others, which requires great timing and skill. For a campaign to have impact, all of its elements must flow harmoniously, one right after another. Each element must be structured to stand on its own, to be successful by itself, and to enhance all the other elements.

*We would like to thank and acknowledge David Thalberg of the Susan Magrino Agency in New York City for his great help in writing and reviewing this chapter. David formerly worked with Rick as senior vice president of New York City's Planned Television Arts.*

To make your campaign work, create a timeline. Your campaign may include all of the right ingredients; it can be well planned, researched, and targeted, but without a timeline, it probably won't work or return your investment.

A timeline is a list of each strategy you intend to employ in your publicity campaign and the date when you must initiate each tactic. A timeline forces you to think about:

- Every tactic in your campaign.
- How long it will take.
- When it must start.
- Who will perform it.
- The resources needed.

"Your timeline must be more than just a general or tentative plan," David Thalberg, of New York City's Susan Magrino Agency, explains. "It must be a detailed outline of the precise strategy you intend to take. When your campaign is rolling, your timeline can always be tweaked. For example, if a certain tactic is working well, you can decide to do more of it, or if another part bombs, you could decide to scrap it completely."

For first-time authors, timelines can be especially critical because publishers typically don't give first books much of a publicity push. Writing a timeline can awaken novice writers to all the strategies that they can take to inform the world that their book has been published. Timelines can help them firm up their publicity budgets and give them a logical, well-thought-out schedule that they can easily follow. They can show authors what they can do themselves and where they need help.

As we discuss timelines, we will touch upon lots of publicity tactics, more than you will include in your campaign. Some of these tactics we have previously addressed, so please excuse any repetition. However, we think it's essential for you to see the big picture, an overview of just how many strategies you can employ in a publicity campaign and how critical the timing can be.

As you read about timelines, please refer to the chart provided at the end of this chapter. This chart was prepared for an actual promotional campaign for a book that was written by a top corporate leader, which accounts for why it is so extensive. Its comprehensiveness and the fact that the campaign was hugely successful make it an ideal reference tool for this book. Adapt the timeline chart for your book's publicity campaign. Select those tactics that you think will work well for you and then investigate them. Learn what implementing and coordinating them will take and what's involved in a book publicity campaign.

## Getting Started

Start early. As soon as you know your book will be published, begin planning your publicity campaign. If you wrote a promotion plan as a part of your book proposal, reread it and think about how to implement it. If you didn't create a promotion plan, write one now. For detailed information on writing a book promotion plan, see our book *Author 101: Bestselling Book Proposals*. Give yourself plenty of time to prepare your campaign timeline. Start as soon as you know that your book will be published, even if you don't know precisely when. Don't wait, because planning and coordinating all your publicity strategies is an involved and time-consuming process. Begin by:

- Deciding which specific strategies you might employ. For example, book signings, approaching book reviewers, going on a speaking tour, and so on.
- Investigating each strategy by finding out:
  *How it works*
  *If it could be good for your book*
  *How long it would take*
  *Its cost*
  *The help you would need*
  *When you should start*

- Determining which strategies you could do on your own and which will require help.
- Deciding how to best coordinate all facets of your campaign.
- Identifying when each segment will start.

First decide what you want to do; identify the strategies that you think will work for your book. Then, create a preliminary timeline.

### Create a Timeline

When you write your timeline, concentrate on how long each strategy will take to prepare, execute, and complete. Also clarify the people and resources you will need. Determine when you will need them, and check whether they will be available on those dates.

Set dates to start working on each item listed on your timeline and when each will launch. For example, on March 15, begin to draft the press release you plan to mail on April 15. Build in enough time to write the release and have it edited, critiqued, and sent. If you're booked to speak at the Adventurer's Club on April 18, list the dates when you

---

**Author 101 Advice**

When you request endorsements, make the endorsers' lives easier by providing samples that they can adapt and e-mail back to you. Find endorsements in other books, copy your favorites, adapt them, and send them as samples to potential endorsers. Write testimonials of your own that include points you would like stressed. For example, "Rick Frishman is a book-promotion giant" or "Robyn Freedman Spizman is always ten steps ahead of the pack."

Make the endorsements truthful and decide if you want them to endorse you or your book. If you receive endorsements after the deadline, hang on to them because they could be squeezed in, especially if they're from big names, or you could use them for promotional materials, subsequent books, or future editions of your book.

must order copies of your book, have handouts printed, and arrange to be videotaped.

Although the dates on your timeline can be tweaked, try to stick to your schedule. Only make changes for emergencies or those rare opportunities that come only once. When you start making changes, it can weaken your timeline because you no longer consider deadlines critical. Constant or last-minute changes can also alienate the media, organizers, and hosts, which will kill future opportunities. In contrast, religiously meeting your target dates will give your campaign direction and discipline.

## Preparing Materials

Create a list of all the elements that will be involved in your campaign and then start working on those that will take longest to achieve. Keep in mind that everything will take longer than you initially expect, especially those items that will require you to rely on others or be out of your control. When people don't deliver when promised, promptly follow up and give them a gentle nudge.

Major items for which you should prepare include:

### Endorsements
Publishers need the endorsements for your book early so that they can include them in your book and their promotional materials. They will give you deadlines for endorsement submissions. Usually, they want them at least three or four months before the book's publication date.

Begin working on endorsements early because they rarely arrive when promised; something always seems to pop up to slow down or derail the process, especially when you have to deal with celebrities and go through their handlers. With endorsements, always try to:

■ Get endorsements from the most well-known and accomplished people you can reach. If you're a professional, seek out the top people in your professional organizations. If you're a businessperson, approach the leaders in your industry. If you're a novelist, try to get endorsements from the most popular novelists.

■ Ask your agent, editor, and publisher to help you get endorsements from their authors.

■ If anyone ever offered to help you, this is the time to call in that chit. Ask them for endorsements.

### Press Kit Materials

Assembling the pieces of a press kit early is often advantageous because you can use all or various pieces with different promotions. For instance, when you send reviewers galleys of your book, which usually occurs about four months before the publication date, you can send the entire press kit or just parts you select, such as your press release, Q&As, your biography, and your photo.

If you create your press kit early, you may want to rewrite some pieces from time to time. Since news stories are constantly breaking, you might be able to link your book to some of them. Over time, materials and authors grow stale: writing about new slants can recharge and enliven you. Review your press release and Q&As frequently to keep them fresh and newsworthy.

If you look good, take advantage of it. Send your photo with your promotional materials to show the media what you look like. Better yet, scan a professionally taken photo on all your promotional materials, but don't let it dominate the page. If you have an interesting photo that relates to your book, such as monuments described in your book, soldiers during battle, or the dog that saved your life, be sure to include that also.

### Press Releases

The number one mistake that authors make in getting publicity for their books is that they wait too long, according to Paul Hartunian, the nation's leading authority on showing business owners and entrepreneurs how to get publicity. "They wait until their book is either just about to come out or has already been released before they start getting publicity.

If a book on repairing cars is coming out in October, authors usually wait until September or October to start getting publicity. Unless they send press releases, the media won't know who they are. Instead, they should start regularly sending press releases in January and send a different release on something about car repairs every week or so, even though the book doesn't exist, to build name recognition," Hartunian advises. "They must give the media the opportunity to find out who they are."

"Then, when the book comes out in October," Hartunian notes, "the media will recognize the author's name and know that he or she has great advice on car repairs. So, it will read the press release and may try to find out more about the book and/or the author.

"If you think you want to write a book, if you have a dream of writing a book, even if it's just something you casually mention to your family one day, start sending press releases to begin getting publicity on that topic. Establish yourself as an authority, if not the authority, in that field," Hartunian adds.

To build name recognition and perception of you as an expert, send press releases weekly, but at the least, every other week. Don't worry about having enough to say. Think of the problems that readers have and answer them. If you find that you truly don't have enough to say, reconsider whether you can write an entire book.

### Speaking Engagements

Set up your speaking engagements months in advance. For most organizations that book speakers, four to six months prior isn't uncommon. The largest, most high-powered organizations will hire speakers a year or more in advance.

Host organizations frequently have long lead times and many want to fill out their rosters as early as possible. Closing deals with organizations that host speakers often involves red tape because they have planning committees, program committees, and publicity committees that need information on you and your speech as early as possible so they can prepare their promotional materials. Then, their legal people may also want to get into the act.

Even smaller local organizations such as religious, business, and community organizations need lead time. And the more lead time you can give them, the more smoothly the event will run and the more publicity you usually will receive.

Approach organizations and try to book your speaking engagements early so you can coordinate them with the publication of your book and any follow-up media events. For example, if your speech in Miami is well received, you probably will want to return to Miami on your media tour or to give workshops and seminars. Chances are that you can drum up media coverage for your return appearances on the basis of your prior success. If you will be making future visits, plug them during your speech and tell your audience where those interested can sign up. If, at events, you will be giving handouts or using visual aids or any type of technology:

- Arrange for all materials to be on hand when you arrive.
- Obtain advance information on the venue, such as its size, dimensions, configuration, sound quality, and lighting.
- Arrange with the organizers to visit the venue before you are scheduled to appear, to check all equipment.

Before you speak at engagements, arrange for copies of your book to be available for sale. At these events, you should be able to sell copies of your book, so coordinate how those books will be sold. The ideal scenario is to build the cost of your book into the admission fee for the event. If the regular fee for the event is $20, the host would charge $39.95 and include a copy of your book, which guarantees you sales. However, this arrangement can be a hard sell with many host groups.

More often, host organizations will permit you to set up a table in the back of the room to sell copies of your book. Set a time, preferably right after you speak, to meet purchasers and sign the copies they buy.

As a condition to appearing at engagements, obtain approval of the host organization to sell your book and your other products. Then have everything else you sell available at the engagements: audiotapes and videotapes, CDs, workbooks, and products. To make these items more attractive, create a special price for this event. If all of your products normally sell for $125, sell them at the special price of $79 for this event.

"Don't give out ordering information for your book. You want people to buy there," David Thalberg advises. "You don't want people to have time to bring something home and think about it. It's spur of the moment. If you're a dynamic speaker, they're going to buy whatever you have to sell. And if you offer the 'special only-at-this-event discount,' you'll increase the likelihood of sales."

Pitch local media at least six to eight weeks in advance of the date you would like to be covered. If you're going on a road tour, booking signings or events in other cities, try to generate coverage by their local or regional newspapers, morning shows, and news programs. Pitch the major, most important outlets first. If you start early enough, you will still have time to approach backups if your first choices say no.

When you land an appearance or an interview by a top outlet, use it to get additional media coverage. Tell your number two, three, and four targets that you're booked on number one, which can help make you more attractive to them.

Whenever you travel, try to get media coverage. For instance, if you're scheduled to be in Philadelphia on a business or family trip in early March, contact the top media right after the first of the year. Work from the top down and contact as many outlets as possible to maximize the amount of publicity you could get.

Reserve your flights and hotels at least a month in advance. Better yet, book earlier, but always buy refundable, changeable tickets. Everything always changes with the media. Big shows suddenly drop out or you're offered a last-minute booking. If, after a morning-show appearance, you're invited to do a spot on the evening news, your ticket shouldn't stop you. Look at the additional price of a changeable ticket as the cost of insurance. And it's usually tax deductible.

Road tours, which formerly were a central part of most publicity campaigns, now occur far less often. Publishers no longer routinely pay for them. In fact, they usually offer them only to their biggest, bestselling authors or authors with established, national platforms.

Authors of real estate and finance books frequently go on tour to promote their upcoming seminars and workshops, where they are virtually guaranteed to sell lots of their books from the back of the room. Occasionally, traditional publishers send authors whom they hope to break out—especially those who write fiction—on tour. Usually, they schedule those authors for readings at key bookstores.

If you want to underwrite your road tour, coordinate it with your publisher. Although they may not pay for your expenses, they may advise you on the cities, bookstores, and venues to visit; connect you with important people; and try to get you media bookings.

Conclude your road tours in your hometown and invite the local media. Work the local hometown angle, and the fact that you were just on tour will provide a hook that the local media can use. The fact that you're a first-time author can also give the media another hook.

Don't overlook local bookstores, even if they're chains, discount, or warehouse operations. Many of them love the local-author connection and want to be seen as being community-friendly. They may schedule readings and events, recommend your book, and give it prominence on the shelves or in displays. Some also have local-author sections and host local-author readings. Many place a special tag on local authors' books.

Offer to sign copies of your book for local booksellers. Signed books sell well and they can't be returned to your publisher.

### Author Questions and Answers

Concentrate on preparing questions and answers (Q&As) that will inform the media about the most important content in your book. Write questions that go straight to the heart and soul of the book and bring out its greatest strengths. Compose questions that reveal the most interesting, controversial, earth-shattering, innovative, shameful, and shocking information. Provide emotionally charged answers that are powerful, hard hitting, moving, insightful, and shocking.

**Robyn Says**

Customize your galley list to hit publications and sites that review books on your subject. If you write a business book, approach *BusinessWeek*, the *Wall Street Journal*, or Fast Company. If it's chick lit, send it to girls' and women's magazines, or if it's a diet book, to health and fitness publications.

Request that your publisher prepare and send ARCs. Most are usually willing to send between 50 and 100 copies. If your publisher balks, have it send copies to those you both agree could be most helpful to your book. If it won't send any, arrange to send a few to the most important outlets at your own cost.

Your Q&A is an ideal way to let media outlets hear your voice and learn about your book without having to read it, which most of them simply won't do. In two pages, you can answer twelve to fifteen questions that will give the media a solid understanding of your book and interest it enough to want to learn more. The media can get a sense of your personality above and beyond the book and of how you answer questions.

- Keep each answer to one brief paragraph that runs no more than three or four sentences.
- Try to limit your Q&A to two pages, but in no cases exceed four—the media won't read that much.

The idea is to give the media quick hits of information, a taste of your book's flavor, and a sense of your personality.

As we've previously stressed, interviewers, program hosts, and other media people will often ask you the exact questions that you wrote for your Q&A. So, make your questions and answers terrific because they can play a long and crucial part in your publicity campaign.

If you encounter trouble coming up with messages to stress in your Q&As or you have too many messages, consider taking media training before you write your Q&A. Media training can help because it teaches you to deliver your most important messages.

## Advance Review Copies

Approximately four months prior to the publication date, publishers send advance review copies (ARCs), which are also called review copies and bound galleys, to print publications. This process involves a number of steps, which include the following.

1. Preparing a list of reviewers to whom ARCs will be sent.
2. Writing a galley letter, which is similar to a one-sheet press release, to accompany the review copies (see the sample galley letters on pages 219–222).
3. Following up.

Review copies must be sent well in advance of publication because book editors need lead time to screen submissions and then assign those they decide to have reviewed to writers, who are frequently freelancers. The reviewer must then read the book and write the review so that it will be published just as the book hits stores.

Your editor and publisher will have a basic list of trade publications that will receive ARCs: *Publishers Weekly*, *Kirkus*, *Library Journal*, *Booklist*, and book-review Web sites. For links to book-review sites, see *www.complete-review.com*. To find book-review blogs, see *www.beatrice.com*, *bookangst.blogspot.com*, and *artsjournal.com/beatrix/*. When appropriate,

**Rick Says**

A significant, but often overlooked, advantage of hiring a firm or consultant who specializes in publicizing books is the fact that it follows up. Following up is hard, repetitive work that many people hate. Publishers' in-house publicists rarely follow up; they're too busy and simply don't have time to call reviewers and ask if they're interested in reviewing books.

When you sign a contract with an independent publicist or book publicity firm, specify that the publicist will place follow-up phone calls to each reviewer who receives a review copy.

review copies will also be sent to the big media outlets such as the *Today* show, *Good Morning America*, the *Early Show*, the *Oprah Winfrey Show*, *60 Minutes*, *20/20*, the *New York Times*, the *Wall Street Journal*, *USA Today*, and major magazines.

If your publisher is not planning to send ARCs, get permission to photocopy your manuscript and send it to the publications listed above and your hometown media. "We've been told numerous times that rubber banded photocopies are fine ARCs," David Thalberg says. "Just be sure that your manuscript pages are numbered and that your name, contact information, and the book's title are printed on every page in case the rubber band snaps."

Give your publisher the names of local publications or sites that might review your book. Patti Thorn, book editor of the *Rocky Mountain News*, recommends that local authors place a Post-it stating "Local Author" on the cover of review copies so she won't overlook it.

Send a galley letter or a press release with the review copies of your book. A galley letter is a personalized one-page editorial letter that highlights what's in the book. Since reviewers are flooded with so many book-review requests, they only have time to quickly scan the accompanying letters, so just say, "You will find the following information in this important new book, which will be published on November 14 by Adams Media." Then, bullet the major points that you want reviewers to know. Even if reviewers don't read your letter, they can scan it to find out what your book is about.

When publishers or editorial directors feel strongly about a book, they may send a letter saying, "Although I usually don't send letters of this kind, I really feel that this is a very special book and I hope you will read it." Let us stress that these letters are rare and are seldom sent more than once a year per house.

Book editors may send galleys that they think could make good feature stories to other editors. Feature articles usually provide more publicity than book reviews do because more people read features than reviews. However, don't discount the value of book reviews, and try to land both, which could be even more beneficial.

If you follow up yourself, wait about a week after they should have received your book before you call. Give them time to see your book. Chances are that you won't get to speak with them and they probably won't respond to your calls. However, your call could prompt them to look for your book in the stack by their desk.

Should you reach a reviewer, don't ask if he or she got your book. Instead, inquire whether he or she needs more information on *Bestselling Book Publicity*, or ask if he or she is "considering reviewing *Bestselling Book Publicity*." State your book's title. The mere fact that you are following up could induce a reviewer to look for and consider your book.

## SAMPLE GALLEY LETTER NUMBER 1

January 23, 2006

Greetings—

Ask some people what they think of when you say the word "Wal-Mart" and you're sure to elicit a wide variety of reactions. Investors might think of it as a steady performer with a strong track record. Labor leaders may view the company as an antiunion juggernaut that limits workers' rights. Retail analysts look at it as a model for growth and expansion. Consumers simply think of the retailing giant as a great place to get a wide variety of items at prices that other stores simply cannot match.

And for years—since Sam Walton's death over a decade ago—Wal-Mart's corporate leadership, both past and present, have been quiet on all of these topics . . . until now.

Don Soderquist started at Wal-Mart Stores, Inc., in 1980, and twenty-five years later has written the only true insider account of Wal-Mart's business-practices since Walton's autobiography in 1993. He began his career with the company as an executive vice president and before his retirement in

*continued*

*continued*

1999 would eventually become chief operating officer and senior vice chairman. He now provides the first true insider account of how Wal-Mart achieved its incredible success, and can discuss a variety of topics regarding the company, including:

- What his views are on claims that Wal-Mart is looking to kill off mom 'n' pop stores
- What he thinks about critics who call Wal-Mart antiunion
- How the company continued to grow exponentially even after the death of Walton, its visionary
- Which aspects of Wal-Mart's business practices should be emulated by all companies, large and small
- How Wal-Mart can continue its success well into the future if it continues to follow the twelve principles that got it to where it is today

Enclosed you'll find a galley copy of Don's new book, *The Wal*Mart Way* (Nelson Business, April '05). If you like what you see and would like to schedule an interview with Don to discuss his experiences at Wal-Mart, how businesses can use the lessons of the retailing behemoth to their advantage, and what his views are regarding critics' attacks on Wal-Mart, please feel free to give me a call and I'll make the proper arrangements.

If you are a book reviewer and plan on running a review of *The Wal*Mart Way*, please let me know if you would like a final copy of the book and/or electronic images of Don and the book cover art. Thank you for your time and consideration, and I look forward to speaking with you soon!

Best,
Jared B. Sharpe
Publicist
Planned Television Arts
p: 212-593-6467
e: sharpej@plannedtvarts.com

January 23, 2006

Greetings,

With a historic sell-off finally over and the stock market rallying with renewed confidence, the top equity analyst at the globally recognized investment research firm Morningstar has put together a no-nonsense, step-by-step guide to picking great stocks, understanding market sectors, and successfully investing like a pro.

Pat Dorsey, Morningstar's Director of Stock Analysis and weekly guest on Fox News Channel's *Bulls & Bears,* delivers comprehensive research and proven strategies in the new book *The Five Rules for Successful Stock Investing: Morningstar's Guide to Building Wealth and Winning in the Market.* With his energetic and down-to-earth style, Pat presents a 360-degree view of market trends, evaluating stocks, and running your portfolio like a business.

After nearly 80 million people lost more than $7 trillion, the time for get-rich-quick guides and hot tips is over. This book is written for the serious investor who wants to understand how the market actually works, how professional investors recognize winning fundamentals, and how to avoid common mistakes that lead to big losses. *The Five Rules for Successful Stock Investing* stands out by providing a strategic, easy-to-follow plan for minimizing risk and maximizing profit based on sound, informed decisions, not on predictions or conjecture.

Among the aspects of Dorsey's book that sets it apart from the rest:

- Its cold-shower approach to investing. Dorsey explains that a level head and a deep breath are the first lines of defense protecting investors from bad investments.

*continued*

*continued*

- Its introductory lessons on accounting that help investors follow the money trail and understand if they're putting their money into a solid company.
- A detailed "Guided Tour of the Market," which illustrates the various factors affecting thirteen different sectors of the market, including health care, energy, retail, software, and consumer goods.
- Finally, the unparalleled research and knowledge of Morningstar, one of the most trusted and respected names in global investment research and analysis.

Enclosed you will find a copy of *The Five Rules for Successful Stock Investing* as well as numerous fact sheets that you may find useful for future articles. If you are interested in speaking with Pat Dorsey about the book and how investors can start making more informed and successful choices of stocks, or if you plan on possibly reviewing the book, please feel free to contact us at the numbers and e-mail addresses listed below.

Thank you very much for your time and consideration. We hope that you enjoy the book and look forward to speaking with you soon.

Sincerely,
Jared Sharpe  212-593-6467 / sharpej@plannedtvarts.com
Scott Piro  212-593-6439 / plros@plannedtvarts.com

## Campaign Elements

Not every element that follows may work for every book or platform, but the ones listed below are good cornerstones.

### Media List

Your media list includes the names of those who will receive a copy of the sale version of the book. It will include those who received review copies of your book plus national media outlets and local media in your area, the areas you plan to visit, and those where you have special contacts.

To find sources, go to the library and leaf through Bacon's publications such as Bacon's *MediaSource*. Although you can pay for the same information on the Internet, at libraries, it's free. However, the information may be dated because media people move frequently. Your best bet is to do your initial research at the library and collect a bunch of names and contact information. Then call or check Web sites to verify what you found and to get the most current information.

Also check the Harrison guides, *Radio-TV Interview Report* for national broadcast media information. Call media outlets and ask who you should send your material to. Try to get an actual person's name, not simply an e-mail address to "info@."

### Internet Marketing

When people hear about you or your book, they go to the Internet to get more information. They Google you, read about you, and visit your Web site; they look for your book on Amazon.com. So, as an author, it's essential to have a strong Internet presence.

■ The first step in your Internet marketing plan is to put up a memorable Web site. Your Web site must be great-looking and reflective of the impression you want to convey. For example, you may want it to appear authoritative, lighthearted, elegant, colorful, hip, scholarly, or goofy. Or, it could have a theme related to your book or your area of expertise. Your site must also be up to date and easy and intuitive to use, and all links must work.

■ Register your site with all the major search engines under your name, your book's name, and every conceivable variation of them. That way, when people misspell your name and don't get your book's title exactly right, they will still get to your site.

■ Include in your Web site everything that's in your media kit. See Chapter 4 to review exactly what you need. Your site should allow visitors to read a sample chapter, order your book, enter into exchanges with you, and view your upcoming events and appearances. It should link to other complementary sites and to your strategic partners. Your site must have a press room with the latest articles on you and your book.

■ In addition to your site, start your own blog, newsletter, or e-zine.

Numerous firms can be hired to handle your Internet book-marketing campaigns. These firms know all the components that can be included in your campaign. They can create an Internet campaign that may include creating a Web site for the book, sending your book to relevant Web sites, and sending it to blogs. These firms have lists of Web book reviewers; will syndicate your content on the Web; or will set up chats, downloads, newsgroups, and mailing lists.

In cyberspace, podcasting seems to be the next frontier. Podcasting is making material from your book available on iPods. Audiobooks can now be downloaded onto iPods and soon, experts predict, so will interviews, articles, and excerpts of your book. From your Web site, people could download a chapter of your book and then buy the rest if they like it. In the process, you're capturing their name and e-mail address, which you can use in the future.

A subspecies of Internet marketing is the e-mail blast or Amazon blast, which was discussed in detail in Chapter 11. Essentially, Internet blasts are when you send targeted e-mail to everyone on your list, and to everyone on your friends' and associates' lists and lists you buy.

### Newspaper and Radio Releases

You can write feature articles, or articles can be written under your byline, that will be sent to over 10,000 newspapers across the nation. Similarly, radio features also can be written and sent to hundreds of radio stations nationwide.

Services including North American Precis Syndicate (NAPS; *www.napsnet.com*) and News USA (*www.newsusa.com*) will write, produce, and distribute these features. They can put the cover of your book on them, link them to your Web site, and distribute them to news outlets. Feature articles can be produced as professional-looking two-column articles that newspapers will pick up and use without change.

Similarly, radio features can be produced and sent to radio stations throughout North America. They can write scripts and record an interview that will be sent to hundreds of stations. Through these services, your message about your book can be delivered widely without your constantly having to give interviews.

Newspaper and radio feature services also give PR firms that specialize in publicizing books discount prices, which many pass on to their clients. So, it is often more cost effective and efficient for authors to go through their publicists than to do all the work involved to write and distribute these features.

### Media Training

Many of us are petrified of publicly speaking or being interviewed. We wish that we could speak as smoothly, effortlessly, and articulately as all those people we see on television. Well, surprise, surprise—all those accomplished speakers you see and hear are either trained actors or they have gone through extensive media training. If you hope to publicize

**Rick Says**

Although independent companies specialize in producing and distributing radio features, those of us who are book publicists, as a part of our jobs, supervise and work closely with these firms. We know from long experience the companies that we can trust to deliver the best results. We also review the content of articles and scripts, provide editorial input, and make sure that services cover all essential points. Then we coordinate their release and distribution with the rest of your campaign.

Since we work with these services so often, we get a special price, which we pass on to our clients. So, it's usually cheaper for you to go through us than to deal directly with radio feature distribution services.

**PUBLICITY TIMELINE**  *Created by Planned Television Arts*

| | 12/15 | 1/1 | 1/22 | 2/12 | 3/5 | 3/12 | 3/19 | 3/26 | 4/2 PUB DATE | 4/9 | 4/16 | 4/23 | 4/30 | 5/7 | 5/14 | 5/21 | 5/28 |
|---|---|---|---|---|---|---|---|---|---|---|---|---|---|---|---|---|---|
| 1. Create overall promotional plan | XX | XX | | | | | | | | | | | | | | | |
| 2. Create timeline | XX | | | | | | | | | | | | | | | | |
| 3. Solicit expert endorsements | | XX | | | | | | | | | | | | | | | |
| 4. Preparation of press material | | XX | | | | | | | | | | | | | | | |
| 5. Q&A with author | | XX | | | | | | | | | | | | | | | |
| 6. Initial galley media list prepared | | | XX | | | | | | | | | | | | | | |
| 7. One-sheet for galleys written | | | XX | | | | | | | | | | | | | | |
| 8. Galley one-sheets approved by JH | | | | XX | | | | | | | | | | | | | |
| 9. Galleys sent out to long lead media | | | | XX | | | | | | | | | | | | | |
| 10. Follow-up calls to galley mailing | | | | XX | XX | XX | | | | | | | | | | | |
| 11. Create media list | | | XX | XX | | | | | | | | | | | | | |
| 12. Press kit material finalized | | | | XX | | | | | | | | | | | | | |
| 13. Press kit material approved by JH | | | | XX | | | | | | | | | | | | | |
| 14. Begin mailing to media | | | | | XX | | | | | | | | | | | | |
| 15. Internet marketing campaign | | | | | | XX | XX | XX | | XX | XX | XX | XX | XX | XX | XX | |
| 16. Draft newspaper feature release | | | | | XX | | | | | | | | | | | | |
| 17. Draft radio news release | | | | | XX | | | | | | | | | | | | |
| 18. Approval on NFR & RNR by JH | | | | | XX | | | | | | | | | | | | |
| 19. Follow up with national and local media; interviews scheduled | | | | | | XX | XX | XX | XX | XX | XX | XX | XX | XX | XX | XX | |
| 20. Media training | | | | | | | XX | | | | | | | | | | |
| 21. National media interviews occur | | | | | | | | | XX | XX | XX | XX | XX | XX | XX | XX | |
| 22. Local 5-city media tour | | | | | | | | | XX | XX | | | | | | | |
| 23. Satellite television tour® | | | | | | | | | XX | | | | | | | | |
| 24. Morning drive radio tour® | | | | | | | | | | XX | | | | | | | |
| 25. NFR & RNR distributed | | | | | | | | | XX | | | | | | | | |

your book, media training is essential. Good publicists won't allow their clients to appear before the media until they've had media training.

For a full discussion of media training, see Chapter 9.

## Publication Date

The first two or three weeks after a book is published are critical because booksellers only want books that move quickly. The giant retailers must receive a certain dollar amount from every square foot of their shelf space, so if your book doesn't make an immediate splash, they may pull it and replace it with titles that will. Since the first few weeks in the life of a book are so vital, be ready to jam your heart, soul, and guts into an intensive, nonstop blitz to publicize your book.

By the time your book comes out, you should have much of your campaign in place: Some reviews of your book should be in hand and your Web site should be online. Your kickoff party, road tour, book signings, national bookings, newspaper and radio feature releases, Internet blast, etc., should be ready to go within those first weeks.

Time your publicity blitz to hit on the publication date and run the week thereafter. Don't start too early, to "seed the public's interest," because the public will forget or someone else will steal your thunder. Tell everyone—your friends, family, and network; your publisher's sales reps, distributors, and in-house publicists—about all the publicity that will begin on the pub date. On the pub date, start your road tour, your Morning Drive, Satellite Media Tour, your radio tour, and your Internet blast. Morning Drive and Satellite Media Tours, which are described in Chapter 14, entail giving interviews at a single session that are then distributed to various media outlets. By running your Internet blast early, you can make your book a bestseller and say that it's a bestseller in the rest of your campaign. Oddly enough, Internet blasts also seem to generate bookstore sales on or around the target dates.

Another option is not to jam all your publicity efforts in during the first week or so after the pub date, but to dole them out more gradually. The advantage of this approach could be that the book will continue to move more steadily rather than making a big hit and then falling off. Both approaches have worked successfully.

## *Review Plan*

Six to eight weeks after the publication date, when the dust has cleared and you've been released from the asylum, review your promotion plan. Examine and evaluate your campaign point by point. Be ruthlessly honest and objective.

- Was your campaign successful?
- What worked?
- What didn't work?
- What do you want to try again or differently?
- What could be done better?
- How could it be done better?

Decide if you want to recontact media outlets that turned you down or to approach them differently. Conditions change; it may be a slower news time now. When you initially pitched them, they could have been involved in other stories that left no time for you. Something may have occurred subsequently that might awaken their interest in you.

Contact your agent, editor, and your publisher's in-house publicists. Ask for evaluations and get their input. Ask what continuing publicity measures they would recommend, additions you should make, and portions you should change.

Keep the fires burning by continually giving ongoing radio and print interviews. Give interviews even if they're in small markets, to keep your campaign alive and try to generate new interest. Build your platform and your profile around your book, with a steady stream of speeches, appearances, workshops, and columns.

Stay alert for developments that could revitalize your campaign; new stories or events that you could connect to your book and use in a new push. When these opportunities arise, quickly write new press releases that link your book to the news. Always try to keep interest in your book alive. Meet new people, continue to get new endorsements, and build new relationships. Constantly look for new opportunities to promote your book.

## Action Steps

1. Name three items that a timeline forces you to think about.
2. When should you start preparing the timeline for your campaign?
3. How far before your book's publication date should review copies be sent?
4. List three important items in establishing an Internet presence for your book.
5. Name four key questions that you should ask when you review your campaign.

### Remember

▲ **Have a solid blueprint.** Every element in a book promotion campaign must be carefully planned, shaped, and coordinated to work with all of the others. This requires great timing and skill and all the pieces must flow harmoniously, one right after another. Each part must be successful by itself and enhance all the other campaign elements.

▲ **Get ahead of the book.** When your book comes out, it's critical to have your campaign in full swing because booksellers want to see that books are moving quickly. So, time an intensive, nonstop publicity blitz to hit on your publication date and run a week or two thereafter. Don't start too early or the public will forget or someone will slip in to steal your thunder.

Concentrate all your thoughts upon the work at hand. The sun's rays do not burn until brought to a focus.

*Alexander Graham Bell*

# How to Hire the Best Publicist

**THIS CHAPTER COVERS:**

▶ Your alternatives
▶ Finding publicists
▶ How publicists work
▶ Before you sign
▶ Interviewing
▶ Your involvement

AFTER THEY'VE SIGNED with a publisher, most authors are surprised to learn that they may have to spend their own money to publicize their book. For authors, hiring a publicist has become more the rule than the exception because publishers can't be counted on to publicize their books. And book publicity is a bottomless pit; you can never get enough!

Hiring a publicist can be a costly and risky venture. You may get great publicity that doesn't translate into enormous book sales. But if publicity brings you fame rather than fortune, it could still be beneficial to you as an author. The point is, publicity may not be beneficial to you or your book, and if it is, the rewards may not always be immediate and clear.

The fact is that without word of mouth, books rarely sell. While exceptions do exist, the key to being a bestselling author is that you must be a relentless promoter! Remember, a book is a business—how else will you let customers know you've arrived!

Sometimes, you just can't publicize your book by yourself; it takes too much time and work. Deep down, you may also feel that you don't know enough about publicity to get the results you want because every time you try, your publicity campaign sputters and doesn't get off the ground.

Often, it's smarter and more cost effective to call in a professional to help with all or parts of your campaign. If you hire a publicist, you can concentrate on your business, what you really do best, while the pro keeps your campaign humming.

Now that you've read the information in this book and understand more about publicizing books, it should be easier for you to find the right publicist and for you to work with them. You will have a better understanding of the language, your options, and what a publicity campaign involves. You may even have ideas on how you should proceed and be able to make valuable contributions that could make your publicity campaign go more smoothly.

## Your Alternatives

When you want to publicize your book, you have three basic options: hiring a firm, hiring a consultant, or doing it yourself. Let's look at some of the pluses and minuses of each.

One word of warning: When you hire a publicist, even for just part of a campaign, stay involved! Publicists, including the best of us, are not miracle workers, and we usually can't get the best results with uninvolved clients. We need cooperative clients; clients who become our partners by giving us information, insights, and help in achieving their objectives. However, as we will get into later in this chapter, don't interfere, disrupt, or try to micromanage your publicist. Don't make your publicist dread your constant calls.

### PR Firms

PR firms are one option. If they're large and well established, you probably will be paying top dollar, which will include sums for their overhead and reputation. However, they may also have great know-how and fabulous contacts, which could make them well worth the price. Smaller firms may cost less, have lower overhead, and provide more personal service. The key when hiring any firm is to evaluate its client list, determine its level of understanding of your book, and see if you are a good fit. Size does not matter; we've seen small, well-connected firms make a book soar; we've also seen large firms with offices across the world network do zilch. Smaller firms are often run by experienced pros who worked for bigger firms or corporations. Make sure to understand the firm; find out who will do the daily work on your account and what contacts, skills, and services they will provide. PR firms usually work on monthly retainers but may agree to run your campaign

Hire a firm that's rich in your niche. Since book publicity is such a specialized field, look for PR firms that specialize in or have extensive experience publicizing books and consider hiring those that know and have experience in your topic. Usually, they will provide better, more targeted results. Most experienced book publicists have vast knowledge and close contacts that they've developed over the years. Often, they can accomplish more with one well-placed phone call than non-book specialists can achieve in weeks—if at all.

Overall, book publicity specialists tend to be creative and open to new ideas and approaches; they know firsthand that the most offbeat promotions can work wonders, so they love to devise and try the unusual in the hope of creating big hits. Professional publicists also are aware that they're in the relationship business, so they're normally easy to work with.

for a project price. The culture of each PR firm is as different as the results that can be achieved, so get involved up front, during the hiring process—that's the time to find out what you can expect.

Avoid agencies that do publicity on the side or it's not their main focus; they rarely promote books well. Examples of these agencies are advertising or branding firms that also offer PR services. Chances are that they haven't successfully promoted many books. Naturally, exceptions to the rule exist, but working with a firm that focuses on authors and books usually produces the best results.

Usually, it's preferable to hire experienced book publicists, but don't discount those who have never dealt with books because they can contribute brilliantly to your campaign. Although they may not have the best book publicity contacts, they may have fabulous, inventive, and innovative ideas. A foray into books may rejuvenate them and stimulate their enthusiasm, drive, and creative flair. They may import ideas or tactics that are foreign to book promoters and bring a new vision that sees what others might have missed or were too close to see.

When you truly believe in a publicist, go with him or her. When you find yourself being swept up by an individual's vision, energy, or excitement, follow it through. Publicity is a business of sparks; lots of little sparks can ignite a campaign, send it roaring, soaring and do wonders for you and your book.

### Consultants

These freelancers usually work on their own, without staffs. Most worked for PR agencies or businesses before they decided to go it alone, so their experience and abilities will vary. Check their backgrounds and credentials thoroughly. Consultants may not be any less expensive than agencies, but they usually have less overhead. They may be more flexible in what they charge and agreeable to working for a stated fee to promote your book. Consultants usually have networks that they use to perform specialized tasks, so you may have to incur additional costs.

*Being Your Own Publicist*

Okay. Although we've advised you to beware of running your own book publicity campaign, we would be remiss not to mention that option. Regardless of whether they hire professionals, all authors must be their own books' publicists. The best authors are involved authors. Some authors excel at representing themselves; they have fabulous contacts and the time, inclination, and energy to tirelessly promote their books. If this sounds like you, you could pull it off.

When authors decide to publicize their books, few have the same contacts and knowledge as PR firms or consultants. Should you decide to be your book's publicist, build your contact and knowledge base.

If you go it alone and discover you're lost or barely making a dent, you obviously need some help. If you still want to be hands on, consider breaking down the effort into smaller chunks and hiring a professional to handle matters in which they excel and/or in which you may be weak.

## *Finding Publicists*

Find the names of and obtain information about PR firms in *O'Dwyer's Directory of Public Relations Firms*. This annual directory, which has been published since 1970, lists over 2,900 of the largest firms worldwide. It is available in a bound volume or online. You can check *O'Dwyer's* at no charge and find a listing of firms at *www.odwyerpr.com*. It reports on PR firms geographically, by size and eleven specialty areas. Membership is required to access information, but print versions are available at many libraries. Check online sources such as:

- *PRWeek's www.prweekcontact-directory.com* (all content is available only to subscribers)
- *http://dir.yahoo.com/Business_and_Economy/Business_to_Business/Corporate_Services/Public_Relations*
- *http://directory.google.com/Top/Business/Marketing_and_Advertising/Public_Relations*

The latter two sites require a fee to be listed in specific areas.

Ask your literary agent, your editor, and other members of your publisher's staff to recommend book publicists. Go directly to the head of publicity for your publisher. Ask for the names of four or five publicists with whom he or she had good experiences.

Ask the media. Members of the local media know the great publicists; they know with whom they like to work. They may be reluctant to recommend a specific firm, so ask for several names. Also, contact the local press club for recommendations.

Contact all your network members. Ask if they know and can introduce you to people in local media, especially those who report on books. Talk to authors and literary agents for recommendations of firms or consultants that could run your publicity campaign or parts of it. If they don't know of any, ask if they know of other people who might. Ask your network contacts to introduce you or get permission to use their names.

If you've taken writing classes, workshops, or seminars, try to get referral recommendations from your teachers, leaders, or fellow students. Also ask people who run or work in your local bookshops and libraries.

Ask everyone you know for names and leads; the most unlikely people may have the best contacts. Understand that it may take time to finally connect with people who can help you. However, if you keep asking, you will eventually find the names of those who have actually hired professionals to publicize their books.

Book publicists also have subspecialties. For example, some specialize in cookbooks, business books, books of faith, books of fiction, Spanish-language books, and so on. Find those that are right for your book. When you speak with individuals who have worked with book publicists, ask them:

- How would the firm's or consultant's performance rate on a scale of 1 to 10, with 10 being the highest?
- What tasks did the firm or consultant perform best?
- What tasks did the firm or consultant perform worst?
- How much did the firm or consultant charge?
- Did the firm or consultant deliver at the agreed-upon price? If not, why and how far off were they?
- Was the firm or consultant accessible to you?
- How promptly did the firm or consultant return your phone calls and e-mails?
- Were your questions always satisfactorily answered?
- Was the firm or consultant pleasant to work with?
- Was the firm or consultant always professional?
- Can you give me the names of others whom I could contact and may I use your name when I contact them?
- Would you hire the firm or consultant again?

## How Publicists Work

Publicists work under a number of fee arrangements. The two most popular are the retainer approach and the menu approach, which we will discuss below. Some publicists insist on contracts for stated periods of time or the duration of a campaign. Others charge on a pay-as-you-go basis, with no minimum time.

In most cases, fee arrangements, contract duration, and the services to be provided can be negotiated.

### The Retainer Approach

Most PR firms work on a retainer basis. That means that each month, you pay the firm a fee that buys you a stated block of its time. Fees are based on the firm's estimate of how much work will be required on your account and how long your campaign will take. They usually require you to sign up for a minimum number of months.

When you work under a retainer, find out how much time your fee buys you for each tier of publicists who will work on your account. For example, at some agencies, senior publicists bill at a higher rate than their juniors and you may be entitled to less of their time. Also ask how you will be charged if you use more than your allotted time—are you surcharged, and at what rates?

In addition to fees, you will be billed for expenses that are incurred on your account. Reasonable expenses include those for printing and reproducing promotional materials and media kits; postage, overnight shipping, and delivery services to send your book and promotional materials; and telephone calls to the media. Expenses for meals and entertainment should require your approval. A ceiling can also be put on expenses that requires the firm to get your approval before incurring costs over a set amount.

Some firms charge a percentage of your retainer to cover the administrative or processing work they do on your account. Others mark up their reimbursable expenses for their administrative efforts.

For your fee, you are entitled to know what is happening with your book. You should receive weekly or bimonthly updates, which Rick calls a "Yes, No, Maybe" list. For example, if he sends your book to 100 newspapers, all 100 names will be listed, as will the facts that the *New York Times* said yes, the *Wall Street Journal* passed, and the *Chicago Tribune* is on the fence.

PR professional Willy Spizman adds, "The Spizman Agency encourages constant communication and keeping clients informed. The key is to read the reports you receive from your publicist and give him or her ample time to make your PR work. Creating national hits takes time and you don't just get instant bookings on the top shows. While it can happen when the timing or topic is right, it's important to have clear expectations. Most clients rarely read their updates and it's important for them to do so. An informed client is the best client and it takes time to fully digest the scope of what publicists are doing because the great ones invest an enormous amount of time in catapulting you to success. When you sign on with a PR firm, a written agreement is usually executed that states the duties and responsibilities of each of the parties."

### The Menu Approach

Some firms, including Planned Television Arts (PTA), work on a menu basis. That means that their clients can choose to have PTA provide specific PR services and they pay only for those they want performed. Under the menu system, publicists walk authors through the list of available services and they decide which will be best for each campaign. The menu approach also helps authors exercise more control of their budgets because they only pay for the services they select.

Publishers often underwrite or share in the expenses of one or more menu services. They generally do so only for the biggest, most well-known authors, but it never hurts to ask.

Publicists offer a wide menu of services, so ask them about the specific services they provide. Some of the services that publicists provide include the following.

- **Material preparation.** Publicists will write, develop, and place a number of promotional materials. A comprehensive press kit may be prepared with a press release as its centerpiece. Other press kit items include: the author's biography, the author's photograph, suggested interview questions, story-ready information, byline articles, relevant background materials, and more.
- **Morning Drive Radio Tours.** In a single morning, an author, from his or her home or office, gives a minimum of eighteen

radio interviews that generally reach at least 10 million listeners. Morning Drive Radio Tours target national radio programs that have the appropriate demographic and format for each author.

- **Satellite TV Media Tours.** In one morning from a single location, authors give eighteen to twenty back-to-back news interviews with local television stations across the country. Each interview runs four to six minutes and is run on morning news shows that reach millions of targeted viewers.
- **Newspaper feature releases.** Items about your book are sent to 10,000 newspapers across the country. Clients receive hundreds of tear sheets that are generated by this service.
- **TelePrint conferences.** A one-hour news conference with an author and reporters throughout the country. Anywhere from ten to twenty reporters can participate in the call, which follows a press conference format and can be used to reach specific audiences by targeting newspaper sections such as technology, lifestyle, book review, business, religion, women's, and others.
- **Magazine and print campaigns.** Placements with national and local magazines, dailies, and newswires as well as specialized trade media that are of importance to the author. Major broadcast bookings often result from high-profile feature articles. Feature articles quickly establish an author's credibility and greatly enhance his or her future media and marketing efforts.
- **National TV and radio campaigns.** Authors are booked for appearances on the most visible and influential television and radio shows. Getting national bookings is increasingly competitive and requires experienced media relations experts who have developed personal relationships with key producers.
- **E-mail blasts.** Lists of names are gathered from a number of sources, and e-mails are sent to those names, offering them incentives to purchase an author's book from a specific online bookseller on a certain day. Since online booksellers compile their bestseller lists on an hourly basis, the objective of the blast is to make the book a bestseller with an online bookseller.

- **Road tours.** Authors are sent to major cities where they can appear on a variety of outlets ranging from 6:00 to 7:00 A.M. news programs that lead into the *Today* show or *Good Morning America*, local Fox morning shows that air from 7:00 to 9:00, midday and noon news programs, daytime talk programs, taped public affair programs, and evening news programs. Media road tours also include print and radio interviews. Training, travel, escorts, updates, and the top television, radio, and print placements are provided in every market. Arrangements are made for booksellers to sell books at all events.
- **Media training.** Authors are taught how to identify their books' most important and interesting messages and how to clearly and entertainingly discuss them. They are also instructed on how to deal with journalists, editors, producers, and hosts and how to handle themselves in interviews and public appearances.

## *Before You Sign*

Choose four or five firms or consultants to interview. Before you contact them, formulate some basic ideas on what you want them to do and the results you hope to receive. However, be open to their suggestions because as experienced professionals, they probably will suggest better, more productive tactics than you had in mind.

Also be realistic. We know that your hopes are deeply attached to your book, but all books won't be mega-sellers, especially authors' first books. As much as you believe in your book, don't expect a publicist to be able to make it *Tuesdays with Morrie*; it could happen, but the odds will be long.

Decide how much you are willing to spend. Discuss pricing with your agent. Most firms have set fees for specific services, so calling and saying you have $5,000 to spend isn't the best approach. Instead, explain your book's focus and your expectations, and ask what it will take to launch your book.

Publicity is an investment, and at first, the cost might surprise you. Investments always entail risks, so if you're not willing to invest, don't put firms or consultants through the entire selection process. Don't waste their time. Wait until you're ready and willing to spend.

Meet and interview each firm and consultant in person. Go to their offices, look around and into their eyes.

- Get a sense of the atmosphere and how they work. Is it relaxed, tense, efficient, well organized, or chaotic? How do they dress and answer phones? Do they look and act professional and would you want them to represent you?

- Trust your instincts, your gut feelings. How do you feel? Are you comfortable, on edge, intimidated, or unimpressed? Do you like and trust them? Do you believe what they're saying? How much interest do they seem to have in your account?

- Ask who will perform the actual work on your campaign and for details on his or her experience. Make sure to meet that person and to look for signs of his or her energy, enthusiasm, excitement, and creativity. Find out who will be supervising your account and to what extent he or she will be monitoring it.

- How did the people you met react to your book? Do they want to read it? Do they seem excited by it or even interested in it? Is it just another job to them?

- Are they good listeners? Do they seem to understand you and your needs? Do they genuinely seem interested in helping you or are they just selling you?

- Do they have good ideas, energy, and a twinkle? Are they people who can get others excited enough to really get behind your book?

- What results do they claim? Who are their clients? Ask for a list of their clients and permission to contact them. Ask specifically for the names of those that worked with the people who will be handling your account. Call them. Don't just call the three or four clients that the firm selects; request their entire client list and then decide whom to call. When you reach the firm's clients, ask them the questions listed in "Finding Publicists" above.

- Be wary of formulaic campaigns that follow repetitive formats. While some successful tactics may be worth repeating, they can quickly grow old. Repetition often stifles creativity and causes publicists to be inattentive or to merely go through the motions, which can sap the life and energy from campaigns.

- Ask each firm or consultant what it will bring to your account. Is it creativity, experience, contacts, large agency backing, personal service, attention to detail, entrepreneurial background, media placement, booking speaking engagements, and more? Make them sell themselves to you.

- Find out if publicists are members of the Public Relations Society of America (PRSA) and associations specific to publishing, such as the Small Publishing Association of North America (SPAN) or the Publishers Marketing Association (PMA). Since publicity is a business of contacts, your publicist should have solid connections within the industry in which he or she works.

- Visit all candidates' Web sites. If publicists don't promote themselves with great Web sites, they probably won't do a good job of publicizing your book. Their Web sites should include testimonials, titles they represented, case studies, and staff biographies.

Ask candidates for references from authors they represented. Verify them by speaking personally with their authors. Don't merely settle for written testimonials that praise a candidate, check them. Be wary of publicists who want you to contact only certain authors. Instead, get a copy of their entire client list and decide whom you want to call. Try to speak with authors they have recently represented and those who are long-standing clients. When you call, ask authors the questions listed in the section "Finding Publicists" above.

# Interview Checklist

Personally interview every firm or consultant that you are considering. At the least, ask them the following questions:

- How long have you been in business?
- How many books do you publicize each year?
- What kinds of books are your specialty?
  *Which do you do best?*
  *Which don't you handle well?*
- What is your plan for my campaign?
- What is the timeline for my campaign?
- What fees would you charge for my campaign?
- How much in expenses should I expect to incur for my campaign?
- How much access will I have to the strategists who design my campaign?
- How much input will I have in my campaign?
- Will I receive weekly communications on my campaign?
- How often will I get updates on my campaign?
- How many calls will be made on my campaign?
  *Weekly? Monthly?*
- What specific results can I expect to receive?
  *In one month? In three months?*
  *When my project is completed?*
- How do I measure results?
- What can I do if I don't receive the results promised?
  *Can I fire you?*
  *Will you refund fee payments? If so, how much?*
  *Will I receive extra work at no charge?*
- What results have you created for similar clients in the past?
  *Who are they? May I contact them?*
- What are your strong points, your advantages over other agencies or consultants?

For PR firms:

- Who should I contact to get information about my account?
- Who in the firm has the ultimate responsibility for my account?
- Who runs the division or group that will be handling my account?
  *What is his or her experience and expertise?*
- Who will lead my account?
  *What is his or her experience and expertise?*
  *How much time will he or she spend on my account?*
- Who is the person whom I will work with?
  *What is his or her experience and expertise?*
  *How much time will he or she devote to my account?*
  *Who will be under him or her; how many people?*
- Who will supervise the work on my account?
  *What is his or her experience and expertise?*
  *How much time will he or she put in on my account?*

If publicists claim that they can get you on *Oprah*, the *Today* show, *Good Morning America*, or *Larry King Live*, run the other way! No one can guarantee those appearances.

## Your Involvement

Some authors have great difficulty allowing publicity professionals to run their campaigns. Their books are their babies; they're the culmination of their visions, and their long, hard labor brought them to life. Frequently, they've fought like mad for them and have trouble stepping back or letting go. They insist on being involved in every aspect of their book's campaign because they feel that no one knows or cares as much about their book or has as much riding on its success as they do.

Clearly, when you work with a publicity firm or consultant, you must be involved, but where do you draw the line? Start by entering into a written agreement that defines each party's duties and responsibilities. Have the agreement prepared by or reviewed by an attorney. Give either party the right to terminate the agreement by giving the other party thirty days' written notice. State that the agreement can be cancelled for any reason or no reason at all.

In the agreement, get the right to make all final decisions that exceed a particular amount of money, for example, $250. Agree that within ten days of signing the agreement, you will receive a detailed promotion plan for your book and that you will be given regular weekly or bimonthly updates on your account. Regular updates will tell you whether your campaign is proceeding on schedule and what problems arose, so you can address them before they get out of hand.

Clarify in the agreement the amount of fees the firm or consultant will be paid and when they will be due. State what expenses will be reimbursable and when they should be paid. Put a ceiling on the expenses the firm or consultant can incur without obtaining your consent. Specify who owns all property created for the campaign, including original artwork.

Keep in communication with your publicist so you know what's going on. Let your publicist know how you feel about the progress on your campaign. If you're not pleased or have a legitimate concern, schedule a time to address it with your publicist. Make sure that you fully understand every explanation your publicist gives you.

Resist the urge to control every aspect of the campaign. Your interference with publicists will make it harder for them to do their jobs. So don't meddle or micromanage.

Confine your involvement to the bigger issues, concepts and goals. Leave the details and the means of accomplishing them to the professionals you employ. If you really want to help, step back and let those you hire do their jobs. Respond promptly to their requests and try to make their work easier. Understand that they know more about publicizing books than you do. So, get out of their way and give them the leeway and support they need to do their jobs excellently.

If you're a control-a-holic—an individual who must approve everything that involves you—either find a PR firm that appreciates your style or consider hiring a consultant. During the interviewing process, make it clear to the firm or consultant that you intend to be a hands-on employer, who will be fully involved with every detail of your campaign. If the consultant agrees to this arrangement, you may be able to create a solid and productive working relationship.

## Action Steps

1. Explain the advantages of hiring a publicist that specializes in promoting books.
2. Name a print and online directory that lists public relations firms.
3. List five questions that you should ask authors who have worked with professional publicists.
4. List five questions that you will ask a publicist during an interview.
5. What should you do if you tend to micromanage those whom you employ?

### Remember

▲ **Seek professional help.** It's often wise and cost effective to hire a professional to help with all or parts of your campaign. When you need help in publicizing your book, you have two basic options: hiring a firm or hiring a consultant. Usually, it's preferable to hire a firm or consultant that has experience publicizing books.

▲ **Research publicists to find candidates that you could hire.** Create a list and visit each of their offices to get a sense of the atmosphere and how they work. In making your hiring decision, consider how they reacted to your book—if they were good listeners who seemed to understand your needs and were genuinely interested in helping you. Also factor in whether they had good ideas, enthusiasm, and energy.

**CHAPTER 15**

*Publicity is easy to get. Make yourself so successful you don't need it and then you'll get it.*

*Anonymous*

# Summing Up

WE HOPE THAT after reading this book, you understand the importance of publicizing your book and know how to make that experience enjoyable and productive. Don't let the job intimidate you; adopt a new, positive approach. Although creating and running a publicity campaign will take planning and focus and will require you to coordinate innumerable steps, it can be the highlight of your writing experience.

Publicizing your book can be enormously rewarding. Speaking about what you know, think, and feel is marvelously satisfying. Being recognized for your knowledge can be dizzying, and sharing and exploring it with the brightest and best minds in your field can be dazzling. When you're with the best, it can lift you to levels that you didn't know existed.

Take the abilities that you mastered to write your book and focus them on getting publicity for it. Shift gears, alter your direction, and refocus your efforts. Plan, organize, execute, and coordinate. Create a campaign that positions you to reach the top.

Give your campaign authenticity by having it reflect you—your personality, sense of humor, drive, thirst for knowledge, love of people, and approach. Incorporate in it what you do well.

## The Tools

Investigate the tools that can help build your campaign. Write a great silver bullet that clearly and convincingly delivers your message lickety-split. Practice writing press releases with knockout headlines, headlines that will jump off the page and captivate readers.

Create a book title that will make people react, something that makes them want to learn what your book is about. Come up with ideas for a striking, eye-catching cover and submit them to your publisher. On your cover, list problems your book will solve.

Learn the art of slicing and dicing—using material you have already created to promote your book. Include it in your speeches and presentations, workshops, seminars, and other writing. Post it on your Web sites; use it in your products.

Become a media expert. Learn how the media works and then start building media relationships. Focus on people who cover your area of interest and then become resources for them. Feed them information, leads, and contacts. Make yourself available to give them your expert opinion and analysis.

Master the techniques of interviewing. Don't give any interview unless you know your material cold. Prior to each interview, decide upon the main points that you want to address. Then, control the interview and use it as an opportunity to make your points.

## Special Areas

Learn how to deal with the media by taking media training. Find out how to identify your book's message and the hooks that you can use to attract the media's attention. Media training will also teach you how to be a successful media guest and interview subject.

Authors must have Internet presence because their sites are the first place the media will visit to obtain information about them. Create a great site that shows you and your book in the best light. Make it good to look at and easy to use. Provide a welcoming home page, your biography, a list of your books or writing, a press room, an endorsements sections, and questions and answers. Also include the cover art from your book on every page, your photograph, ordering information for your book, and links to other sites and strategic partners.

Make your book a bestseller with an online bookseller by conducting an e-mail blast. Find partners who will let you contact the names on their lists and will contribute items that will make your offer more attractive. Send a sales letter that offers recipients a bonus package if they buy your book on a certain date from a specified online bookseller.

## Final Thoughts

Now that you have learned about publicizing books, your campaign must be tightly planned and coordinated. Since book publicity campaigns involve so many elements, you must find out how long every stage will take, when it must be started, who will perform it, and what resources will be needed. Then a timeline must be created so all the elements of your campaign will run smoothly. Start writing timelines as soon as you know that your book is going to be published.

Book publicity plans can be exhaustive, so you may want to hire professional book publicists to handle some or all of your campaign. Since promoting books is such a specialty area, find a publicist or firm that has experience publicizing books and has established great media contacts. Get recommendations and references from other authors and your network members. Personally interview all candidates as well as those who recommended them to determine who you think will serve you best.

# Resource Directory

IN CREATING THIS DIRECTORY, we have tried to include the best resources and the most up-to-date information about them. However, resources continually change: They move, merge, refocus the direction of their business, and even shut down. In addition, when you refer to this list, it may be long after we compiled it, so some information may not be current. To be on the safe side, check the resource directory on our Web site, *www.author101.com*, which should have the latest information.

**LEGAL NOTICE:** This list is provided strictly as a resource guide and to inform you of the resources that may be available to you. Readers should independently check all information about these resources before using them. The authors and publisher specifically assume no liability for the use of this resource directory, nor do they guarantee its accuracy.

**PMA: Independent Book Publishers Association,** 627 Aviation Way, Manhattan Beach, CA 90266; Tel: (310) 372-2732; Fax: (310) 374-3342. E-mail: *info@pma-online.org*. Runs the PMA Publishing University, which is usually held the two days before the annual BEA trade show begins. *www.pma-online.org*

**BestSeller Mentoring,** Randy Gilbert and Peggy McColl, 398 E. Eaglewood Lane, Mt. Jackson, VA 22842; Tel: (540) 856-3318. E-mail: *support@bestsellermentoring.com*. *Make Your Book an Online Best Seller.* Learn how to sell tons of books online and get onto the bestseller list for Amazon.com, Barnes & Noble, Books-a-Million, 800-CEO-READ, etc. *www.BestSellerMentoring.com*

**PR Leads,** Daniel Janal, P.O. Box 130, Excelsior, MN 55331; Tel: (952) 380-1554. E-mail: *dan@prleads.com*. *www.prleads.com*

**Planned TV Arts,** Contact: Rick Frishman, 1110 Second Avenue, New York, NY 10022; Tel: (212) 593-5845; Fax: (212) 715-1667. E-mail: *Frishmanr@plannedtvarts.com*. PTA is one of the leading book publicity firms in the United States, specializing in radio, print, and national TV and radio placements for all authors. They work with major publishers (Random House, Simon & Schuster, Rodale, etc.) and love small publishers, too! *www.plannedtvarts.com*

**Rick Frishman.** You can get Rick's Million Dollar Rolodex at *www.rickfrishman.com*.

**The Spizman Agency,** Contact: Willy Spizman, Atlanta, GA; Tel: (770) 953-2040. E-mail: *willy@spizmanagency.com*. The Spizman Agency is a full-service public relations firm that specializes in marketing, promoting, and publicizing books, products, and leading-edge experts. They have worked with many bestselling authors and publishers as well as with first-time authors launching their books and literary careers. The Spizman Agency oversees the Think About It program at Turner Broadcasting and serves as the Atlanta affiliate of Planned Television Arts. The agency focuses on print and broadcast placement, book development, and comprehensive book consultation.

*www.spizmanagency.com*

**AceCo Publishers,** Alex Carroll, 924 Chapel Street #D, Santa Barbara, CA 93101; Tel: 1-877-733-3888. E-mail: *Alex@RadioPublicity.com.* Web: *www.1shoppingcart.com/app/aftrack.asp?afid=29117. Alex Carroll's Radio Publicity Home Study Course.* The ultimate in learning how to get yourself booked on the largest radio shows.

*www.RadioPublicity.com*

**North American Precis Syndicate,** Jim Wicht, Empire State Building, 350 Fifth Avenue, 65th Floor, New York, NY 10118; Tel: 1-800-222-5551. E-mail: *jimw@napsnet.com.* NAPS National Newspaper Feature Service. Covers 10,000 newspapers nationwide. A great way to get feature stories on your product or book published in daily and weekly newspapers throughout the country . . . at very low cost. Tell Jim that Rick Frishman sent you, to get a special bonus.

*www.napsnet.com*

**Metro Editorial Services,** 519 Eighth Avenue, New York, NY 10018; Tel: (800) 223-1600; Tel: (212) 223-1600. E-mail: *mes@metro-email.com.* Prepares and sends a feature news story to more than 7,000 newspapers monthly. Also sends out themed material to targeted audiences.

*www.metroeditorialservices.com*

**PR Newswire,** 810 Seventh Avenue, 35th Floor, New York, NY 10019; Tel: (212) 596-1500; Tel: (800) 832-5522. Sends news releases to targeted or all media nationally and internationally.

*www.prnewswire.com*

**Bradley Communications,** 135 E. Plumstead Avenue, P.O. Box 1206, Lansdowne, PA 19050-8206; Tel: (610) 259-1070; Tel: (800) 784-4359; Fax: (610) 284-3704. *Radio-TV Interview Report.* Sends a description of your expertise and media pitch to more than 4,000 media outlets.
✍ *www.rtir.com; www.freepublicity.com*

## BOOK PRODUCTION CONSULTANTS

**Pneuma Books, LLC.** 327 Curtis Avenue, Suite Five, Elkton, MD 21921; Tel: (410) 996-8900; Fax: (410) 996-8901. The premier book development, design, and marketing solution for publishers; not a subsidy publisher or vanity press.
✍ *www.pneumabooks.com*

**Foster Covers,** George Foster, book cover designer, 104 S. Second Street, Fairfield, IA 52556; Tel: (641) 472-3953; Tel: (800) 472-3953; Fax: (641) 472-3146. E-mail: *foster@lisco.com.*
✍ *www.fostercovers.com*

**RJ Communications,** Ron Pramschufer, 51 East Forty-Second Street #1202, New York, NY 10017; Tel: (800) 621-2556; Fax: (212) 681-8002. E-mail: *Ron@RJC-LLC.com.* Has thirty-plus years in the business, specializing in all areas of the design and manufacture of fiction, nonfiction, and children's picture books. Free e-mail and telephone consultation.
✍ *www.BooksJustBooks.com*

**Penelope Paine,** 817 Vincente Way, Santa Barbara, CA 93105; Tel: (805) 569-2398. E-mail: *PPPennyP@aol.com.* Specializes in children's books and selling to school systems.

**Jane Centofante,** 10616 Rochester Avenue, Los Angeles, CA 90024; Tel: (310) 475-9758; Fax: (310) 474-0814. E-mail: *jfcento@aol.com.* Editor of nonfiction bestsellers; edits manuscript for content and structure so it's publisher-ready.

**Media + (Media Plus),** Judith Kessler, 828 Westbourne Drive, West Hollywood, CA 90069; Tel: (310) 360-6393; Fax: (310) 360-0093. E-mail: *jude001@earthlink.net*. Award-winning writer/creative consultant in all forms of media, including book proposals and media training.

**Quinn's Word for Word,** Robin Quinn, 10573 West Pico Boulevard #345, Los Angeles, CA 90064; Tel: (310) 838-7098; Fax: (same). E-mail: *quinnrobin@aol.com*. Copyediting, writing, proofreading, manuscript evaluation, and ghostwriting. We make your ideas sparkle.

**Cypress House,** Cynthia Frank, 155 Cypress Street #123, Fort Bragg, CA 95437-5401; Tel: (707) 964-9520; Fax: (707) 964-7531. E-mail: *qedpress@mcn.org*. Editing, production, and promotion services for new publishers. Personalized and reasonable.

### GHOSTWRITERS

**Mark Steisel,** Tel: (415) 454-9161, (415) 454-0125. E-mail: *msteisel@earthlink.net*. Rick's favorite ghostwriter.

**Tim Vandehey.** E-mail: *tim@pacificwhim.com*.

**Word Wizard,** David Kohn, 3117 Lake Shore Drive, Deerfield Beach, FL 33442; Tel: (954) 429-9373. E-mail: *WordWiz@gate.net*. Award-winning ghostwriting, editing, manuscript analysis, coaching. Twenty-five years of experience.

**Mahesh Grossman,** Tel: (561) 434-9044. E-mail: *getpublished@authorsteam.com*.

### COPYRIGHT AND PUBLISHING ATTORNEYS

**Lloyd Jassin, Esq.,** The Actors' Equity Building, 1560 Broadway #400, New York, NY 10036; Tel: (212) 354-4442; Fax: (212) 840-1124. E-mail: *Jassin@copylaw.com*.
*www.copylaw.com*

**Charles A. Kent, Esq.,** 1428 de la Vina, Santa Barbara, CA 93101; Tel: (805) 965-4561.

**Law Offices of Jonathan Kirsch,** 1880 Century Park East, Suite 515, Los Angeles, CA 90067; Tel: (310) 785-1200. E-mail: *jk@jonathan kirsch.com.*

**Ivan Hoffman,** Attorney at Law, P.O. Box 18591, Encino, CA 91416-8591; Tel: (818) 342-1762; Fax: (419) 831-2810. E-mail: *ivan@ivan hoffman.com.*
✑*www.ivanhoffman.com*

**Venable,** Jeff Knowles, 1201 New York Avenue NW #1000, Washington, DC 20005; Tel: (202) 926-4860. E-mail: *jdknowles@venable.com.*
✑*www.venable.com*

**Joel Berman, Esq.,** 780 Third Avenue, New York, NY 10017; Tel: (212) 583-0005. E-mail: *joel@joelsberman.com.* Every type of legal issue. Wills, estates, and if you need to sue someone.

### CLIPPING SERVICES
**Bacon's Clipping Bureau,** 332 S. Michigan Avenue #900, Chicago, IL 60604; Tel: (312) 922-2400; Tel: (800) 621-0561; Fax: (312) 922-3127.
✑*www.bacons.com.*

**BurrelleLuce Press Clipping Service,** 75 E. Northfield Road, Livingston, NJ 07039; Tel: (973) 992-6600; Tel: (800) 631-1160; Fax: (973) 992-7675.
✑*www.burrellesluce.com*

**BurrellesLuce Press Clippings,** 589 Eighth Avenue, 16th Floor, New York, NY 10018; Tel: (212) 279-4270; Fax: (212) 279-4275.

**Canadian Press Clipping Services,** 2206 Eglinton Avenue E. #190, Toronto, Ontario M1L 4T5, Canada; Tel: (416) 750-2220, ext. 203.

**Newsclip Clipping Bureau,** 363 W. Erie Street, Chicago, IL 60610; Tel: (800) 544-8433; Fax: (312) 751-7306. E-mail: *clip363@aol.com.*
✐*www.newsclip.com*

**Freebies,** 1135 Eugenia Place, P.O. Box 5025, Carpenteria, CA 93014-5025; Tel: (805) 566-1225; Fax: (805) 566-0305. E-mail: *freebies@aol.com* or *freebies@earthlink.net.* Linda Cook, editor. Published five times a year with a circulation of 350,000 paid subscribers.

### MEDIA DIRECTORIES

**Information Today, Inc.,** 143 Old Marlton Pike, Medford, NJ 08055-8750; Tel: (609) 654-6266; Fax: (609) 654-4309. E-mail: *custserv@infotoday.com. Literary MarketPlace* (*LMP*) has lists of book reviewers and talk shows as well as publicists. The first place to check out media directories is at your library. See what they offer and how much they cost, and then decide how to get what you need.
✐*www.literarymarketplace.com*

**Bacon's Information,** 332 S. Michigan Avenue #900, Chicago, IL 60604; Tel: (800) 621-0561. *Bacon's Media Calendar Directory* lists the lead editorial calendars of 200 daily papers and 1,100 magazines. Important if your book's sales are keyed to a holiday. Includes a free bimonthly newsletter.
✐*www.bacons.com*

**R. R. Bowker,** 630 Central Avenue, New Providence, NJ 07974; Tel: (888) 269-5372; Fax: (908) 771-7704. E-mail: *info@bowker.com.* Publishes *Broadcasting & Cable Yearbook* and *Ulrich's Periodicals Directory.*
✐*www.bowker.com*

**BurrellesLuce,** 75 E. Northfield Road, Livingston, NJ 07039; Tel: (973) 992-6600; Tel: (800) 631-1160; Fax: (973) 992-7675.
✍ *www.burrellesluce.com*

**Adweek Directories,** 1515 Broadway, New York, NY 10036.
✍ *www.adweek.com*

**The Yellow Book Leadership Directories.** Leadership Directories, 104 Fifth Avenue, New York, NY 10011; Tel: (212) 627-4140. Directories of media, associations, law firms. The Web site has media and industry news.
✍ *www.leadershipdirectories.com*

**AceCo Publishers,** Alex Carroll, 924 Chapel Street #D, Santa Barbara, CA 93101; Tel: (805) 962-7834; Fax: (805) 564-6868. E-mail: *Alex@RadioPublicity.com*. *Alex Carroll's Radio Publicity Home Study Course.* Offers a database of radio stations as well as a course on getting publicity via radio phone interviews.
✍ *www.1shoppingcart.com/app/aftrack.asp?afid=29117*

**Media Distribution Services,** 307 West Thirty-Sixth Street, New York, NY 10018-6496; Tel: (212) 279-4800; Tel: (800) 637-3282. Has lists for all media. Will blast-fax, print, and mail.
✍ *www.mdsconnect.com*

**Infocom Group,** 5900 Hollis Street #L, Emeryville, CA 94608; Tel: (510) 596-9300; Tel: (800) 959-1059. E-mail: *info@infocomgroup.com*. *National PR Pitch Book* and *Bulldog Reporter's MediaBase* custom lists.
✍ *www.infocomgroup.com*

## NEWSLETTERS

**"The Tip Sheet"**—Monthly newsletter by Planned TV Arts, 1110 Second Ave., New York, NY 10022; Tel: (212) 593-5820. To sign up, go to *www.plannedtvarts.com*.

**Open Horizons,** P.O. Box 205, Fairfield, IA 52556; Tel: (641) 472-6130; Tel: (800) 796-6130; Fax: (641) 472-1560. E-mail: *info@book market.com*. *Book Marketing Update.* A twice-monthly newsletter about promotion. Editor-in-Chief John Kremer, author of *1001 Ways to Market Your Books.* Provides marketing tips and techniques, Internet sources, and media contacts.
✍ *www.bookmarket.com*

**Infocom Group,** 5900 Hollis Street #L, Emeryville, CA 94608-2008; Tel: (800) 959-1059. E-mail: *Bulldog@infocomgroup.com*. *Bulldog Reporter.*
✍ *www.bulldogreporter.com*

**Partyline,** 35 Sutton Place, New York, NY 10022; Tel: (212) 755-3487. E-mail: *byarmon@ix.netcom.com*. New media, interview opportunities.
✍ *www.partylinepublishing.com*

**Speaker Net News,** 1440 Newport Avenue, San Jose, CA 95125-3329; Tel: (408) 998-7977; Fax: (408) 998-1742. E-mail: *editor@speakernetnews. com.* A free weekly newsletter aimed at speakers. Also provides valuable ideas for writers.
✍ *www.speakernetnews.com*

**Ragan Communications,** 316 N. Michigan Avenue, Chicago, IL 60601; Tel: (800) 878-5331. *Ragan's Media Relations Report.* Provides information on trends, media tips, and interviews.
✍ *www.ragan.com*

## CONFERENCE RESOURCES

**How to Build a Speaking and Writing Empire,** a seminar run by author Mark Victor Hansen (of the *Chicken Soup for the Soul* series). For a brochure, call (800) 423-2314.

*Literary Market Place* and the May issues of *Writer's Digest* and *The Writer* magazines list writers' conferences.

**ShawGuides**—*www.shawguides.com/writing*

**Maui Writer's Conference**—*www.MauiWriters.com*

**Rick's Cheap Domains.** Get domains for $8.95.
✍*www.rickscheapdomains.com*

Besides workshops, the following organizations provide a wealth of information, online and offline, about publishing and promotion.

**The Jenkins Group,** Jerrold Jenkins, 400 W. Front St., Traverse City, MI 49684; Tel: (231) 933-0445; Tel: (800) 706-4636; E-mail: *jenkinsgroup @bookpublishing.com.*
✍*www.bookpublishing.com*

**Open Horizons,** John Kremer, P.O. Box 205, Fairfield, IA 52556; Tel: (641) 472-6130; Tel: (800) 796-6130; Fax: (641) 472-1560. E-mail: *info@bookmarket.com.* John is the author of *1001 Ways to Market Your Book.* He also edits the *Book Marketing Update* listed above and conducts three-day Book Marketing Blast-Off Seminars.
✍*www.bookmarket.com*

**Para Publishing,** Dan Poynter, P.O. Box 8206-146, Santa Barbara, CA 93118-8206; Tel: (805) 968-7277; Tel: (800) PARAPUB; Fax: (805) 968-1379. E-mail: *info@parapublishing.com.*
✍*www.parapublishing.com*

**PMA: Independent Book Publishers Association,** Jan and Terry Nathan, 627 Aviation Way, Manhattan Beach, CA 90266; Tel: (310) 372-2732; Fax: (310) 374-3342. E-mail: *pmaonline@aol.com.*
✍*www.pmaonline.org*

Appendix **I** Resource Directory

259

**Small Publishers Association of North America (SPAN),** 1618 West Colorado Avenue, Colorado Springs, CO 80904. Tel: (719) 471-2182. *✎www.spannet.org*

**BestSeller Management Consulting,** Greg Godek, 5641 La Jolla Hermosa Avenue, La Jolla, CA 92037; Tel: (858) 456-7177; Fax: (858) 456-7155. Works with two clients per year in getting them on the bestseller lists.

**Cross River Publishing Consultants,** Thomas Woll, 3 Holly Hill Lane, Katonah, NY 10536; Tel: (914) 232-6708; Tel: (877) 268-6708; Fax: (914) 232-6393. E-mail: *twoll@pubconsultants.com*. Author of *Publishing Profit*. Consults on general management issues, publishing economics, editorial analysis, etc.
*✎www.pubconsultants.com*

## "BACK OF THE ROOM" BOOK SALES
**Fred Gleeck.** Tel: (800) FGLEECK.
*✎www.fredgleeck.com; www.theproductguru.com; www.selfpublishingsuccess.com; www.infoproductsseminar.com*

**Media and Back of the Room Sales Training.** Joel Roberts, media trainer extraordinaire. Tel: (310) 286-0631.

## VIDEO MEDIA TRAINING
**Book Marketing Works,** 50 Lovely Street, Avon, CT 06001; Tel: (860) 675-1344; Tel: (800) 562-4357. E-mail: *info@strongbooks.com*. *You're on the Air*, a must-have video created by Brian Jud, in which producers for major shows discuss how to prepare for and give interviews. Comes with two companion books by Jud: *It's Show Time: How to Perform on Television & Radio* and *Perpetual Promotion: How to Contact Producers and Create Media Appearances for Book Promotion*. He offers other videocassettes and audiocassettes.
*✎www.bookmarketingworks.com*

# Index

## About the Authors

*Photo by Robbi Frishman.*

**Rick Frishman,** president of Planned Television Arts since 1982, is one of the most powerful and energetic publicists in the media industry. In 1993 PTA merged with Ruder Finn, where Rick serves as an executive vice-president. While supervising PTA's success, he continues to work with many of the top editors, agents, and publishers in America including Simon & Schuster, Random House, HarperCollins, and Penguin Putnam. The authors he has worked with include Stephen King, President Jimmy Carter, Mark Victor Hansen, Henry Kissinger, and Jack Canfield.

Rick is a sought-after lecturer on publishing and public relations and is a member of PRSA and the National Speakers Association. He is cohost of the weekly radio show *Taking Care of Business*, which airs on WCWP in Long Island, New York *(www.tcbradio.com)*. Rick and his wife Robbi live in Long Island with their three children, Adam, Rachel, and Stephanie, and a cockapoo named Rusty.

Rick is the coauthor of *Guerrilla Marketing for Writers* and of the national bestseller *Guerrilla Publicity*. His book *Networking Magic* was released by Adams Media in 2004 and immediately went to number 1 at Barnes&Noble.com.

Starting in 2006, he joins coauthor Robyn Spizman to travel the country under the banner of Author 101 University *(www.author101 .com)*. You can e-mail Rick at *frishmanr@plannedtvarts.com,* or call him at (212) 593-5845. Visit *www.rickfrishman.com* for his Million Dollar Rolodex.

## ABOUT THE AUTHORS

**Robyn Freedman Spizman** is an award-winning author of dozens of inspirational and educational nonfiction books, including *Make It Memorable, The GIFTionary, The Thank You Book,* and *When Words Matter Most.*

A seasoned media personality and consumer advocate for twenty-five years, she has appeared repeatedly on NBC *Today*, CNN, and is featured regularly on the NBC's Atlanta affiliate WXIA-TV and the top-rated afternoon show on Star 94 with "The Giftionary Show" with Cindy and Ray. Named one of Atlanta's leading women in business by *Business to Business* magazine, her advice and books have been featured extensively in the media, including the Discovery Channel, CNNfn, *Family Circle, Woman's Day,* the *New York Times, USA Today,* and more.

Robyn is the coauthor of *Secret Agent* (with Mark Johnson), which is her first novel for young adults, as well as the coauthor of *Women for Hire's: The Ultimate Guide to Getting a Job* (with Tory Johnson and Lindsey Pollak) and *Women for Hire's: Get Ahead Guide to Career Success* (with Tory Johnson). Johnson and Spizman's newest book for women, titled *Take This Book to Work,* is scheduled for release in Fall 2006.

A popular speaker nationally on book writing and motivational topics, Spizman is considered one of the most dynamic how-to experts in the country. In addition to her writing, reporting, and speaking, she is the cofounder of the Spizman Agency, a highly successful public relations firm specializing in book publicity in Atlanta, Georgia, which her husband owns and runs.

Nominated for a Book for a Better Life Award, the *USA Today* Family Channel Award, as well as Georgia's Author of the Year Award, Robyn is a woman of many accomplishments. See *www.robynspizman.com* for more information.

Photo by Keiko Guest Photography.